Dialogically Speaking

Dialogically Speaking

Maurice Friedman's Interdisciplinary Humanism

edited by

KENNETH PAUL KRAMER

PICKWICK *Publications* • Eugene, Oregon

DIALOGICALLY SPEAKING
Maurice Friedman's Interdisciplinary Humanism

Pickwick Publications
An Imprint of Wipf and Stock Publishers
199 W. 8th Av.e, Suite 3
Eugene, OR 97401

www.wipfandstock.com

ISBN 13: 978-1-60899-838-8

Cataloging-in-Publication data:

Dialogically speaking : Maurice Friedman's interdisciplinary humanism / edited by Kenneth Paul Kramer.

xxvi + 304 p. ; 23 cm.

ISBN 13: 978-1-60899-838-8

1. Friedman, Maurice S. 2. Buber, Martin, 1878–1965. 3. Psychology and religion. 4. Philosophical anthropology. 5. Interpersonal relations. 6. Dialogue. 7. Religion— Philosophy. 8. Meaning (Philosophy) in literature. I. Kramer, Kenneth Paul. II. Title.

BL48 D51 2011

Manufactured in the U.S.A.

To the memory of Bernard Phillips
"The search will set you free."

Contents

PART THREE: Religion as Dialogue

PART FOUR: Psychotherapy as Dialogue

Contributors

ROYAL E. ALSUP, PhD, is an adjunct faculty member at Saybrook Institute Graduate School and Research Center in San Francisco; is the co-founder of Transpersonal and Existential Psychotherapy Center in Arcata, California, and Mental Health Director of United Indian Health Services, Trinidad, California; and has published numerous articles and book chapters.

PAT BONI, PhD, is a retired Lecturer in Religious Studies, San Diego State University, former director of the Graduate Religion/Human Sciences Program at the California Institute for Human Sciences, Encinitas, California, and co-editor of *Intercultural Dialogue and the Human Image* and *Martin Buber and the Human Sciences.*

KENNETH N. CISSNA, PhD, Professor and Chair of Communication at the University of South Florida, has co-authored with Rob Anderson several books including *Moments of Meeting: Buber, Rogers, and the Potential for Public Dialogue, Dialogue: Theorizing Differences in Communication Studies,* and *The Carl Rogers-Martin Buber Dialogue: A New Transcript with Commentary.*

MAURICE FRIEDMAN, PhD, Professor Emeritus of Religious Studies, Philosophy and Comparative Literature, San Diego State University; he is the author of *Martin Buber: The Life of Dialogue; Problematic Rebel: Melville, Dostoevsky, Kafka, Camus; The Worlds of Existentialism: A Critical Reader; To Deny Our Nothingness: Contemporary Images of Man; Touchstones of Reality; Martin Buber and the Theater; Martin Buber's Life and Work* (Three vols.); *The Healing Dialogue in Psychotherapy; Martin Buber and the Eternal; Abraham Joshua Heschel and Elie Wiesel: You Are My Witnesses; A Dialogue with Hasidic Tales; Encounter on the Narrow Ridge: A Life of Martin Buber; Dialogue and the Human Image: Beyond*

Humanistic Psychology; Religion and Psychology: A Dialogical Approach; A Heart of Wisdom: Religion and Human Wholeness; The Affirming Flame: A Poetics of Meaning.

RICHARD HYCNER, PhD (Canada), is Emeritus Professor of Environmental Policy, Brock University, St. Catherines, Ontario, and is the author of *Between Person and Person: Toward a Dialogical Psychotherapy.*

HAROLD KASIMOW, PhD, is the George Drake Professor of Religious Studies at Grinnell College in Iowa. His works on interreligious dialogue have been published in China, England, India, Japan, Poland, and the United States; he has co-edited *No Religion Is an Island: Abraham Joshua Heschel and Interreligious Dialogue, John Paul II and Interreligious Dialogue, Besides Still Waters: Jews, Christians, and the Way of the Buddha,* and *The Search Will Make You Free: A Jewish Dialogue with World Religions.*

NATHAN KATZ, PhD, is the Bhagwan Mahavir Professor of Jainism & the Religions of India at Florida International University, Miami, and co-founder/co-editor of the *Journal of Indo-Judaic Studies;* he has written numerous books including *Kashrut, Caste and Kabbalah: The Religious Life of the Jews of Cochin, Who Are the Jews of India?, Studies of Indian Jewish Identity, The Last Jews of Cochin: Jewish Identity in Hindu India, Buddhist Images of Human Perfection,* and *Spiritual Journey Home: Eastern Mysticism to the Western Wall.*

PAUL KNITTER, PhD, is the Paul Tillich Professor of Theology, World Religions, and Culture at Union Theological Seminary; his books include: *No Other Name?; One Earth Many Religions: Multifaith Dialogue and Global Responsibility; Jesus and the Other Names: Christian Mission and Global Responsibility; Introducing Theologies of Religions;* and *Without Buddha I Could Not Be A Christian: A Personal Journey of Passing Over and Passing Back.*

KENNETH PAUL KRAMER, PhD, is Professor Emeritus of Comparative Religious Studies at San Jose State University; he is the author of *Redeeming Time: T. S. Eliot's Four Quartets, Martin Buber's I and Thou: Practicing Living Dialogue, Death Dreams: Unveiling Mysteries of the Unconscious Mind, The Sacred Art of Dying,* and *World Scriptures: An Introduction to Comparative Religions.*

BARBARA R. KRASNER, PhD, is the Director of the Center for Contextual Therapy and Allied Studies, King of Prussia, PA; she is co-author with Ivan Boszormenyi-Nagy of *Between Give and Take: A Clinical Guide to Contextual Therapy*, and co-author with Austin Joyce of *Truth, Trust and Relationships: Healing Interventions in Contextual Therapy*.

DONALD J. MOORE, S.J., PhD, is Professor Emeritus of Theology at Fordham University. Since January 2000 he has been dividing his time between New York and the Pontifical Biblical Institute in Jerusalem where he is involved in interfaith dialogue and work for justice and peace. He is the author of *Martin Buber: Prophet of Religious Secularism* and *Abraham Joshua Heschel: Hallowing the World*.

RICHARD D. STANTON, PhD, is a licensed clinical psychologist in Bourbonnais and Kankakee, Illinois, and Allied Health Professional in Watseka, Illinois; he has published several articles and book chapters including "Maurice Friedman's Philosophy of the Human Image: The Foundation for His Critique of Contemporary Psychology" in *Contemporary Psychology: Revealing and Obscuring the Human* by Maurice Friedman.

JOHN RAPHAEL STAUDE, PhD, is a Lecturer of European History, Philosophy and Psychology at the Osher Institute for Continued Learning at University of California, San Diego; he has published several books which include *Wisdom and Age: The Adventure of Later Life; Consciousness and Creativity;* and *Max Scheler 1874–1928: An Intellectual Portrait*.

ELIE WIESEL, PhD, is the Andrew W. Mellon Professor in the Humanities, and Professor of Philosophy and Religion at Boston University. For his literary and human rights activities, he has received numerous awards including the Presidential Medal of Freedom, the U.S. Congressional Gold Medal and the Medal of Liberty Award, and the rank of Grand-Croix in the French Legion of Honor. In 1986, Elie Wiesel won the Nobel Prize for Peace. He is the author of more than forty books of fiction and non-fiction, including *Night, A Beggar in Jerusalem, The Testament,* and *The Fifth Son*.

Preface

Aperson does not spend his whole life polishing a single lens unless doing so quickens awareness, hones perspectives, and releases a continuity of significant discoveries. Not shackled by the imperatives of classical pedagogy, Professor Maurice Friedman's intellectual career (spanning fifty years of study, teaching, writing, speaking, traveling, mentoring, and co-founding the Institute for Dialogical Psychotherapy) has engendered grammars of genuine dialogue. With illuminating range, he has applied Martin Buber's philosophy of dialogue to the human sciences. At the same time, his own thought has branched off in new forms that challenge not only what we know, but how we know. From the standpoint of Jewish philosophy, writing as a philosophical anthropologist, Friedman's central subject has been to establish the *I-Thou* relationship as an alternative way of knowing beyond individualism and collectivism.

At once a world-renowned translator, interpreter, editor, and biographer of Buber, Friedman is as well a constructive philosopher and comparative religionist. Friedman's inestimable contribution to Buber scholarship is embodied in his life-long focus on Buber's philosophical anthropology and expressed, not only in his teaching, but also in his writings. Friedman's genius, as Rollo May has noted, lies in his capacity to enter into Buber's mind and spirit, which he accomplished in his three volume *Martin Buber's Life and Work*. While Elie Wiesel calls Friedman's work an "overwhelming contribution," and Emil Fachenheim calls it "a masterpiece," Martin Marty has written that all subsequent work on Buber must build on Friedman's foundation. Like Buber, Friedman has tirelessly pointed not toward abstract philosophical systems, but toward a life of encounter on "the narrow ridge" of genuine dialogical engagement.

Yet, rather than reading his own interpretations into Buber's work, or being merely a conduit through whom Buber's thoughts flow unchanged, one of Friedman's main contributions has been to articulate *how* dimensions (religious, literary, existentialist, sociological, and psychological) of

Buber's thought have and could still help to reshape the human sciences. Throughout Friedman's work, it becomes clear that describing dialogical behaviors between persons in social situations has no reducible meaning—it is meaningful in itself. Trying to define its significance would be like attempting to define the meaning of a line of poetry, or of an artistic image. At the same time, this "direct, reciprocal, present" relationship between unique persons is necessary if the wholeness, and uniqueness of a person is to emerge. Although "genuine dialogue" evades conceptualization, requisite principles for communicating meaningfully, for Friedman, include:

- turning toward others courageously, and trustingly;
- being "fully" present to another's self-disclosure;
- listening attentively both to what is spoken and unspoken;
- imagining what the other is thinking, feeling, experiencing;
- responding responsibly without withholding oneself; and
- confirming the other as your dialogical partner.

The central significance of genuine dialogue for Friedman is its spokenness, or rather our being spoken through it. Indeed, the title of this book—*Dialogically Speaking: Maurice Friedman's Interdisciplinary Humanism*—was selected specifically to emphasize the central significance of living speech for human existence on the one hand and for Friedman's interdisciplinary methodology on the other. It is through dialogical speech between persons that we are confirmed as selves, and that we build language that becomes actual in spokenness and within which we think, communicate, and create. For Buber, and for Friedman, the true civilizing tool is a cosmos built upon *logos*—the common speech-with-meaning—which joins us in a mutually encountered togetherness. Because of the spoken nature of dialogue, therefore, readers of this book become readers-as-listeners, readers who open themselves to being addressed by a voice. A speaking voice cannot be read as an object, does not allow itself to be reduced to one-sided ideas, and demands a uniquely personal response.

Friedman's contributions, however, are not limited to epistemological and pedagogical possibilities emerging from his applications of Buber's thought to disciplines within the Humanities and Social Sciences.

Closer to the "lived concrete," they also lie in his emphasis on "existential courage" and "existential trust." With fear and anxiety, distrust and emptiness impeding human interactions, the antidote—genuine dialogue—demands trusting in existence and having the courage to meet and interact with the vicissitudes of each new moment. "Existential trust," and its corollary "existential grace," generate the courage to address and the courage to respond even in the face of separation, miscommunication, and pseudocommunication. Trusting enables us to live moment-to-moment, and to listen deeply to the other, both to what is spoken and to what is left unspoken. Accordingly, meaningful self-disclosure, for Friedman, cannot remain rhetorically one-sided within the content of one's own experience, but rather involves two-sided interactions between persons or between a person and a text.

Friedman's particular concern for more than fifty years—why he remains relevant—has been to delineate not merely an intellectual perspective on human life, but a total, living attitude that expresses and extends our humanity. Unlike cultural anthropology or any of the other social and human studies such as sociology, psychology, and economics, Friedman's work has always pointed toward the totality of the human person—what makes the human *human*, that is, what is essential to our existence as human persons in direct and indirect relationship with one another and with the environments in which we live. For Friedman, therefore, to avoid viewing the human being as a summation of parts, both objective (the known) and subjective (the knower) "one must be a participant who only afterward gains the distance from one's subject matter that will enable one to formulate the insights one has attained."[1]

Although the term "existentialist" or "philosophical anthropologist" might well be used to describe Friedman's life work, the term "humanist" more adequately indicates his dialogical approach to the wholeness and uniqueness of the human. Yet since understandings of the word vary, what kind of humanist is he? Many secular humanists, for instance, reject belief in God and are guided by reason and ethical principles. Based on this view, the ultimate source of meaning is the individual. In using "Maurice Friedman's Interdisciplinary Humanism" as a subtitle of this book, I am taking the word "humanism" out of its theological and religious context and giving it a broader meaning than an ideological approach to human

---

1. Friedman, *Buber and Human Sciences*, 16.

experience—namely, the way in which a person humanizes the concrete situations of existence. Friedman's larger humanism is defined not by the negation of transcendence but precisely by the fact that it negates nothing that is fully human and is open to the concrete and unique, even when manifested, as William James puts it, in the very dirt of private fact.

In contrast to secular humanists, Friedman affirms a "believing humanism" in which, humanity and faith penetrate each other. As Buber suggested in his significant public address to accept the Netherlands Erasmus Prize in 1963, "our faith has our humanity as its foundation, and our humanity has our faith as its foundation."[2] Rather than viewing the human as a self-conscious reflection of Being in itself (e.g. from Hegel to Heidegger), for Friedman what makes us authentically human arises in our direct and faithful response to everyone and everything we encounter. Faith, or better put, existential trust means perseverance in relationship to God's hidden yet self-revealing presence in every authentic interaction, every genuine dialogue, with whomever or whatever is encountered. The content of his believing humanism is not, therefore, the content of absolute objective principles (whether theological or philosophical), nor is it a phenomenological analysis of existence. It is instead the wholly particular content of each moment's lived dialogue in which the reality encountered is neither subjectivized nor objectivized but responded to responsibly.

If the content of his thought is open and accessible in the lived concrete, its interdisciplinary form witnesses to the full interpenetration of faith and humanness and provides a testimony to how each finds one's deepest ground in the other. I recall from graduate seminars hearing him once describe being interviewed by the president of Swarthmore College because the department of philosophy wanted to hire him. "I know that this is the wrong question to ask a polymath," the president said, "but is there any one thing that you are interested in?" Friedman realized that the president saw him as made up of departments. He could not imagine, for example, that Friedman's central focus was on the image of the human that provided a vital unity to all his interests. He could only see that philosophy was here, literature over there, religion in the next room, and in this place was psychology. Friedman recognized early in his career, thereby, that many people who become specialists "play certain language

---

2. Buber, *A Believing Humanism*, 117.

games and can no longer really hear and do not want to hear what others are saying."[3]

Though important distinctions between methods and approaches remain, the foundation shared by academic disciplines for Friedman emerges from a common ground that integrates and reveals deepest aspects of our humanness. It is because no particular discipline can ever hope to exclusively capture the wholeness of the human, and because human uniqueness can never be encapsulated by a general description of human behavior, that dialogues between and within fields are necessary to deepen understandings of authentic humanness.

The interface of four disciplines and four main concerns, more than others, shape the dialogical lens through which Friedman's relation to being and meaning is expressed. Part One, "Philosophy as Dialogue," sets the book's backdrop by describing the interhuman dynamics of becoming uniquely human from an ontological perspective; Part Two, "Literature as Dialogue," introduces the first of Friedman's two interrelated methods for studying human experience, the human image; Part Three, "Religion as Dialogue," describes and exemplifies his other major interpretive approach, touchstones of reality; and Part Four, "Psychotherapy as Dialogue," demonstrates the healing outreach of genuine dialogue, dialogical psychotherapy. If Part One provides the dialogical foundation upon which this book is situated, and Parts Two and Three focus on Friedman's central interpretive approaches to the human sciences, Part Four, drawing upon the findings of the first three, provides therapeutic applications of interhuman dialogue. Engaging live options of human expression across the humanities and social sciences, Friedman points readers toward a meaningful self-disclosure which steers between broad relativism and narrow exclusivism.

Herein lies the distinguishing feature of this text. Each part, forming a kind of "intertextual compass" for navigating the theory, methods, and applications of Friedman's thought, contains both an essay by Friedman, embodying one of his major themes, along with solicited essays from former students and colleagues familiar with his work, essays that make plainly evident the difficult choice of living on "the narrow ridge" between failure and success, inauthentic and authentic behaviors. Like a *Festshcrift*, solicited essays address specific aspects of Friedman's thought.

---

3. Friedman, *Intercultural Dialogue and Human Image*, 110.

However, unlike a *Festschrift* these essays have been arranged to embody and engender a pluralistic structure for meaningful dialogical communication. In this way, the significance of Friedman's philosophy is presented both directly by Friedman himself in the Introduction, the lead chapter of each Part, and the Conclusion—forming, as it were, a book within this book, one that encapsulates his own life-long scholarly perspective—and then through dialogical responses to his thought, which highlight and apply his interdisciplinary, existentialist humanism.

Initiating the dialogical essays embodied in this text, each contributor was given a copy of Friedman's introductory essay "My Dialogue with Dialogue" to read before writing their response to one theme in his work. Setting a tone for the book, in the Introduction Friedman clarifies essential elements of Buber's life work on "genuine dialogue" and then addresses the necessary relationship between dialogue and dialectic in the human sciences. In this spirit, individual chapters address issues endemic to dialogical aspects of becoming *human*, such as: the development of the Buber-Friedman relationship, the existential choice between meaning and non-meaning, the covenant of peace, the significance of interior dialogue, the interaction of trust, revelation, and prayer, mysticisms of the particular, Indic-Jewish interreligious dialogue, the problem of genocide, Hasidic teaching, dialogical psychotherapy, contextual therapy, and confirmation and disconfirmation.

In Part One, "Philosophy as Dialogue," chapters on Buberian, existentialist, and theistic sources of Friedman's thought help to frame his originality. Friedman's own chapter lays out a basic distinction between one-sided observation and becoming aware in relation to another person. He addresses what it means to become authentically human, not as a universal precept, but in direct mutual relationship with another for whom I am responsible and to whom I respond genuinely. That is, we become ourselves through each particular action and we choose ourselves in each act of becoming. Stanton provides an overview of Friedman's unique 'apprenticeship' with Buber as his main English translator, interpreter, and editor. Staude's essay is representative in its blending of anecdotal and commentarial methods employed by most authors in the volume and serves to introduce the thinker, Friedman.

Part Two, "Literature as Dialogue," focuses on literary images of the human not as defined or determined realities, but as an "image" shaped and re-shaped by one's experience in dialogue with others. Friedman's chapter asserts that the most fruitful approach to literature is to take seriously its full address to the reader as a whole human person and to discover in our encounter with it that image of authentic human existence implicit in the very style of most great literature. In its very particularity, the image of the human (a highly personal unique life-stance embodying a dialogical attitude and a willingness to respond responsibly), in literature gives us the wholeness of the human as more abstract disciplines cannot. This image is not static but dynamic, a direction of movement, providing a thread which links various occasions and instances of dialogical existence. Boni's essay demonstrates how Friedman connects this image to his reading of literary classics. Kramer's essay points out how "characters" drawn from all sources serve to "mediate" between subject and object, private and public, and how the significance of inner dialogue (intralogue) especially with those with whom one shares public conversations, enter into future encounters.

Part Three, "Religion as Dialogue," considers how religions persist from the past and move into the future through present "touchstones of reality." Friedman's chapter asserts that *homo religiousis* is *homo dialogus*. It is a lived reality that is ontologically prior to its expression in creed, ritual, and group. At the same time, it is inseparable from touchstones of reality, those centrally significant life-events with which I continue to have a dialogue and which I bring into new relationships. Moore's essay ties Friedman's thought to Buberian theology, and graciously criticizes its rejection of traditional creeds and rites. Katz's essay combines scholarly precision with a kind of anti-metaphysical pragmatism in his recounting of Friedman's revealing reading of Asian religious texts. Kasimow's essay presents a comparison among and between the influences of Buber, Abraham Heschel, and Friedman in his own thought. Alsup's chapter offers a gripping tale of how disparate touchstones of reality both constrain dialogue and make it possible. Part Three concludes with Elie Wiesel's riveting essay on Reb Uri of Strelisk, which is framed by a fascinating discussion about Hasidism between Wiesel and Friedman. Through story and not through scholarship, the figure of Reb Uri, known for his great power of ecstatic praying, makes perhaps the most Buberian and Friedman-like point—that "any human being weighs more than all the books in the world."

Part Four, "Psychotherapy as Dialogue," then shifts attention to the nurturing and restorative power of dialogue, especially as it takes place through the practice of dialogical psychotherapy and confirmation. Specific insights from the "human image" and from "touchstones of reality" are applied to areas across family, community, and society. The wide breadth of Friedman's range of interests and their impact on other scholars is largely registered in this Part. Friedman's chapter demonstrates how dialogical psychotherapy is not a school of therapy but a movement that has had its representatives and pioneers in many major schools of psychotherapy. By dialogical psychotherapy, Friedman means therapy that is centered on the *meeting* between the therapist and his or her client or among family members as the central healing mode, whatever analysis, role-paying, or other therapeutic techniques or activities may also be used. Hycner's essay points to Friedman's capacity to break down barriers and "start afresh," providing opportunities for moving in new directions. Krasner's work in "contextual therapy" is one such example. Cissna's essay indicates how "dialogue is not an ideal concept but a practical accomplishment enacted within constraints on each occurrence." He offers a challenging account of how productive even a strained dialogue may turn out. The volume concludes with a critical essay by Paul Knitter questioning Friedman's dialogue of touchstones in light of conflict along with Friedman's response.

Intriguingly, the warmth of encounter between the contributors and Dr. Friedman—their informal, anecdotal nature, their personal stories and tributes—performs the kind of dialogue that they thematize, making the scholarship at once refreshing and challenging. A special feature of this book is found at the end of each Part, which provides interactive, interpretive exercises under the caption "Dialogical Knowing." Because a person becomes uniquely and wholly authentic, according to Friedman, through concretely meaningful responses to the other (person/place/thing), readers-as-listeners can knowingly interact with suggested questions such as: How do you respond to Friedman's dynamic interaction with human wholeness? Does it (and, if so, how) affect your life in observable ways? To understand, challenge, and/or apply Friedman's ideas, readers can also engage Friedman's thought by participating in four stages of thinking or writing that he assigned to his students as a personal academic journal to facilitate dialogical knowing.

As a former student of Professor Friedman (in a PhD program in "Religion and Literature" that he founded and directed at Temple University in the late sixties, and early seventies), I have continued to study and deeply appreciate his works along with the writings of Martin Buber through him. This book therefore aims to demonstrate the high degree of relevance of dialogical philosophy—its teaching and its practice—for the present day. In summation and anticipation of what follows, we cannot do better, I think, than to begin with a slice of conversation taken from a May 1st, 1996 dialogue with Maury in an interdisciplinary seminar at San Jose State University. In response to my question about the limits of dialogue, Friedman remarked:

> There are several limits: one is time; one is hunger; and one is that you do what you can in a situation. There are even tragic situations where there are simply not the number of resources on either side for the genuine meeting to take place. You don't insist on the dialogue and you don't assume it will always happen—you are simply open for it. If I could make dialogue happen, that wouldn't be dialogue. That would be willfulness. So I have my radius. I can prevent it, though. There can be a one-sided prevention of dialogue. I can do it simply by saying—"nothing's going to get through to me." But when there's a *willingness* for dialogue, then—and you used the word earlier—one must "navigate" moment-by-moment. It's a listening process.

Kenneth P. Kramer
Santa Cruz, CA
Passover—Easter 2010

Acknowledgment

E ACH OF US, TOGETHER and in our own ways, with varying intensities and for unique reasons, wishes to acknowledge our deep gratitude to Martin Buber (1878–1965) for his life of unreserved dialogue. What we inherit from Buber is a profound caring for how best to respond openly, honestly, immediately to each person's unique address. Buber's life-work gave one such expression—authentic dialogue—which, as he said, is part of our birthright as human beings. For this reason in a time when we are in danger of losing our birthright, Martin Buber has pointed us again to "the touch of the other."

Introduction

My Dialogue with Dialogue[1]

MAURICE FRIEDMAN

MY MEETING WITH MARTIN BUBER

MY DIALOGUE WITH DIALOGUE probably began in 1944 or 1945 when I returned to Martin Buber's *I and Thou* and read it not for its resemblance to non-dualistic Hinduism but for what it said in itself: "All real living is meeting." My 600-page doctoral dissertation on the whole of Buber's thought that I had access to was certainly another step along the way, and equally important was my dialogue with Buber himself—first by letter and later in person. Even before he had read my dissertation Buber wrote me saying he would like to help me and asked me to write him about myself without holding back but "please, no analyses." He liked my way of narrating but complained that I communicated how I felt about others but did not enable him to see the persons themselves.

When I first met him in person in October 1951, Buber told me that he was not mainly interested in me because I was writing a book

---

1. Kenneth Kramer, in addition to his long and selfless task of editing this book over more than ten years, has gone through my writings and selected passages that fit the title of this essay "My Dialogue with Dialogue" as well as repeating the process for my other essays used at the beginning of each part: "Becoming Authentically Human: the Consciousness of Dialogue," "A Poetics of Dialogue; the Human Image," "Religion and the Religions: Touchstones of Reality," and "Healing Through Meeting: Dialogical Psychotherapy." What is more, in places he has added a few sentences of his own. For all of this I am most grateful.

1

on him but as a person. "My books are snake skins that I throw off," he said. "They are not what is important to me." He told me he had met T. S. Eliot five days before in London, that he was a shy person but one who was really frank. When I asked him if he did not find important differences between Eliot's thought and his own, Buber replied, "When I meet a person, I am not interested in his opinions but in the person."

THE ONTOLOGY OF THE BETWEEN

The fundamental fact of human existence, according to Martin Buber's philosophical anthropology, is person with person. But the sphere in which person meets person has been ignored because it possesses no smooth continuity. Its experience has been annexed to the soul and to the world so that what happens to an individual can be distributed between outer and inner impressions. But when two persons "happen" to each other, then there is an essential remainder which is common to them, but which reaches out beyond the special sphere of each. That remainder is the basic reality, the "sphere of the between." The participation of both partners is in principle indispensable to this sphere. The unfolding of this sphere Buber calls "the dialogical." The psychological, that which happens within the souls of each, is only the secret accompaniment to the dialogue. The meaning of this dialogue is found in neither one nor the other of the partners, nor in both taken together, but in their interchange.

AS I SAY THOU I BECOME I

The fundamental fact of human existence, according to Martin Buber's philosophical anthropology, is person with person. But the sphere in which person meets person—the "between"—has been largely ignored because it possesses no smooth continuity. Its experience has been annexed to the soul and to the world so that what happens to an individual can be distributed between outer and inner impressions. If it is the interaction between persons which makes possible authentic human existence, it follows that the precondition of such authentic existence is that each overcomes the tendency toward appearance, that each means the other in her/him personal existence and makes her/his present as such, and that neither attempts to impose her/his own truth or view on the other. It would be mistaken, therefore, to speak of individuation alone.

Individuation is only the indispensable personal stamp of all realizations of being human.

In the dialogical view we become persons in what Buber calls the "I-Thou" relationship—the direct, reciprocal, present relation between the person and what comes to meet him or her as opposed to the indirect, nonmutual relation of "I-It." I-Thou is a dialogue in which the other is accepted in his or her unique otherness and not reduced to a content of my experience. I-It is a monologue, the subject-object relation of knowing and using that does not allow the other to exist as a whole and unique person but abstracts, reduces, and categorizes. In I-It, only a part of one's being—rational, emotional, intuitive, sensory—enters into the relation; in I-Thou, the whole being enters in.

When two persons really "happen" to each other, then there is an essential remainder which is common to them, but which reaches out beyond the special sphere of each. That remainder is the basic reality, the "sphere of the between." The participation of both partners is in principle indispensable to this sphere. The unfolding of this sphere Buber calls "the dialogical." The psychological, that which happens within the souls of each, is only the secret accompaniment to the dialogue. The meaning of this dialogue is found in neither one nor the other of the partners, nor in both taken together, but in their interchange.

WHOLENESS, DECISION, AND DIALOGUE

True decision can be made only with the whole being, and it is decision in turn that brings the person to wholeness. Yet this wholeness is never a goal in itself but only the indispensable base for going out to meet the Thou. Decision is made *with* the whole being, but it takes place *in* dialogue. The person who decides continually leaves the world of It for the whole if dialogue in which I and Thou freely confront each other in mutual effect, unconnected with causality. It is in dialogue, therefore, that true decision takes place. Decision within dialogue is a corollary of personal unification; for it means giving direction to one's passion.

In their dialogue with others and in their life with the community it is possible for persons to divert fear, anger, love, and sexual desire from the casual to the essential by responding to what comes to meet them, to what they become aware of as addressing them and demanding from them an answer.

CONFIRMATION

True confirmation means that one confirms one's partner as this existing being even while one opposes her. I legitimize her over against me as the one with whom I have to do in real dialogue, and I may then trust her also to act toward me as a partner. To confirm her in this way I need the aid of what Buber calls "imagining the real." This imagining is no intuitive perception but a bold swinging into the other which demands the intensest action of my being, even as does all genuine imagining, only here the realm of my act is not the all-possibly but the particular, real person who steps up to meet me, the person whom I seek to make present as just so and not otherwise in all her wholeness, unity, and uniqueness. I can only do this as a partner, standing in a common situation with the other, and even then my address to the other may remain unanswered and the dialogue may die in seed.

INDIVIDUATION

If it is the interaction between person and person which makes possible authentic human existence, it follows that the precondition of such authentic existence is that each overcomes the tendency toward appearance, that each means the other in her personal existence and makes her present as such, and that neither attempts to impose her own truth or view on the other. It would be mistaken to speak here of individuation alone. Individuation is only the indispensable personal stamp of all realization of human being. The self as such is not ultimately essential but the created meaning of human existence again and again fulfills itself as self. The help that persons give each other in becoming a self leads the life between persons to its height. The dynamic glory of human beings is first bodily present in the relation between two persons, each of whom in meaning the other also means the highest to which this person is called and serves the fulfillment of this created destiny without wishing to impose anything of her own realization on the other.

THE SIGNS OF ADDRESS

If we shut off our awareness to "the signs of address," we are shutting off our awareness of the address of God, for the One who speaks in these signs is the "Lord of the Voice," the "eternal Thou." To escape responsibility for this life, we turn existence into a system of hideouts, every person hides, like Adam, to avoid rendering accounts. This lie displaces the undivided seriousness of being human with others in all its manifestations and destroys the good will and reliability on which our life in common rests. Further, the external conflict between person and person has its roots in the inner contradiction between thought, speech, and action. One's failure to say what one means and do what one says "confuses and poisons, again and again and in increasing measure," the situation between oneself and the other person. Unaware that the roots of the conflict are within our inner contradiction, we resist beginning with ourselves and demand that the other change at the same time. But just this perspective in which one sees oneself only as an individual contrasted with other individuals, and not as a genuine person whose transformation helps toward the transformation of the world, contains the fundamental error.

To the extent that the soul achieves unification, in contrast, it becomes aware of "direction" and of itself as sent in quest of it. This awareness of direction is ultimately identical with the awareness of one's created uniqueness, the special way to God that is realized in one's relation with the world and with others. The person who knows direction responds with the whole of one's being to each new situation with no other preparation than one's presence and one's readiness to respond. Direction is not meeting but going out to meet. It is not identical with dialogue, but it is, along with personal wholeness, a prerequisite of any genuine dialogue. It is also a product of dialogue in the sense that the awareness of direction comes into being only in the dialogue itself. One discovers the mystery waiting for one not in oneself but in the encounter with whom or what one meets. Although "the one direction of the hour towards God . . . changes time and again by concretion," each moment's new direction is *the* direction if reality is met in lived concreteness.

GENUINE DIALOGUE

Essential to the life of dialogue is the realistic trust that recognizes the strength of the tendency toward seeming yet stands ready to deal with the other as a partner and to confirm her/him in becoming her/his real self. This life is a part of our birthright as human beings, for only through it can we attain authentic human experience. But this birthright cannot be simply inherited, it must be earned. We must follow Buber in not underestimating the obstacles to the life of dialogue, but we must also follow him in refusing to magnify them into an inexorable fate.

In genuine dialogue the experiencing senses and imagining the real work together to make the other person as whole and one. For this dialogue to be real, one must not only mean the other, but also bring oneself, and that means saying at times what one really thinks about the matter in question. One must make the contribution of one's spirit without abbreviation and distortion: everything depends here upon the legitimacy of what one has to say. Not holding back is the opposite of letting oneself go, for free speech involves thought as to the way in which one brings to words what one has in mind. A further condition of genuine dialogue is the overcoming of seeming. Because genuine dialogue is an ontological sphere that constitutes itself through the authenticity of being, every intrusion of seeming can injure it.

Genuine dialogue can be either spoken or silent. Its essence lies in the fact that "each of the participants really has in mind the other or others in their present and particular being and turns to them with the intention of establishing a living mutual relation between himself and them." The essential element of genuine dialogue, therefore, is "seeing the other" or "experiencing the other side." Only through a quite concrete imagining of what the other is thinking, feeling, and willing can I make the other present to myself in his or her wholeness, unity, and uniqueness.

This "imagining the real" is not "empathy" as it is commonly understood, for it does not mean giving up one's own standpoint in order to enter that of the other. Rather it is a living partnership in which I stand in a common situation with the other and expose myself vitally to her share in the situation as really her share. Without forfeiting anything of the felt reality of my own activity, I at the same time live through the common event from the standpoint of the other. This "inclusion" of the other takes place most deeply and fully in marriage, the "exemplary bond," which, if it is real, leads to a "vital acknowledgment of many-faced otherness— even in the contradiction and conflict with it." In all human relations, in fact, the responsible equality of one's decision will be determined by the degree to which one really experiences the side of the other and makes the other present to one.

THE IMAGE OF THE HUMAN

Based on my study of Buber's life and works, I have developed two essentially dialogical approaches to human existence and meaning: "the image of the human" and the "touchstones of reality." To use one obvious connecting point between my two metaphors, if religion derives from and rests upon our touchstones of reality, it also embodies and expresses our image of the human, our image not only of what human life is but also of what it can and ought to be. Each metaphor describes interlinked hermeneutical activities for signifying human meaning and value. These methodological approaches to human existence and meaning were developed independently of each other and at different times. Each grew out of his concern for communicating the interdisciplinary and intercultural significance of dialogue. Though not synonyms, they point to the concrete, lived reality of becoming authentically human. Both metaphors emphasize open dialogue with what is met; both emphasize discontinuity; and both emphasize events. Yet the image of the human speaks of a gradual building up of our human attitude, as much unconscious as conscious, whereas touchstones of reality come to us in sequence like a rock path across a lake, such as one sees at a Zen Buddhist temple in Kyoto.

The image of the human and personal wholeness are mutually entailed if we understand the image of the human aright—not as some universal model or ideal that we all can or ought to adopt but as a highly personal unique life-stance that every one of us chooses again and again as our personal way of being human. The image of the human means a meaningful personal and social direction that gives us some guidance in choosing between our potentialities and finding a way forward in the present that leads organically into the future. It is the expression of what we are in our uniqueness and in our humanity. The universality that is talked of here is one that exists only in and through the concrete, the particular, the unique.

The pole of the unique and the pole of the human stand in fruitful tension with each other: in each situation I must be concerned with what is authentic human existence and what is authentic existence for me in particular. These two can never be divided from each other, nor can they be identified. What we mean by "human" is at once something we take for granted and something we do not know and must constantly discover and rediscover. That we are all "human" is the commonest presupposition of social intercourse. What the human is, can be, and ought to become is continually changing, however, not only with each new culture and period of history, but also with each new individual. It is precisely in one's uniqueness, and not in what one has in common with others, that each person realizes what the human can become in one. The image of the human is an embodiment of an attitude and a response. Whether it is an image shared by only one person or by a society as a whole, the individual stands in a unique personal relation to it. One's image of the human is not some objective, universal Saint Francis, but the Saint Francis who emerges from one's own meeting with this historical and legendary figure.

TOUCHSTONES OF REALITY

"Touchstones of reality," as I use that phrase in my book of that title, is not a definition: it is a metaphor. I use this metaphor in conscious contrast to all those ways of thinking that try to deal with reality in objective terms: metaphysics, philosophy of religion, theology. But I also use it in contrast to the subjective approaches that explain "reality" away, whether in terms of Freudian psychology, or Sartrian existentialism of choice— the invention of values—or the linguistic analyst who says this is what you prefer or postulate and the rest is just an unwarranted inference from your emotions, the deconstructionist or constructivist reduction of everything to social context, or any of the other cultural relativizing or subjectivizing approaches.

In contrast to both the objective and the subjective, I claim that in our lives we do have certain events that become for us touchstones of reality. We bring them with us into other life events so that they affect the way we enter these life events, and they are themselves modified in the process. While I cannot define what reality is apart from our touching, in touching we do come in contact with something really "other" than ourselves, with some otherness that has its unique impact upon us. I do not mean by touchstones of reality merely subjective experience, therefore, but what transcends our subjective experience even though we are fully part of it.

Our image of the human and our personal wholeness go together not only because each person's image of the human is unique but also because our wholeness as persons is inseparable from the unique direction that we take, the attitude and life-stance that we bring to our response to the demand placed on us by the persons and world with which we stand in dialogue. Thus our individuation and our integration cannot be an end in itself, divorced from the unique direction that our image of the human and our touchstones of reality embody. These images and touchstones are our way of going out to meet what comes to meet us. We cannot use everything else merely as a means to the end of our personal integration, as sometimes seems to be the goal of Jungian therapy, or Joseph Campbell's "follow your bliss" without concern for the partnership of existence.

A DIALOGICAL THEORY OF KNOWLEDGE

Underlying both the image of the human and touchstones of reality, as I use these terms, is a dialogical approach to knowledge that holds that it is in the immediacy of contact that we know and that our objective knowledge is derived from this I-Thou knowing. This means that in our approach to the human sciences as a whole we must be concerned with the dialectical alternation between I-Thou knowing and I-It knowledge or, to put it another way, between dialogue and dialectic.

Dialogue recognizes differences and never seeks for simple agreement or unanimity. Dialectic, in contrast, begins with the categories of "the same" and "the other," but excludes the reality of "the between" and with it the recognition of real otherness as that which can be affirmed even in opposing it. Thus both the original assumption and the goal of dialectic is a unified point of view. The dialectician's faith in logic as the arbitrator and common denominator not only of his inner reflections but also of the dialogue between person and person is essentially single-voiced, monological, and pseudo-universal.

This contrast between dialogue and dialectic has much to do with the importance of the spokenness of speech in which the between becomes real in the relationship of two persons or more. When the word really becomes speech, when it is really spoken, it is spoken in the context of relationship, of the meeting with what is other than us, of mutuality. It takes its very meaning from the fact that it is said by one person and heard by another. The hearer adds a different dimension and relationship to the word that is spoken, even as he or she stands on a different ground from the speaker. One must keep in mind, therefore, the genuinely two-sided and dialogical character of the word as the embodiment of the between when it is spoken.

The mystery of word and answer that moves *between* human beings is not one of union, harmony, or even complementary, but of tension, for two persons never mean the same thing by the words that they use, and no answer is ever fully satisfactory. The result is that at each point of the dialogue understanding and misunderstanding are interwoven. From this tension of understanding and misunderstanding comes the interplay of openness and closedness and expression and reserve that mark every genuine dialogue between person and person. Thus the mere fact of the difference between persons already implies a basic dramatic situation as an inherent component of human existence as such that drama only reproduces in clearer and heightened form.

DIALOGUE AND DIALECTIC IN THE HUMAN SCIENCES

I once had the notion of writing a book on dialogue and dialectic in the human sciences in which I would show this dialectical alternation in such fields as psychology and psychotherapy, sociology and anthropology, literature and religion. Human existence necessarily and properly alternates between the immediate and the mediate, the direct and the indirect. Both dialogue and dialectic imply the alternation between two different points of view. In the case of dialogue, this also means real meeting with the unique otherness of an other, whereas in the case of dialectic the alternation may take place within the head of a single thinker, and the points of view may remain disembodied and hypothetical.

The tendency of by far the largest and most dominant methodology in most human sciences today is to begin with dialectic and to examine dialogue as a part of that dialectic. Putting this in Buber's terminology, it means that the mutual knowing of the I-Thou relationship is subsumed under the subject-object knowledge of the I-It relation. A radical reversal of this perspective would not mean any rejection of dialectic, which remains essential to the whole human enterprise of connected thought from one generation to another. What it does mean is a shift in emphasis toward understanding dialogue as the source of knowing and dialectic as an elaboration of that source. "The corrective office of reason is incontestable," wrote Martin Buber. "It can be summoned at any moment to adjust the incongruity between my sense perception and what is common to my neighbors. In the I-It relation what is received in the I-Thou is elaborated and broken up. Here errors are possible which can be corrected through directly establishing and comparing what is past and passive in the minds of others. But reason, with its gigantic structure of general concepts, cannot replace the smallest perception of something particular and unique, cannot by means of it take part in the grasping of what here and now confronts me."

DIALOGUE AND DIALECTIC IN PHILOSOPHY

Starting with the philosophy of dialogue, we can say that the I-Thou relationship is a direct knowing that gives one neither knowledge about the Thou over against the I nor about oneself as an objective entity apart from that relationship. It is, in Buber's words, "the genuine reciprocal meeting in the fullness of life between one active existence and another." Although this dialogical knowing is direct, it is not entirely unmediated. The directness of the relationship is established not only through the mediation of the senses in the concrete meeting of real living persons, but also through mediation of the world. That means the mediation of those fields of symbolic communication, such as language, music, art, and ritual, that enable human beings ever again to enter into relation with what comes to meet them. The word may be identified with subject-object or I-It knowledge while it remains indirect and symbolic. However, it is itself the channel of expression of I-Thou knowing when it is taken up into real dialogue.

Subject-object or I-It knowledge is ultimately nothing other than the socially objectified and elaborated product of the meeting that takes place between the person and her Thou in the realms of nature, social relations, and art. As such, it provides those ordered categories of thought that are, together with dialogue, primal necessities of human existence. But as such, also, it may be, like the indirect and objective word, the symbol of true dialogue. It is only when the full meaning of the symbolic character of subject-object knowledge is forgotten, or remains undiscovered, as is often the case, that this knowledge ceases to point back toward the reality of direct dialogical knowing and becomes instead an obstruction to it.

In his classic work *I and Thou* Martin Buber used Socrates as an illustration of the I that is made real by virtue of sharing in the dialogue between person and person. Yet Socrates is not, for all that, an adequate image of the life of dialogue. Socrates went forth to people, trusted them, met them, never suspended dialogue with them. Yet his emphasis upon dialectic thought often put him in the position of the essentially monological thinker whose dialectic, even when it brings in other people, is little more than a moving forward through the opposition and interaction of different points of view, rather than an interaction between really other persons.

Martin Buber's friend, the Jewish existentialist philosopher Franz Rosenzweig, said that the reason why most philosophical dialogues, including those of Plato, are so tedious is that there is no real other who speaks. In a real dialogue the other person has not only ears but also a mouth and can say something that will surprise you. That is why real dialogue takes place in time. You cannot know the answer in advance the way Socrates teases the geometrical proposition out of the slave boy in the *Meno*.

DIALOGUE AND DIALECTIC IN SOCIAL PSYCHOLOGY AND SOCIOLOGY

The alternation between dialogue and dialectic also applies to social psychology and sociology, as I shall illustrate with some thoughts from my book *The Confirmation of Otherness: In Family, Community, and Society* (Friedman, 1983). We need to be confirmed by others. They make us present, and this, as Martin Buber points out, induces our inmost self-becoming. One of the paradoxes of confirmation that I elaborate is that we are all too often confirmed with strings attached. Another is that we do and must live in a world in which we have both personal uniqueness and social role. Everyone has to play a social role as a basic prerequisite not only to economic livelihood, but also to relations to other people and families in society. Yet we cannot resolve this tension between personal uniqueness and social role by sacrificing personal confirmation; for that results in an anxiety that can only become greater and greater. To stand in this tension is to insist that one's confirmation in society also be in some significant sense a confirmation of oneself as a unique person who does not fit into a social category.

To be confirmed in personal uniqueness is to be confirmed directly. That is dialogue. To be confirmed only as a certain social role is to be confirmed indirectly. That is dialectic. Both are necessary. We cannot altogether dispense with the idea of social role, though we can guard ourselves against taking it as a reality in itself. We must see it, instead, within the interaction between more or less static conceptions of roles and the actual dynamic of our relationship to them. We cannot deny the specialization of labor. Neither can we deny the continual rationalization of that specialization in terms of job descriptions and problems of decision-making and authority. This includes the obvious need to call for people not as the unique persons that they are but as abstractions, such as professor, secretary, machinist, crane operator, doctor, or bank clerk.

What we need not accept is that the convenient label and the social role exhaust the reality of the person for the hours during which she works. On the contrary, her own unique relationship to her work is of crucial importance not only for the success or the meaning of the work but for the human reality that here becomes manifest as event. What is more, we can recognize the necessity for a continual critique of abstractions, to make them more and more flexible and more and more in line with the actual situation at any one time.

In terms of this critique, it is a part of the task of man and woman alike to reject the unfair burden of always responding to a situation in a catalogued way. This means rejecting the life in which the human has been all but smothered under the weight of technical, social, and bureaucratic abstractions.

DIALOGUE AND DIALECTIC IN PSYCHOLOGY AND PSYCHOTHERAPY

Dialogue and dialectic are also central to psychology and psychotherapy. Even the patients' sicknesses are part of their uniqueness, for even their sicknesses tell us of the unique life directions to which they are called. If, instead, therapists make patients into objects to themselves, the therapists will have robbed the patients of part of their human potentiality and growth.

This is not a question of choice between scientific generalization and the concrete individual, but of which direction is the primary one. Is the individual regarded as a collection of symptoms to be registered in the categories of a particular school, or are the theories of the school regarded as primarily a means of returning again and again to the understanding of the unique person and his or her relationship with his or her therapist?

An increasingly important trend in psychotherapy suggests that the basic direction of movement should be toward the concrete person and her uniqueness, and not toward subsuming the patients' symptoms under theoretical categories or adjusting them to some socially derived view of the ideal. This trend emphasizes the *image* of the human as opposed to the *construct* of the human. The image of the human retains the understanding of human beings in their concrete uniqueness: it retains the wholeness of the person. Only a psychotherapy that begins with the concrete existence of persons in their wholeness and uniqueness and with the healing that takes place in the meeting between therapist and client will point us toward the image of the human. In the last analysis, the issue that faces all the schools of psychotherapy is whether the starting point of therapy is to be found in the analytical category or the unique person, in the construct or the image of the human.

The therapist with years of experience and the knowledge of the many case histories that are recorded in the literature will naturally think of resemblances when a client tells her something. But if she is a good therapist, she must discover the right movement back and forth between her patient as the unique person he is and the categories and cases that come to her mind. She cannot know through scientific method when a particular example from case histories, her earlier clients, or even her own experience applies. This is where true intuition, where imagining the real, or "inclusion," comes in.

Martin Buber is probably best known around the world as a philosopher of religion. It's true that his philosophy of God as the "eternal Thou," along with his dialogue with Taoism, Zen Buddhism, and Hindu thinkers, and our I-Thou relationship to God has had a revolutionary impact on many religions. And of course that's been important for me too as a philosopher of religion, as a professor of religious studies, as someone concerned with the history of religions. Yet in some ways as I grow older the aspect that speaks more and more to me is Buber's philosophical anthropology.

The task of the philosophical anthropologist, as Buber put it forth in his essay "What is Man?" in *Between Man and Man*, was to discover the uniqueness and wholeness of the human. What makes humans different from other animals? To be a philosophical anthropologist one has to be able to bear solitude; one has to delve into the human from within; one has to become a problem to one's self; and then one must discover all the varieties of behavior in different cultures. This activity is not the same as that of the cultural anthropologist; it is concerned more broadly with the human, yet it is not like the eighteenth-century thinker concerned with a universal human nature.

What is Man?

> The most formidable statement of the task set to philosophical anthropology was made by Kant . . . He distinguishes between a philosophy in the scholastic sense and a philosophy in the universal sense. He describes the latter as "the knowledge of the ultimate aims of human reason" or as the "knowledge of the highest maxim of the use of our reason." The field of philosophy in this [latter sense] may, according to Kant, be marked off into the following questions. "1. What can I know? 2. What ought I to do? 3. What may I hope? 4. What is man? Metaphysics answers the first question, ethics the second, religion the third, and anthropology the fourth."[2]

> A legitimate philosophical anthropology must know that there is not merely a human species but also peoples, not merely a human soul but also types and characters, not merely a human life but also stages in life; only from the systematic comprehension of these and of all other differences, from the recognition of the dynamic that exerts power within every particular reality and between them, and from the constantly new proof of the one in the many, can it come to see the wholeness of man . . .

> Philosophical anthropology is not intent on reducing philosophical problems to human existence and establishing the philosophical disciplines so to speak from below instead of from above. It is solely intent on knowing man himself. This sets it a task that is absolutely different from all other tasks of thought. For in philosophical anthropology man himself is given to man in the most precise sense as a subject. Here, where the subject is man in his wholeness, the investigator cannot content himself, as in anthropology as an individual science, with considering man as another part of nature and with ignoring the fact that he, the investigator, is himself a man and experiences his humanity in his inner experience in a way that he simply cannot experience any part of nature . . .[3]

> The fundamental fact of human existence is man with man. What is particularly characteristic of the human world is above all that something takes place between one being and another the like of which can be found nowhere in nature . . .

2. Buber, *Between Man*, 119.

3. Ibid., 123.

The view which establishes the concept of "between" is to be acquired by no longer localizing the relation between human beings, as is customary, either within individual souls or in a general world which embraces and determines them, but in actual fact *between* them.

"Between" is not an auxiliary construction but the real place and bearer of what happens between men; it has received no specific attention because, in distinction from the individual soul and its context, it does not exhibit a smooth continuity, but is ever and again re-constituted in accordance with men's meeting with one another; hence what is experienced has been annexed naturally to the continuous elements, the soul and the world.[4]

This reality, whose disclosure has begun in our time, shows the way, leading beyond individualism and collectivism, for the life decision of future generations. Here the genuine third alternative is indicated, the knowledge of which will help to bring about the genuine person again and to establish genuine community.

This reality provides the starting point for the philosophical science of man; and from this point an advance may be made on the one hand to a transformed understanding of the person and on the other to a transformed understanding of community. The central subject of this science is neither the individual nor the collective but man with man. The essence of man which is special to him can be directly known only in a living relation . . . The philosophical science of man, which includes anthropology and sociology, must take as its starting-point the consideration of this subject, "man with man." . . . Consider man with man, and you see human life. Dynamic, twofold, the giver and the receiver, he who does and he who endures, the attacking force and the defending force, the nature which investigates and the nature which supplies information, the request begged and granted—and always both together, completing one another in mutual contribution, together showing forth man.[5]

BIBLIOGRAPHY

Buber, Martin. *Between Man and Man*. Translated by R.G. Smith. New York: MacMillan, 1948.

4. Ibid., 203.
5. Ibid., 205.

PART ONE

Philosophy as Dialogue

"MY PARTICULAR CONCERN AS a philosophical anthropologist is for the wholeness and uniqueness of the human. I am not concerned merely with describing values and ideals but with what makes the human human, what is essential to our existence as human persons in direct and indirect relationship with one another and with the environments in which we are set."

—Maurice Friedman

1

Becoming Authentically Human

The Consciousness of Dialogue

Maurice Friedman

"The limits of the possibility of dialogue are the limits of awareness."
—Martin Buber, *Between Man and Man*

B ECOMING AUTHENTICALLY HUMAN IN the truest sense of the word is our becoming as persons. Situated within the tension of the "is" and the "ought" in our personal, communal, and social existence, one comes to awareness as a self, not just through one's individuality and not just through one's differences from others but in dialogue with others. Because one lives as a separate self, yet in relation to other persons and to society, present, past and to come, we need an image of authentic humanness to direct us toward finding a meaningful way of life. Whether it is an image shared by only one person or by a society as a whole, the individual stands in unique personal relation to it. One's image of authentic humanness is not some objective, universal Saint Francis or Gandhi, but the Saint Francis or Gandhi who emerges from one's own meeting with this historical and legendary figure.

AUTHENTICITY

The image of authentic humanness does not mean some fully formed, conscious model of what one should become—certainly not anything simply imposed on the individual by the culture, or any mere conformity with society through identification with its goals. Rather, for each one of us it is made up of many images and half-formed images, and it is itself constantly changing and evolving. It proceeds and develops through every type of personal encounter we have; a friend stands by us in a crisis; a poet speaks to us through his poems; a great historical figure affects us through the impact she had on those among whom she lived; the characters of novels and plays seize our imaginations and enter into our lives through a dialogue we carry on with them in the wordless depths of our being. Even when it occurs through ideal types such as the knight, the courtier, the Roman citizens, the Spartan, and the saint, the image of authentic humanness implies a more concrete representation of what the human is and should be rather than abstract, philosophical concepts. We cannot understand authentic humanness through some general conception of human nature, but again and again *through the concrete* uniqueness of single persons who realize their humanity by becoming what only they can become.

The image of authentic humanness therefore distinguishes between our potentiality and the direction we give to our potentiality. Such terms as self-fulfillment, self-expression, and self-realization are comforting to many in our age who vaguely feel that they are living without expressing themselves; yet they offer little real help toward an image of authentic humanness, for they leave unanswered the question of what direction one must take in order to "realize" or meaningfully "express" the self. If we had only one set of potentialities, then the question could be simplified to one of realizing them or not realizing them. But our potentialities are, in fact, legion. To give our potentialities direction means to decide— not consciously, but again and again through the response of one's whole being—what is the more and what is the less authentic choice in a particular situation, what is the more and what is the less authentic response, and in what way is it ours because it is true for us and we have committed ourselves to be true to it. We become ourselves through each particular action; we choose ourselves in each act of becoming.

For this reason, it is becoming authentically human and not my universal precept that enables me to say, "Nothing human is alien to me." Becoming authentically human enters into and forms that attitude which makes me ready to meet and respond to any persons whatever as a human being with human dignity, someone I stand open to know, to respect, perhaps even to love. Thus becoming authentically human plays an essential role in linking one moment of realized dialogue with another. It is, often, the very form in which dialogue remains potential, awaiting its actualization.

THE CONSCIOUSNESS OF DIALOGUE

Buber's classic presentation of his philosophy of dialogue is his poetic book *I and Thou*. Here he distinguishes between the "I-Thou" relationship that is direct, mutual, present, and open, and the "I-It," or subject-object, relation in which one relates to the other only indirectly and non-mutually, knowing and using the other. What is decisive is the relationship itself—whether it is sharing or possessing, imposing on the other or helping her to unfold, valuing the relationship in itself or valuing it only as a means to an end.

Buber's I-Thou philosophy is concerned with the difference between mere existence and authentic existence, between being human at all and being more fully human, between remaining fragmented and bringing the conflicting parts of oneself into an active unity, between partial and fuller relationships with others. It is only in a direct, mutual relationship that I grasp concretely the unique value of the other, experience the other's side of the relationship. From one moment of meeting to another, I carry the other with me, as it were, as one for whom I am responsible, one to whom I am ready to respond when we meet again. No one ever fully becomes a "whole person." But one may move in the direction of greater wholeness through greater awareness and fuller response in each new situation.

As the I of the I-It is different from the I of I-Thou, so is the consciousness of the I-It relation and the I-Thou relationship. The consciousness of I-Thou is not only fuller than that of I-It; it is also qualitatively different. Only in I-Thou is the unique known of and for itself; only in I-Thou is there real presence and presentness; only in I-Thou is the ineffable "suchness" of the particular met and recognized in itself.

THE INTERHUMAN

"The inmost growth of the self does not take place, as people like to suppose today," writes the great Jewish philosopher Martin Buber, "through our relationship to ourselves, but through being made present by the other and knowing that we are made present by him."[1] The sphere in which person meets person has been ignored because it possesses no smooth continuity. Its experience has been annexed to the soul and to the world, so that what happens to an individual can be distributed between outer and inner impressions. But when two individuals "happen" to each other, there is an essential remainder that is common to them but that reaches out beyond the special sphere of each. That remainder is the basic reality, the "sphere of the between." In an essential relation the barriers of individual being are breached and "the other becomes present not merely in the imagination or feeling but in the depths of one's substance, so that one experiences the mystery of the other being in the mystery of one's own." This is the heart of true friendship and of genuine love. The two persons participate in one another's lives not merely psychologically, as images or feelings in one another's psyches, but ontologically as a manifest, even if not continuous, reality of the between.

In us something takes place that takes place nowhere else in nature. One person turns to another as this particular being in order to communicate with the other in that sphere of the between that reaches out beyond the special sphere of each. In that sphere what happens cannot be exactly distributed between an "outer" event and an "inner" impression. This realm of the between exists on the far side of the subjective and on this side of the objective "on the narrow ridge where *I* and *Thou* meet." This sphere of the interhuman is where the human comes into being, and it is our contact with the really real.

Since "the between" is not a fixed object but a reality that comes and goes, it cannot be objectified. The psychological, what happens within the soul of each, is only the secret accompaniment to the dialogue. The meaning of this dialogue is found in neither one nor the other of the partners, nor in both added together but in their interchange. What is essential is not what goes on within the minds of the partners in a relationship but what happens *between* them. For this reason, Buber is unalterably opposed to that "psychologism" that wishes to remove the reality of relationship into the separate psyches of the participants. This distinction between the "dialogical" and the "psychological" constitutes a radical attack on the psychologism of our age.

The meeting between persons is hardly a mere going outward; for in its depth such meeting includes our penetrating to the very heart of

1. Buber, *Knowledge of Man*, 61.

the other by what Buber calls "imagining the real"—a bold swinging to the life of the other so that to some extent one concretely imagines what the other is thinking, feeling, and willing. Only from such a meeting, in fact, can we know that there is not just one inner—myself—, and one outer—others. Only if we can get beyond this deep-seated prejudice of inner and outer can we understand the sense in which our existential meetings—whether with persons, animals, plants, or rocks—are, in their betweenness, meeting with the reality that can be known only in the between. As every electron has a finite center and an infinite circumference, so we each have our own ground yet meet each other from that ground. Our existences interpenetrate. Inner versus outer is thus not only a distortion of the primordial human wholeness of the person, but also a distortion of the reality of our existence as person *with* person.

There is a decisive difference between the revelation in dialogue of the uniqueness of a human and a non-human existing being. The latter, whether it be a tree or an animal, will not hide from us by a conscious act of will. The human being, in contrast, cannot and will not allow another to "see into his soul" if one senses that the other comes merely as objective observer, scientifically curious analyst, or prying manipulator.

BECOMING AWARE

It might appear from the epigraph that I have placed at the head of this essay that if the limits of dialogue are the limits of awareness, all we need to attain dialogical consciousness is that very enhancement of awareness that so many have striven for from the nineteen-sixties until now. It is not so. In contrast to the observer and the "onlooker," according to Buber, is that knowing or consciousness in which I allow the person before me to say something *to me*, to claim my attention and demand my response, not by anything the other intends but by the other's very being.

What characterizes all knowing by rule, from the crudest superstition to the highest reaches of gnosis, is that it has one universal meaning. The true signs of address, in contrast, are unique. They stand in the stream of "happening but once." "Lived life is tested and fulfilled in the stream alone." They speak to me in my life, but not in such a way that they can be interpreted or translated, explained or displayed. They are inseparable, incomparable, irreducible—what Buber in an earlier essay called the "bestowing side of things" that blazes up to meet us if we bend over it with our fervor. "It is not a *what* at all, it is said into my very life; it is no experience that can be remembered independently of the situation, it remains the address of that moment and cannot be isolated, it remains the question of a questioner and will have its answer."[2]

INCLUSION OR IMAGINING THE REAL

Is there really such a thing as dialogical consciousness apart from or in addition to that individual consciousness with which we are all so familiar that we take it for granted?

To answer this question we must look at three central concepts in Buber's philosophy of dialogue and his philosophical anthropology. The first of these is inclusion, or "imagining the real." By inclusion Buber means a remarkable swinging over to the side of the other with the most intense activity of the being so that one to some extent experiences concretely what the other person is thinking, feeling, and willing. Buber also calls this experience "imagining the real," for in contrast to the free play of the imagination this fantasy is directed to the concrete other to whom one says Thou. This other can be perceived in her wholeness, unity, and uniqueness only as a partner and not at all as an object.

Inclusion, as a result, must be distinguished from every type of intuition that sees through a person and finds out what makes that person "tick." Inclusion means a reversal of the single instinct. It is a bipolar reality. Unlike both identification and, in the narrow sense of the term, empathy, inclusion means remaining on one's own side and at the same time going over to the side of the other.

Buber placed inclusion and "imagining the real" at the center of his mature philosophical anthropology. In "Distance and Relation" he defined imagining the real as "the capacity to hold before one's soul a reality arising at this moment but not able to be directly experienced." This capacity is essential to making the other present, which is essential, in turn, to confirmation—a principal factor in the life between persons:

> "Imagining" the real means that I imagine to myself what another is at this very moment wishing, feeling, perceiving, thinking, and not as a detached content but in his very reality, that is, as a living process in this man. . . . I experience . . . the specific pain of another in such a way that I feel . . . this particular pain as the pain of the other. This making present increases until . . . the pain which

2. Buber, *Between Man*, 12.

I inflict upon him surges up in myself, revealing the abyss of the contradictoriness of life between man and man. [3]

In "Elements of the Interhuman" Buber focuses again upon inclusion and imagining the real in the section entitled "Personal Making Present." In this section Buber asserts that to be aware of a person means to perceive her wholeness as a person determined by the spirit—the dynamic center that stamps her every utterance, action, and attitude with the recognizable sign of uniqueness. Such an awareness is impossible so long as the other is a separated object of contemplation or observation, and it is particularly hindered by the analytical, reductive, and deriving look that prevails today and that threatens radically to destroy the mystery between person and person.

This implies, of course, that a person's wholeness and uniqueness can only be perceived in dialogue, in which, in contrast to monologue, one allows the other to exist in her otherness and not just as a content of one's experience. But this dialogical perception demands that Cinderella gift, one day to become a princess, that Buber calls "imagining the real." Buber describes imagining the real here as "a bold swinging—demanding the most intensive stirring of one's being—into the life of the other." It is not, again, the all-possible that is imagined, but just the particular real person who confronts me and whom I can make present only in this way.

Inclusion is not a possession of a spiritual élite. On the contrary, it is a gift that every human being has, even though it mostly sits by the ashes of the fireplace and seldom goes out to the ball where there is intercourse between human beings. It is evident from what we have said above that it is just such an extension of consciousness beyond the individual as we hypothesized might be the case with dialogical consciousness. Most people imagine that we are imprisoned within our individual experience and find it hard to believe that Buber's imagining the real can actually enable us to make our own what the other experiences.

THE ESSENTIAL WE

Although Buber is most famous for the "I-Thou" relationship, the heart of his essay "What Is Common to All" is what he calls "the essential We." He does not deny the validity of ordinary individual consciousness in

3. Buber, *Knowledge of Man*, 60.

this essay, but he extends the human beyond that to what the pre-Socratic philosopher Heraclitus spoke of as "the common" that one should follow. If by "the common" Buber means only some moral obligation to serve the community or society, it would no more modify the individual character of our consciousness than Jeremy Bentham's assumption that making laws according to the utilitarian calculus of maximizing pleasure and minimizing pain would result in a harmonious society. But to Buber, as to Heraclitus before him, it means far more than that.

We learn at the outset that the heart of the essay's concern is maintaining unmixed the oppositeness of two states of human consciousness—that of waking and that of sleeping. This in itself demonstrates the essay's significance for our investigation of the consciousness of dialogue. "The waking have a single cosmos in common," says Heraclitus in one of his aphorisms, providing a clue to what I found missing in the Hindu contrast between waking and dreaming and between superconsciousness and waking. They were regarded as three states of individual consciousness, I pointed out above. But in waking consciousness we have the possibility of becoming a co-worker in building the common cosmos as we do not in dreaming or in superconsciousness.

Particularly important here is the fact that Buber speaks of the full mutuality of human being-together as "a spiritual reality." This spiritual reality only comes into existence, writes Buber, if human beings "do not sleep while waking and spin dreamlike illusions which they call their own insight." The pure duty and responsibility of waking togetherness that Heraclitus places upon us means the rejection of "that dreamlike refusal of the We through whose illusion the common day is broken asunder."

This task of establishing in common a common reality clearly implies that there is a consciousness of the We, the common, that is more than the sum of individual consciousnesses. That this is so Buber makes clear by contrasting Heraclitus' teaching with Chuang-tzu's idealist version of Taoism and with the ancient Hindu teaching of identity—*tat twam asi.* In the latter discussion he makes fully explicit how "the ancient Hindu 'That art thou' becomes the postulate of an annihilation of the human person." The identification of the other with oneself has as its corollary the devaluing and destruction of the uniqueness of the person—"the affirmation of the primally deep otherness of the other."

Once during the seminars on the unconscious and dreams that Buber gave for the Washington School of Psychiatry in 1957, he remarked that the reason the so-called "normal" person prefers the real world to the world of the schizophrenic is not because it is a better world but only because it is a real world, i.e. it remains in relation to the essential We!

What Buber says of the common logos adds to our understanding of the common consciousness that is attained through the We. The logos does not attain to its fullness in us but rather between us. It is the eternal chance for speech to become true between human beings and in this sense it is common to them. Persons who genuinely think with one another because they genuinely talk to one another existentially effect the communal guarding of meaning. Thus logos is not law or word to Buber nor even simply meaning. It is the interhuman event of speech-with-meaning, the sensuous meaningful human word in which human talk becomes true.

Through our common logos the cosmos becomes the shaped world of human beings—a total order formed and revealed. "Only through our service to the logos does the world become 'the same cosmos for all.'" This working together, however, is not that of a team hitched to the great wagon. It is, rather, a tug of war in which each from the ground of his or her uniqueness contributes to building the common order. "This cosmos from which we come and which comes from us is, understood in its depth, infinitely greater than the sum of all special spheres of dreams and intoxication into which man flees before the demand of the We."[4]

In the last section of "What Is Common to All" Buber explicitly recognizes that the human being has always had both his thoughts and his experiences with others and with himself as I. It is as I, moreover, that the human being transplants his ideas into the firmament of the spirit. But it is as We that the human being has constructed and developed a world out of his experiences, and it is as We that the human being has ever again raised them into being itself which, in distinction from both the psychic and physical realms, Buber identifies with "the between"—"the mode of existence between persons communicating with one another."

This We begins, to be sure, with the meeting of I and Thou: "He who existentially knows no Thou will never succeed in knowing a Thou." But it does not remain on the one to one of I and Thou. "In our age, in which the true meaning of every word is encompassed by delusion and

---

4. Buber, *Knowledge of Man*, 95.

falsehood, and the original intention of the human glance is stifled by tenacious mistrust, it is of decisive importance to find again the genuineness of speech and existence as We."[5]

THE UNCONSCIOUS

Buber's uncompleted but nonetheless pregnant speculations concerning the unconscious add one more necessary element to our understanding of the consciousness of dialogue. In contrast to Freud and Jung, who held that the unconscious must be psychic since they would not recognize it as physiological, Buber has suggested that the unconscious may really be the ground of personal wholeness before its elaboration into the physical and the psychic.

Buber bursts the bounds of psychologism by recognizing that the division of inner and outer that applies to the psyche and the physical need not apply to the unconscious. Here, in contrast, there might be direct meeting and direct communication between one unconscious and another. Obviously this paves the way for inclusion and imagining the real. Of course, each of the contents of the unconscious can in any moment enter into the dimension of the introspective and thereby be explained and dealt with as belonging to the psychic province.

The physical and the psychical represent two radically different modes of knowing: that of the senses and that of the "inner sense." Pure psychic process is not to be found in the physical. Our memory retains the process, to be sure, but by a new process in time. Physiology deals with things that are to be found, psychology with things that are not to be found. The psychic is pure process in time. In order to grasp the physical as a whole, we need the category of space as well as time. But for the psychic we need time alone.

The unconscious is a state out of which these two phenomena have not yet evolved and in which the two cannot be distinguished from one another. The unconscious is our being itself in its wholeness. Out of it the physical and the psychical evolve again and again and at every moment. The unconscious is not a phenomenon. It is what modern psychology holds it to be—a dynamic fact that makes itself felt by its effects, effects the psychologist can explore.

5. Ibid., 98.

This exploration, as it takes place in psychiatry, is not of the unconscious itself, but rather of the phenomena that have been dissociated from it. Modern psychology's claim that there are unconscious things that influence our life and manifest themselves in certain conscious states is one that Buber, in contrast to the phenomenologists, does not contest.

But we cannot, Buber reminds us, say anything about the unconscious in itself. It is never given to us. The radical mistake that Freud made was to think that he could posit a region of the mind as unconscious and at the same time deal with it as if its "contents" were simply repressed conscious material that could be brought back, without any essential change, into the conscious. Dissociation is the process in which the unconscious "lump" manifests itself in inner and outer perceptions. This dissociation, in fact, may be the origin of our whole sense of inner and outer. The conscious life of the person is a dualistic life. One can have, to some extent, the consciousness of the coming together of one's forces, one's acting unity, but one cannot perceive one's unity as an object.

If the unconscious is not of the nature of the psychic, then it follows that the basic distinction between the physical and the psychic as "outer" and "inner" does not apply to the unconscious. Yet Freud, holding that the unconscious must be simply psychical, places the unconscious *within* the person, and so do all the schools that have come after Freud. As a result, the basis of human reality itself comes to be seen as psychical rather than interhuman, and the relations between person and person are psychologized.

If the unconscious *is* that part of the existence of a person in which the realms of body and soul are not dissociated, then the relationship between two persons would mean the relationship between two non-divided existences. Thus the highest moment of relation would be what we call unconscious. More precisely, the unconscious and the conscious are integrated in the spontaneity of personal meeting. The unconscious should have, may have, and indeed will have more influence in the interhuman than the conscious, Buber insists. Through it there is a direct contact between persons in their wholeness, of which the unconscious is the guardian. This is so because the whole person is not pictured here as divided into a conscious part with which she identifies and a hidden unconscious part which operates as her "shadow" or "not me," to use

Harry Stack Sullivan's term. It is what undergirds and guarantees our wholeness as persons, hence what enters into any act that we perform as whole persons.

THE PHILOSOPHY OF DIALOGUE

Being made present as a person is the heart of "confirmation," which is interhuman, yet is not simply social or interpersonal. Unless one is confirmed in one's uniqueness as the person one can become, one is only seemingly confirmed. The confirmation of the other must include an actual experiencing of the other side of the relationship so that one can imagine quite concretely what another is feeling, willing, and knowing. This "inclusion," or imagining the real, does not abolish the basic distance between oneself and the other. It is rather a bold swinging over into the life of the person one confronts, through which alone I can make that person present in his or her wholeness, unity, and uniqueness.

Setting one another at a distance and viewing each other as independent enables us to enter into relationship as individual selves with those like ourselves. The very essence and meaning of the self is this interrelatedness. Embracing and confronting one another as the unique persons we are called to become gives rise to "the sphere of the *between*." A true event in our lives is neither inner nor outer but takes up and claims the whole of us. In the sphere of the between. I meet you from my ground and you meet me from yours, and our lives interpenetrate. Our very sense of ourselves comes only in our meeting with others.

INDIVIDUAL MYSTICAL CONSCIOUSNESS

In our approach to higher consciousness, we all tend to remain prisoners of Descartes' *cogito ergo sum*. We assume that our individual consciousness is our "touchstone of reality," to use my own phrase, and we proceed from there to discover what we can about altered states and higher levels of consciousness that we see as accessible to the Eastern mystic and to the New-Age Westerner. Although we imagine we are becoming one with the All, we do not, in fact, go beyond the borders of our individual consciousness, deepened and reinforced perhaps by our ideas of Jungian archetypes or transpersonal realms. We accept unquestioningly, as I once did, Gerald Heard's dictum that consciousness is *sui generis*, and we absolutize it.

Strangely enough, this tends to remain true for those who turn from Western psychology to Eastern mysticism. We assume that we have gotten beyond our petty egos to the realization that Brahman is Atman—*tat twam asi*—when, in fact, we are still ensconced in our own consciousness or, still worse, our own world-view.

Many years ago when I was immersed in the *advaitin* Vedanta—the non-dualistic Hindu teaching of Sankaracharya and Sri Ramakrishna—I was struck by the saying that as our dreams are to waking consciousness so is our waking consciousness to *samadhi*—the superconsciousness attained by the enlightened. Only years later, after I had made my own Martin Buber's philosophy of dialogue, did I reflect that all three terms in this equation are individual consciousness, that nowhere is there that coming to the border of one's own consciousness and meeting with others that is the touchstone of reality for the dialogical. To say with Buber that "all real living is meeting" does not mean that everything else is unreal, only that here we touch on what Paul Tillich calls the "really real," or what I call the "touchstone of reality."

> Human life touches on absoluteness in virtue of its dialogical character, for in spite of his uniqueness man can never find, when he plunges to the depth of his life, a being that is whole in itself and as such touches on the absolute . . . This other self may be just as limited and conditioned as he is; in being together the unlimited and the unconditioned is experienced.[6]

Martin Buber's recognition of this meant for him an ascetic renunciation of his natural tendency toward mystic ecstasy in favor of the task of hallowing the everyday. The event that precipitated this renunciation: After a morning of religious ecstasy Buber was visited by a young man with a "question of life and death"—someone in despair for whom, because of his mystic ecstasy, he failed to be present in such a way as to show that in spirte of all there is meaning.

In place of mystical ecstasy with its false conviction of oneness with the all, Buber offered the lived unity of the life of dialogue: "the unity of life as that which once truly won is no more torn by any changes: not ripped asunder into the every day creaturely life and the 'deified' exalted hours. The unity of unbroken, raptureless perseverance in concreteness. in which the word is heard and a stammering answer dared."

---

6. Buber, *Between Man*, 158.

Not only philosophical psychologists such as Jung but mystical philosophers such as Bergson and the mystics themselves may have made a corollary mistake when they assume that it is only in our inwardness that we find our touchstones of reality while the outer, and particularly the social, is relegated to an inferior status.

It should be evident that Buber's philosophy of the unconscious suggests an essential foundation for the consciousness of dialogue that we have discussed in connection with imagining the real and the essential We.

BIBLIOGRAPHY

Buber, Martin. *Between Man and Man.* Translated by R. G. Smith. Reprint, with Afterword translated by Maurice Friedman. London: Routledge, 2002.

———. *The Knowledge of Man: A Philosophy of the Interhuman.* Translated by Maurice Friedman and R. G. Smith. Atlantic Highlands, NJ: Humanities Press International, 1988.

2

Sharing the Narrow Ridge

Maurice Friedman and Martin Buber

RICHARD STANTON

Maurice Friedman's first contact with Martin Buber came through the reading of two of Buber's works in 1944, when Maurice was twenty-four years old. It happened during Friedman's years in Civilian Public Service. Dr. Simon Greenberg met regularly with Maurice at Greenberg's home in Philadelphia; and he loaned Maury an early translation of Martin Buber's *The Legend of the Baal-Shem*. Friedman writes, "I was also greatly attracted by Buber's classic, *I and Thou*, which I read at the same period."[1] Buber was still almost unknown in the United States at this time, as none of his books had yet been published here.[2] Friedman had passed through a period of intense mysticism just prior to encountering these two books of Buber's, as Buber had also gone through his years of mysticism in the years prior to Buber's grounding in the philosophy of dialogue.

In 1944 there was no immediate conversion for Friedman, no easy stepping from secure mystic knowledge to the way of dialogue. It was only after the inevitable breaking asunder of an interim group, "Creative House," which had provided a temporary haven for Friedman in 1945, that Friedman deepened his understanding and appreciation of Buber's works. Later Friedman refocused on Buber's books, *The Legend of the Baal-Shem* and *I and Thou*. Friedman found that the books, "expressed

1. Friedman, *Touchstones*, 52.
2. Friedman, *Narrow Ridge*, 593.

in a way valid for my new experience the reasons for my rejection of solitary contemplation and for my turn to an activist mysticism in the world." Friedman writes that, "I was convinced that I had found in Hasidism the right way of life for me, and I wished to give my life to reviving the Hasidic movement in America.[3] Friedman had familial roots in Hasidism. This part of Friedman's family history (on his mother's side) was not revealed to him until he was in his 20s.

After rejecting a path that would have led him to becoming a rabbi, Friedman entered graduate school, taking his MA in English from Ohio State University in 1947. In the same year, Maurice and Eugenia Friedman were married. As his partner for twenty-seven years, Eugenia would play an important role in the unfolding of Friedman's dialogue with Buber.

Friedman's search for a genuinely interdisciplinary program took him to the University of Chicago. There Friedman studied with Joachim Wach and others, eventually formulating the dissertation for which he received his PhD in the History of Culture in 1950. The dissertation was entitled *Martin Buber: Mystic, Existentialist, Social Prophet—A Study in the Redemption of Evil*. Following four years of further work, this dissertation led to Friedman's first book, *Martin Buber: The Life of Dialogue*.[4] I have long thought that the quotation by Martin Buber, which appears on the rear cover of this book, concisely states Buber's appreciation of Friedman's contribution to the philosophy of dialogue: "To systematize a wild-grown thought as mine is, without impairing its elementary character seems to me a remarkable achievement. On a rather multifarious work Dr. Friedman has not imposed an artificial unity; he has disclosed the hidden one."

Buber's statement indicates how very accurately Friedman had understood him. Their own dialogue was underway. I think that Buber must have received enormous confirmation from Friedman's act of writing as he had done.

Buber's first contact with Friedman came via a lengthy letter, which Friedman wrote to Buber in 1950. In it, Friedman told Buber, "how close I felt to him as a person and a thinker and about the events in [his] life leading up to [his] dissertation."[5] Maurice sent the letter by hand

---

3. Ibid., 78.

4. 1st ed. Chicago: University of Chicago Press, 1955.

5. Friedman, *Narrow Ridge*, 595.

with his mother, who was visiting Israel at the time. Martin Buber, writing in April 1950, replied in English to the letter from Friedman. This was the first of almost three hundred letters which Buber would write to Friedman, roughly one letter every two and a half weeks for fifteen years. In this first direct communication, Buber asked Friedman to send his dissertation to Buber, so that he could read it, and comment on it. Buber also wrote in the letter that he wanted Maurice to write back to him, "about himself, the tale of Friedman's life."

In July, after Friedman had completed the dissertation, he wrote his response to Buber. Buber then wrote back several times in August. The first letter of that month spoke more to the person, and the second wrote of the dissertation, "a really important book," which "deserves indeed to be published and read," according to Buber.[6] A few days after composing that second letter, Buber sent Friedman a third one. It contained "detailed comments and suggestions plus a long bibliography of books and essays about him [Buber] that I [Friedman] did not even know existed."

Buber and Friedman formed their essential relationship over the next four years. I believe that Buber found in Maurice Friedman a worthy disciple who was capable of understanding the full scope of Buber's work, and its context. Friedman was someone who could faithfully convey Buber's mature thought to America and beyond. Buber also found in Friedman, at a late date in his life, a friend, upon whom he increasingly relied to participate in his life work. "Many years of intensive work with Buber, translating, editing and introducing his works," began during that year, 1950.

Writing of the impact on his life, Friedman wrote the following while drafting *Encounter On The Narrow Ridge*, circa, 1990:

> I experienced Buber's response to my dissertation as a turning point in my life, and indeed it was. It was not only a confirmation of my work on him beyond anything I might have dreamed of, but also a confirmation of me as a person that helped give meaning and direction to my life.[7]

Their direct dialogue extended for the next fifteen years, including collaboration on all sorts of projects in addition to the writing. Buber was seventy-two years old when he first heard from Maurice (who was him-

6. Ibid., 596.

7. Ibid., 597.

self twenty eight years old at the time). Their direct dialogue continued until Buber's death in 1965.

During those fifteen years, Friedman and Buber met in America, and in Jerusalem; and they corresponded copiously. Maurice Friedman became Martin Buber's intellectual heir in all but legal reality. In 1954, Buber wrote recommending Friedman to the Columbia University Department of Religion.

> He (Friedman) had to . . . build up something like a system out of what was never intended to become such a thing. This he could do only by true understanding, his best quality indeed. He understands the ideas he meets, and he understands even the persons who thought them, as persons who thought precisely these ideas and not different ones.[8]

My dialogue with Friedman & Buber's dialogue: In October of 1967 I arrived at Pendle Hill, the Quaker Study Center in Wallingford, Pennsylvania, which is outside of Philadelphia. It was then, and remains today, an ecumenical meeting place where persons from seemingly disparate religious traditions as Quakerism, Zen Buddhism, Hasidism and other faiths meet. Psychology, philosophy, art and other subjects within the humanities are also studied regularly there. I came to Pendle Hill as something of a triple refugee: In August, my fellow Peace Corps Volunteers and I had been evacuated from Nigeria. During the months prior to evacuation, truckloads of real refugees, Ibos who had been persecuted in the northern and western regions of Nigeria, had driven past my rural education compound. After a year and a half of simmering, the Biafran war had finally erupted. Perhaps a million and a half people would die before it ended.

Scott Crom, who chaired the Philosophy Department at Beloit College, where I had been an undergraduate, had recommended Pendle Hill. In fact, I was packed and preparing to go there almost two years earlier; but in the morning mail on that Saturday I received my invitation to train for the Peace Corps instead. When, in the fall of 1967, I finally did reach Pendle Hill, I was continuing to look for some ground within psychology where I might feel at home. As a psychology major in a rigidly behavioristic psychology department, I had had to turn to course offerings outside of the department. Philosophy, anthropology, sociol-

---

8. Friedman, *The Later Years*, 202–3.

ogy and the humanities gave me acceptable alternatives to behaviorism, which was then the regnant ideology of psychology. And finally, I was a 'refugee' from a shattered relationship, an engagement that broke apart in 1965. That experience had left me without a strong sense of security: the event of coming apart had changed me.

When classes began at Pendle Hill I first encountered the philosophical anthropology of dialogue. "Dialogue suggests an unreserved communication of one center to another and has less to do with consciousness than with intentionality . . . The human is to be understood in terms of relationships rather than self (person instead of individuality) and . . . that direct, mutual relationship in which I with Thou is primary to I-It."[9] A relationship characterized by dialogue features honesty, openness to otherness, directness of contact, and inclusion or empathy. This capacity for dialogical relating gives special meaning to human existence.

The Pendle Hill of Dan Wilson and Maury Friedman introduced me to a corrective vision, to "a third alternative" as a valid basis for psychological understanding. Neither objectivity nor subjectivity, the uneasy twins of psychology, is sufficient by themselves as approaches from which one can describe and understand human reality. This is so, even though each vantage point does give us some knowledge of the human condition. Yet, even when one holds them in tension in a theory as polar opposites, objectivity and subjectivity fail to exhaust the possibilities. The richness of the between, of meetings and relationship as an "opening way" was made real for me first at Pendle Hill.

Maury and Eugenia Friedman led a weekly Hasidic Tales group in the homelike library of one of Pendle Hill's buildings. It was here, a few years before, that Maury and Eugenia had performed a dramatic reading of Maury's translation of Martin Buber's *Elijah: A Mystery Play.* Eugenia taught a short course during the winter of 1997 on the *Tales of the Hasidim* at Pendle Hill. Between group sessions participants read from Martin Buber's collection of Hasidic Tales, which are separated into tales of the Earlier and of the Later Masters. Then when the group reassembled, members read aloud a tale that had spoken to them, had puzzled them or which had been suggested to them. For the academic year, 1967–1968, Maury served as the guide to my studies at Pendle Hill. I think that he presented an evening series of lectures in the Barn that

9. Stanton, "Dialogue."

year, lectures which were precursors to a book. On occasion, in the spring of 1968, I would ride the train into Philadelphia, and catch a subway to Temple University, where I attended a few of his classes.

The second of the four programs in which I have studied with Maurice Friedman was at Temple University. I was due to begin during the academic year following Pendle Hill. However, my father died in the summer of 1968, so I decided to suspend my plans to start graduate school that fall at Temple. Instead, I remained at home, in Flossmoor, Illinois, and worked as a social worker with the Department of Public Aid on the far south side of Chicago. Then, for two years (1969–1971), I studied in a PhD program at Temple University that Friedman directed. Temple's departments of Religion, Psychology and Psychiatry contributed faculty and course offerings to that program. At the same time, Friedman directed the PhD program in Religion and Comparative Literature, which was also interdepartmental in implementation.

Again, my formal study with Friedman was interrupted. I worked for two years as a Mental Health Specialist for Illinois' Department of Mental Health in an inpatient setting. I directed an Acute Treatment Program, which Maury managed to visit. His teachings concerning the psychological healing that occurs in dialogue, as well as his personal example informed my practice of psychotherapy more than my formal training in psychology. Maurice had visited Carl Rogers' Center for Studies of the Person at La Jolla, as well as having been a resource for other psychological communities in California during the early 1970's. A position was created for him at San Diego State University (combining religion, philosophy and literature) that took him and his family to San Diego. He was also involved with a new program in clinical psychology and, knowing my wish to return to some meaningful graduate program, he suggested that I look into it. From 1973 to 1975 I was a student at California School of Professional Psychology (CSPP) in San Diego. At CSPP I served as Friedman's graduate assistant for a number of courses, as well as becoming involved in the creation of the non-statistical dissertation track and other ventures. Finally, during 1976 to 1978, I completed my formal work with Maury Friedman at Union Graduate School.[10] I wrote my dissertation on Buber, Friedman, and Therapists of Dialogue. That was the central focus that I had carried along from program to program. Assisting Maury in facilitating groups mediated by the Hasidic

10. UGS is now known as The Union Institute.

tales at the Mann Ranch, at an annual convention of the California Psychological Association, and in a few other settings extended my exposure to the role of dialogue in psychology.

Beyond my dissertation, there have been a few other formal products that came from my interest in dialogue. I have made two presentations on Friedman, Buber and dialogue to two conventions of the American Psychological Association. I contributed a chapter to the book, *Contemporary Psychology: Revealing And Obscuring The Human*. And I also wrote, entitled "Maurice Friedman and the Dialogic Human Image in Psychotherapy."[11] I find that even when I write about clinical uses of computers, I set their use in the greater context of dialogue.[12]

It has not been just their words *about* dialogue, which have meant the most to me as I have lived my own life in the soon to be thirty years since first meeting Maurice Friedman and Martin Buber's teachings. Although those "words" have served me well, at times as a lifeline in the sea of psychology, still I owe far more to the voices of Friedman and Buber than I do to some ideas which I borrow from them. Rather, it is the realized dialogue with Friedman, and through him with Buber, which has made a defining difference in my life and work. Buber and Friedman have each lived lives exemplary of dialogue. Over the course of my life, Maury Friedman has had more influence on me—on who I have become—than anyone outside of my immediate family.

When our daughter, Ruth was about ten years old, she expressed real concern over the question, *What was there, before there was God?* My wife Martha and I did not have an answer that adequately spoke to such anxiety, and I mentioned it to Maury during a phone call. He suggested that I read "The Song of Creation" to Ruth. The Song of Creation is a Hymn from the *Rigveda*, a collection of ten books comprising the earliest Aryan scriptures dating back as far as 1,500 BC Running to only fourteen verses, the last two verses go as follows:

> He the first origin of this creation, whether he formed it all or did not form it, Whose eye controls this world in highest heaven, he verily knows it, or perhaps he knows it not. (Book X, 129)[13]

11. *Journal of Humanistic Psychology* 25.1 (winter 1985).

12. "Clinical Computer Use at a CMHC," in *Micropsych Network* 3, no. 6 (August 1988); "Of Modern Inventions," in *Help-Software-a-Guide*, 2d ed. (CATSco, Inc.; July 1991 [4th ed. 1993]).

13. "The Song of Creation," 15–16.

Maury's response brought peace to Ruth's mind, because it replied to a real question with an authority that admits of uncertainty. As the Quakers would say, "it spoke to her condition."

I have had the experience repeatedly as I have studied and worked with Maury in many settings of seeing others enter into dialogues with him, welcomed by the manner in which he presented his materials. He brings his life into the presentation, and this makes it possible for the other to respond in kind. As one who has been at times responsible for getting Maury from one event to the next event in an always very full schedule, I frequently did not have the patience appropriate to those necessarily extended meetings! I note that Buber's ways were not much different, as he wrote to Maury in October 1957:

> For the first time I am not succeeding in coordinating the time *disponible* and the work that must be done before a certain time (in this case, my departure). Of course, much time is taken up by people wanting to talk to me, but I cannot change my way of receiving them all. And all the letters to be answered![14]

Martin Buber's first visit to the United States came late in October of 1951. It provided the opportunity for the first face-to-face meeting that Buber and Friedman had. Friedman writes of that first meeting:

> On October 31, Buber flew to New York from Israel. The seminary put him up at the Hotel Marcy on 96th Street and West End Avenue, where he resided throughout his stay in New York. The first time that I went to New York to see him was perhaps the most memorable of our many meetings over nine years. He received me into his apartment room and looked me searchingly in the eyes while taking my hand. My first response was to how totally "other" this man seemed after I had felt such kinship to him through his writings and letters. He was less than five feet. I am five feet ten. His eyes were of a depth, gentleness, and directness that I have never before or since encountered. He asked me to sit down. "You must not think that I am interested in you mostly because you have written a book on me," he said, and he added, speaking of himself, "my books are not what is important to me. They are like snake skins that I shed when I need to." I spoke to him of my wife: "She is very different from me." "All the better!" he responded. We also talked of women in general. "Someday you will learn that one woman is more than twenty."

14. Friedman, *The Later Years*, 234.

I understood what he meant: into one relationship one may bring one's whole self. Into twenty relationships one brings only fragments of oneself.[15]

This first visit of Buber's to America was a long one. He stayed for approximately six months. Friedman describes the hectic first (two month) portion of Buber's visit:

> Between November 8 and December 21 he delivered twenty lectures in New York, Cleveland, Chicago, and Detroit and at such colleges and universities as Dartmouth, Haverford, Brandeis, Yale, Columbia, The University of Chicago, and Wisconsin. In addition to these lectures, Buber received a stream of visitors, met with publishers, carried on an active correspondence with people all over the world, (and) worked with (Friedman) on translations of his lectures . . .[16]

Maury described his relationship with Buber during this time in the following way, which highlights the differences between Buber's relationships with Maury and with Eugenia Friedman:

> For all his understanding and confirmation of me, I often sensed that I struck Buber as decidedly different from the young persons he was used to. He was for me at that time, in fact, more the prophet of the It than the Thou. "If you do not bring your life into some sort of order, you will be a really unhappy man by the time you are fifty," he once said to me.

In addition to the roles of editor and translator for Buber, Friedman became more of an advisor and confidant during this visit. He also emerged as the keeper of the record:

> I never took a note during or even after my many conversations with Buber, so what has remained of them is only what Buber himself called the work of the "organic selective memory." At his public lectures and in seminars and discussion groups I did take notes.[17]

Buber objected to the presence of recording equipment, even rejecting an offered grant to cover filming of his seminars on *the unconscious* and on *dreams* during his second visit to America, as he felt strongly

15. Ibid., 140–41.
16. Ibid., 143.
17. Ibid, 142.

that such actions interfered with the spontaneity of events. He believed that the barriers to dialogue are already too great to begin with, without introducing such manifest connectedness to future audiences. Between the first and the second visits there were many publications by and about Buber which appeared in America, and his correspondence with prominent figures in the U.S. also was expanded.

Buber's second trip to America came in 1957. Leslie Farber, the third person to chair the Washington School of Psychiatry, proposed bringing Buber to the United States to give the Fourth Annual William Alanson White Memorial Lectures in 1956. Farber asked another faculty member, Maurice Friedman, to act as the go-between with Buber.

Martin Buber and his wife, Paula Buber, flew to Michigan in mid-April. A three-day intercollegiate seminar on his thought was held at the University of Michigan, with scholars taking part on panels. The famous exchange between Carl Rogers and Martin Buber was one of the events of this conference. This "dialogue in public" has been reprinted in several places; and commentary on it continues to appear in print.[18] Maurice Friedman, moderator for the session, notes that:

> After the dialogue, Buber said to me, "I was very kind to him. I could have been much sharper." But he also said that Rogers had really brought himself as a person and that it was because of this that there had been a real dialogue. In fact as a result, he canceled the last paragraph in the manuscript of "*Elements of the Interhuman*" in which he had stated that it was impossible to have a public dialogue.[19]

The Bubers' third visit to America came quickly, in the spring of 1958. Martin Buber had been invited to Princeton on a research fellowship. Princeton was to be a place for work and quiet for Buber, without the distractions of taking off for a week to participate in seminars. Buber did agree to give two public lectures on this journey: one for Princeton and one at the Union Theological Seminary in New York. It was at the house in Princeton, which had been given to the Bubers for the duration

18. Some forty years later, a new book was published during the winter of 1997: *The Martin Buber—Carl Roger's Dialogue: A New Transcript with Commentary*, by R. Anderson and K. N. Cissna (SUNY Series in Speech Communication, edited by: D. Cahn Jr.). In 2002 a book was published by the same authors and the same press and in the same series entitled, *Moments of Meeting: Buber, Rogers and the Potential for Public Dialogue*.

19. Friedman, *The Later Years*, 227.

of their stay that Friedman, and Buber met at great length, extending their collaboration. They worked on several joint projects; and for many hours at a time, through lunch and dinner, spending the night nearby at times, with Malcolm and Barbara Diamond, so as to get back to some project early the next day. Maurice notes in *The Later Years*: "Once Buber remarked to me in the basement where we did our work, 'What did you do to get involved with "*the Buber*"?' and his tone was a mixture of wonder and commiseration." Of course, I believe that Buber and Friedman, for all of their differences, were very much alike! The incident reminds me of an earlier passage in the same book (p. 211), wherein an exchange is recounted that I have heard told before:

> At one point we reached an impasse on the right punctuation to be used in breaking up one of Buber's overlong German sentences. "Grammar is not a subjective matter," Buber said to me and then, turning to Eugenia, who was present, he said, "Your husband is a very stubborn man." "You call *me* stubborn!" I exclaimed, when I finally realized that he was serious. Buber seemed to me by far the most stubborn person I had ever met. As Theodor Heuss expressed it more kindly a year later, in a letter to Buber on his eightieth birthday, "You have always been an inwardly independent man."

Maury dedicated . . . *The Later Years, 1945–1965*, which is the final book of the trilogy, *Martin Buber's Life and Works,* "For Eugenia who shared in my meetings with Martin Buber."

The fruits of the dialogue between Buber and Friedman have continued to appear since Martin Buber died. All but one of Friedman's major books on Buber were written after Buber's death. The serious scholarship that led to the three volume series, *Martin Buber's Life and Work*, took years of research as well as access to remote libraries and collections. That project outlasted many editors. Friedman gives an account of the struggle to produce those three volumes. He would need to travel to Jerusalem twice more, in 1966 and in 1969, for the purpose of accessing the archives on Buber in Israel, and of consulting with Buber's friends, family and other writers on Buber before he was able to write his first drafts. I recall reading an early draft of materials that I think was then in two volumes (or perhaps the second volume was pending, I am not sure) that was on reserve in the Temple University Library. It would have been around 1971. At that time the material was titled, *Encounter on the Narrow Ridge: Milestones in the Life of Martin Buber*, and it had a tentative publication date of fall, 1978. It would eventually become both *Martin Buber's Life and Work*, and *Encounter on the Narrow Ridge*. However one comes to it, the collaboration between Martin Buber and Maurice Friedman has greatly enriched my own field, psychotherapy. The way of response, inherent in the dialogical approach is implicit in many of the therapies that abound today. Even the managed care industry seems to rediscover that if you really listen to people, and then respond they are helped in ways that technique alone will not.

BIBLIOGRAPHY

Friedman, Maurice. *Encounter on the Narrow Ridge: A Life of Martin Buber*. New York: Paragon House, 1991

————. *Touchstones of Reality*. New York: Dutton, 1972.

————. *Martin Buber's Life and Work—The Later Years, 1945–1965*. New York: Dutton, 1983.

Stanton, Richard D. "Dialogue in Psychotherapy: Martin Buber, Maurice Friedman, and Therapists of Dialogue." PhD diss., Union Institute, 1978.

Yutang, Lin, editor. "The Song of Creation." In *The Wisdom of China and India*. New York: Modern Library, 1942.

3

Meaning and Non-Meaning

Maurice Friedman's Dialogue with Existentialism

JOHN-RAPHAEL STAUDE

"Life can only be understood backwards; it has to be lived forwards."

—Søren Kierkegaard

"It is only in the face of death that man's self is born."

—St. Augustine

RECENTLY, WHEN I ASKED Maurice Friedman about the current relevance of existentialism, he read me the following sentence from his introduction to his anthology *The Worlds of Existentialism*: "There is no question that existentialism remains one of the most important philosophical, literary, and psychological movements of the twentieth century—one that will continue to have its impact on centuries to come, whether subsumed under this label or not."

"Yes, but how is it relevant today in light of the discourse of post-structuralism and postmodernism?" I asked. Returning to the same page, Maurice told me of a student who had asked a similar question and read to me his comment: "I wondered at a graduate student's setting his clock by the question of what was intellectually fashionable rather than by the question of what was important to him."

That response set me to thinking and helped me to find my way back towards my own values and intellectual roots. Unfortunately I had almost forgotten them, in my efforts to fit into contemporary intellectual life, rather than having the courage to be myself and to stand by my own beliefs and values, as Maurice has done all his life. I hope this essay does just that, and if it does then once again I have Maurice to thank for guiding me back to myself.

INTRODUCTION

> Human beings are the kind of beings who are always presented with a choice between meaning and non-meaning, between regarding the world and their existence as significant and valuable or feeling them to be meaningless and valueless. This choice is not usually a conscious decision. It is more often a slipping into one or another alternative way of living, alternative realms into which a human being or a whole community can fall.[1]

In the first half of the twentieth century, analytic philosophers banished the question of the meaning of life from rational discourse. Western philosophy until recently has offered at best an ambivalent response to questions about the meaning of life. Anglo-American analytic philosophy for many years dismissed the question of the meaning of life as illegitimate. An extreme point of view developing largely under the influence of logical positivism, held that the phrase "the meaning of life" was actually meaningless.

For analytic philosophers questions reaching beyond empirical knowledge were viewed as attempts at metaphysics. In recent years this hostility to metaphysical questions has diminished and become less doctrinaire and, in conjunction with a renewed interest in consciousness and the mind-body problem, some prominent analytic philosophers have suggested that questions about the meaning of life are intelligible and, in fact, important.[2] The current tendency in philosophy is to reaffirm traditional questions of global meaning, while at the same time avoiding the traditional religious or metaphysical answers, that have been given to the meaning of life in the past.

The force of philosophical argument in our time is to drive a wedge between meaning for an individual life and any wider sense of meaning that could have a rational foundation, reinforcing the split between

---

1. Cahoone, *Dilemma of Modernity*, 283.

2. A few, like Joseph Needleman, have even questioned whether academic philosophical thinking in the analytic tradition is itself somehow debarred from coming to grips with the full existential depth of the question of ultimate meaning in life.

our public and private worlds. Modern analytic thought maintains that objective elements of meaning beyond the self—the meaning of life as a whole—are not necessary or sufficient conditions for the subjective sense of meaning, the meaning of an individual's life. However, some argue that even if the universe as a whole or human history as a whole lacks meaning, nonetheless, *my life* can have a meaning.

Maurice Friedman's dialogical existential philosophy must be understood as a response to the intellectual and cultural disorientation of our time. There is a deep continuity that runs through his writings, evident in his commitment to persons and to interpersonal dialogue as well as in his concern with "the hidden human image." All of these concerns are mirrored in and grew out of his lifelong dialogue with existential philosophy and literature, particularly his dialogue with the life and work of the existential philosopher and religious thinker Martin Buber.

WHAT IS EXISTENTIALISM?

The existential perspective in philosophy has roots that can be traced back to the Greek philosopher. Heraclites, who taught that being alive is to be in flux. This is a cornerstone of the existential perspective. Existentialists argue that we are not set, certain, irrevocable substantial selves. They recognize that we are conflictually defined and are sometimes terrifyingly confused or unclear about who and what we are, even when others are able to give us a clear set of definitions in terms of our complex involvements in role play. They recognize that we can recreate ourselves, but that doing so is often a difficult, non-rationalizable activity with uncertain outcomes. They recognize that who we are, what we are, and what we want is continually in process of becoming and that we ourselves—though we may be able to affect the outcomes of the process of becoming through our continual struggles—are not able to dictate the outcome of this flux. They recognize that we ourselves—our minds our hearts, our society, our bodies—are in constant flux and that uncomfortable as this sometimes makes us feel, flux is crucial in our everyday lives.[3]

As a philosophy and cultural movement in its own right, Existentialism was homologous with the political, social and cultural crisis of Western civilization in the first half of the twentieth century. Its apoca-

3. Compare Douglas and Johnson. *Existential Sociology*.

lyptic sense of doom and crisis was part of the intellectual and cultural response to the collapse of the Old World, specifically the end of the civilization of Old Europe after the First and Second World Wars. It represented a sense of ending.[4]

The central concern of existential philosophy, literature, and art was the meaning of life—or lack thereof—and to understand how to live an *authentic* existence in a world where traditional meanings were no longer convincing. While existential thinkers differed in their answers, most agreed on the importance of the question of the meaning of life, or lack thereof.

In his books Maurice Friedman speaks of it as more of a *mood or style of thinking* than a philosophical school:

> "Existentialism" is not a philosophy but a mood embracing a number of disparate philosophies; the differences among them are more basic than the temper which unites them. This temper can best be described as a reaction against the static, the abstract, the purely rational, the merely irrational, in favor of the dynamic and the concrete, personal involvement and engagement, action, choice, and commitment, the distinction between authentic and inauthentic existence and the actual situation of the existential subject as the starting point of thought. Existential philosophy and literature begins from the concrete lived experience of the person in his historically conditioned life situation. We are beings situated in time and space with a specific individual and cultural life history. [5]

Sartre coined the name "existentialism" in his book *Existentialism is a Humanism* in 1946, though Jaspers had already spoken of a philosophy of *Existenz* in 1930. Existential philosophers reacted against the positivist view that the universe is a closed, coherent, and intelligible system. The existentialists found the resulting contingency of life a cause for lamentation as well as celebration. In the face of an indifferent universe, men like Sartre argued, we are thrown back on our own *freedom,* and are challenged in the process to act *authentically* in the light of the *horizon* or open space of possibilities that the indeterminacy of the world allows.

---

4. See for example Frank Kermode's analysis of existential themes in his book *The Sense of an Ending,* and the essays collected in Jasper and Crowder, eds., *European Literature and Theology in the Twentieth Century.*

5. Friedman, *Worlds,* 2–3.

The existentialists had tried to bring philosophy down to earth again, he said, but like the analytical philosophers they offered only one half of the story. They presented a passionate concern with questions that arise from life, the moral pathos and the firm belief that a philosophy has to be lived. The analytic philosophers, on the other hand, insisted that no moral pathos nor tradition however elevated could be taken seriously if it rested on unanalyzed ideas, murky arguments or the confusion they found in the writings of Nietzsche, Sartre and Heidegger. At the end of his book Kaufmann suggested that "the task of the future is to live and think in the tension between analysis and existentialism."

It was into this contested intellectual field that Friedman had launched his career as a young professor of philosophy and literature at Sarah Lawrence College in 1951. In the anthology *The Worlds of Existentialism,* which he published eight years after Kaufmann's reader, Friedman maintained that since in the interval Existentialism had become better known in America, the time was ripe for a more serious "mature" and comprehensive presentation and evaluation of it. His book, he hoped, would correct the popular distortions, oversimplifications and stereotypes that had grown up around it.

To begin with, he offered an exploration of the multiple worlds of Existentialism, through readings from original sources emphasizing the diversity of the movement. Secondly, by including selections from many "forerunners" he attempted to position Existentialism as a core tradition in Western thought and culture running from Heraclitus, the Hebrew prophets, and Hasidic Rabbis through Christians such as St. Matthew, Meister Eckhart, Pascal, and Dostoevsky, to atheists and militant anti-Christians like Feurbach, Marx, and Nietzsche.

Whereas Walter Kaufmann's 1956 paperback, *Existentialism From Dostoevsky to Sartre,* was designed to introduce a wider public to existentialism. It was organized chronologically by author to tell the story of the development of Existentialism as a movement, Friedman's 562-page reader published in hardback by Random House was a very different proposition. The aim, he wrote in the preface was "to bring out the critical issues that exist among the existentialists in their treatment of such subjects as phenomenology, the existential subject, intersubjectivity, religion, and psychotherapy. In order to accomplish this aim it presents a large number of short selections from the most important existentialist writers and their forerunners." The selections were to be "subsumed under themes rather than presented separately by authors."

Throughout the book, which is organized topically, in contrast to Kaufmann's author-based organization, Friedman stresses the profound and often subtle differences among the existential philosophers. One of his concerns in doing this was to correct the popular stereotype of existentialism derived from Sartre's widely publicized 1946 lecture, "Existentialism is a Humanism" as being exclusively atheistic, pessimistic, and individualistic. "The majority of existentialists," he points out, "are not atheists and there is nothing in existentialism per se that necessitates atheism."[6] This was related to his second objective: to make a place for religious existentialism and particularly for the dialogical existential approach deriving from Camus, Marcel, and Buber, among others.[7]

When I asked Maurice Friedman when and why he first become interested in existential philosophy he replied that it was through a series of random encounters with existential writers and thinkers when he was a young man in the 1940s. "I had read Nietzsche and Dostoevsky when I was still a schoolboy," he told me. In college he read Kafka and Kierkegaard, but only discovered Buber during the war through a fellow Conscientious Objector. Soon after that he read *I and Thou* and *The Legend of the Baal Shem*. "What made Existentialism attractive to me," he said, "was that it was concrete and personal rather than abstract. I appreciated its emphasis on the uniqueness of each individual life. It suited me very well, at the time I discovered it and helped me to find my own voice."

Though there were some profound personal and cultural differences among the Existential philosophers, what they shared that appealed to Friedman was a common concern with the meaning of life and an acceptance of the uniqueness of the individual person including his own unique concrete way of being in the world, his own personal consciousness, will, decision, commitment, alienation, authenticity, subjectivity and intersubjectivity, his own body and his own death. Here he felt he had found a philosophy that sought to do justice to the unique-

---

6. Ibid., 242.

7. "Nothing has so impeded the popular understanding of the complexity of existentialism as Jean-Paul Sartre's essay 'Existentialism is a Humanism,' . . . his facile definition of existentialism as 'existence precedes essence' is not only not true, in that form for most existentialists, but is not even true for Sartre himself" (Friedman, *Worlds*, 239).

ness of the lived experience of each person rather than subsume them into some generalized abstraction as most other philosophies did. From his studies of the Existentialists, Friedman concluded that the task of life is to wrest meaning from the concrete, from the absurd, from the situation in which we find ourselves at the moment.

Often Friedman did not agree with what he read in the Existentialist's writings. For example, he found both Kierkegaard and Heidegger's rejection of society for the lonely relation of the "single one"—whether to God or the self—unsatisfactory. Also, their notion of intersubjectivity, he felt, did not take adequate account of the real nature of dialogue and the healing that can occur through interpersonal encounters between men.

Although he claims that his approach is historical, actually except for half a dozen pages on Heidegger's' involvement with National Socialism, and some generalizations about the alienation of modern man, in his studies of existential philosophy and literature, Friedman eschews any historical analysis of the concrete political-social-cultural context which shaped them. This is unfortunate because the main ideas and values debated among French existentialists like Merleau-Ponty, Sartre and Camus can only really be understood when viewed in the historical context of the intellectual climate of the forties and fifties in which they were articulated.

Let me give an example. What Sartre in 1945 called being "situated in one's times" was something that he and other French intellectuals had felt during the occupation and in the resistance. Intellectuals like Sartre, Camus, de Beauvoir and Merleau-Ponty felt that they had been waiting for such a moment all their lives and welcomed the chance to participate in a romantic crusade and collective commitment whose scope and meaning would transform, transcend, and give a practical impulse to their earlier writings. They felt that whatever happened was their responsibility, even if—especially if—they chose to abstain from choice. Being a part of History gave a meaning to their lives. Being faced with the choice between collaboration and resistance meant taking seriously the idea of evil, and the possibility that human existence hung in the moral balance and must be defended and reclaimed. Their preference for personal embodied engaged action over impersonal objective critical analysis or the disembodied reflection of a transcendental ego must be seen in this historic context.

As an historian of modern France put it: "The dilemma between 'being' and 'doing' which had seemed so significant before the war collapsed. To do was to be: no longer a universal consciousness vested in a singular self, the intellectual was bound within the organic community and there presented with apparently clear and simple choices, all of which entailed action of one sort or another."[8] Only a few actively participated militarily in the resistance, but what was important to these intellectuals was their moral association with the community of resisters, the sense of being part of something larger than oneself—a circle of dissenting writers, a resistance group, a clandestine political organization, or History itself. *Résistantialisme* preceded and provided the context and impulse for *existentialisme.*

French Existentialism was a product of the war experience. Intellectuals who had identified with the Resistance emerged from the war years with a paradoxical sense of themselves and their purpose. It allowed them to identify and even merge themselves for a time with the actions and movement of a whole society. Their experience of war and resistance was important to them precisely to the extent that it contrasted with and seemed to annul their previous sense of alienation and isolation. And their engagement as intellectuals on the side of a historical movement bequeathed to them a special sense of duty and "obligation to articulate and pursue what they understood to be the lessons of the war years, both in politics and in their own professional activities as responsible intellectuals."[9]

THE HIDDEN HUMAN IMAGE

From his first book to his last Friedman was concerned with coming to terms with the plight of modern man, with, as he says, "modern man's hopeless sense of the earth hurtling through the empty space of the heavens on its meaningless progress to extinction, with the apparent meaninglessness and absurdity of human existence. The heartless immensity forces us to realize our own limitedness, our own mortality. When a man loses his limits he has lost that condition that makes human existence possible."[10]

8. Judt, *Past Imperfect*, 34. See also Merleau-Ponty "La Guerre a eu lieu," and his letter to the journal *Action* (74 [February 1, 1946]).

9. Ibid.

10. *Problematic Rebel.* Limitlessness is the enemy of art, as well.

He found that it was not only an awareness of the infinity of time and space that threatened modern man but his own inner dividedness and alienation, his increasing inability to trust existence, and to face life with confidence. "Modern man sees himself less and less as a self with a ground on which to stand, or a center within. He often appears to be drowning and feels lost, confused and terrified. The world to which he must relate seems strange, and without fixed reference points he becomes increasingly disoriented, facing a world he experiences as meaningless, hostile and alien."

Friedman found the ultimate terror of existence he read about in the existential philosophers expressed even more graphically in *existential literature*. Kafka, Dostoevsky, Melville, Rilke, Sartre, and Camus. These were the writers that moved him, that made the ideas of the existential philosophers real for him, that touched his soul. This is probably because, as Milan Kundera wrote in *The Art of the Novel*: "a novel examines not reality but existence. And existence is not what has occurred, existence is the realm of human possibilities, everything that . . . [one] can become, everything . . . [one is] capable of. Novelists draw up the map of existence by discovering this or that human possibility."[11]

At Sarah Lawrence College in the fifties, as the ideas of the existential philosophers began to spread through philosophy and literature departments on U.S. campuses, Friedman expounded on existential themes in modern literature and thought in a course entitled "Images of Man in Modern Literature."[12]

He later elaborated upon the existential despair, alienation and apocalyptic angst of modern man in his trilogy on the image of man in modern philosophy and literature which began with the publication of the first edition of his book *Problematic Rebel: An Image of Modern Man* in 1963. There Friedman sought to illustrate this alienation through many examples drawn from literature and to offer a response to it.

In Dostoevsky's fiction Friedman found already adumbrated the familiar existentialist themes: the awareness of the *angst* of human existence, its anguish and dread, the recovery of man's alienated freedom, the emphasis upon the particular fact and upon the absurd, and the "man-god's" proclamation of self-will in remarkable anticipation of

11. Kundera, "Dialogue," 42.

12. These lectures, along with his master's thesis, formed the basis for his books *Problematic Rebel* and *To Deny Our Nothingness: Contemporary Images of Man*.

Nietzsche and Sartre.[13] Here the anxiety of what Friedman called "the Modern Exile" is manifested in his isolation from other men, inner emptiness, and inauthenticity. The Underground Man, Raskolnikov, Svidrigailov, Kirilov, Stavrogin and Ivan Karamzaov are all essentially isolated from other men and their attempts to break out of this isolation such as Raskolnikov's murder of the pawnbroker woman and Stavrogin's debauchery left them more isolated still. Here Friedman found his own personal answer to the crisis of modern consciousness in the lonely figure of Job, the man of faith who dared to confront God.[14]

Kafka was important for Friedman as a Jew like himself who seriously took upon himself the problematic of facing the absurdity of modern existence, yet not losing faith and hope. In Kafka's *The Trial* we find Joseph K so alienated from life that in trying to handle his case as a business deal he comes to forget it almost entirely and then abandons his position at the bank in favor of futile efforts to circumvent a judgment that he can never comprehend.

All of these examples point to what Friedman calls "the problematic of modern man" a complex balance of personal freedom and psychological compulsion. Existential writers like Dostoevsky and Kafka reveal the discontinuities of a personal existence in which one sometimes acts relatively wholly and spontaneously but more often out of a conditioned reflex or partial compulsion and sometimes in such a way that one cannot tell which.

Influenced by neo-Freudians Erich Fromm and Karen Horney's socio-cultural approach to psychoanalysis, Friedman recognized that the illness of modern man is not just an *individual neurosis* but is the result of *his uprooting from the community in which he formerly lived*, an aspect of his existence as an exile in the modern world. Similarly, the modern man who goes through the crisis of motives in which he can no longer take both other people's motives or his own at face value. This leads to a mutual distrust or mistrust in which people cease to confirm one another which leads to a fragmentation of the self in which each person is incapable of confirming himself or anyone else.

"How can we live in the face of the anxiety in our culture?" Friedman asks. Have we no choice but to accept and embrace those very cultural

---

13. See Friedman, *Problematic Rebel*, 197–208.

14. In his later book, *The Hidden Human Image*, Friedman discussed the life and work of his close friend Elie Wiesel as the "Job of Auschwitz."

forms that help us to repress our anxiety—only to see it break out afresh in new areas intensified and reduplicated? "Not necessarily," he concludes. "It is also possible to revolt against our modern exile rather than to deny or underscore it." But the way we revolt against it makes all the difference. The issue is whether this revolt will result in more anxiety or whether we can hold our own before the anxiety. Only if we can distance ourselves from our anxiety, rather than identifying completely with it, and drowning in it or being paralyzed by it, can we create some margin for a human and even meaningful existence.

Friedman identifies two fundamentally different ways of revolt in modern literature, through the archetypal images of Prometheus and Job. The Modern Promethean, he says, represents a romantic revolt that in the end can only make man subject to the very anxiety he is trying to escape. Examples of Center Prometheans are characters in the works of Dostoevsky, Nietzsche, and Sartre. The Modern Job, on the other hand, represents a sober unprogrammatic revolt that accepts the anxiety of our culture yet [by courageously confronting it] gains real ground in the face of it. Examples of this attitude are embodied in characters in the writings of Kafka, Camus and Eli Wiesel.

Drawing on images from Kafka's novel *The Castle*, Friedman insists that "our task is not to reject the Village for the sake of the Castle or the Castle for the sake of the Village, but to bring the Castle and the Village into fruitful interrelationship with each other. We do not find true existence by leaving the ground of the actual for the ideal or for a solitary relationship with God [as in Kierkegaard]. We find it by 'hallowing the everyday.'"

By neither accepting nor rejecting reality nor cutting ourselves off from the anxiety driving our culture but courageously standing our ground in its midst, [both fighting and dialoging with it and receiving from it] Friedman believes that we may be able to discover and attain the meaning it has to give us. For this is the task of life, in his view, like Jacob to wrestle with the angel and force him to reveal the meaning of the situation in which we find ourselves. The treasure, says Buber, is "here where we stand, where we live a true life." This reality may seem alien and resistant to our ideas and ideals. But, as Friedman says, quoting Camus, "we cannot escape History since we are in it up to our necks. But one may propose to fight within history to preserve from it that part of man which is not its proper province."[15]

15. Friedman, *Worlds*, 16.

If the rhetoric and poetic tone of *Problematic Rebel* often sounds more like literary and cultural criticism than philosophy this is no accident. Many of the leading French existentialists such as Sartre Camus, Malraux, Bernanos and de Beauvoir expressed their ideas through the medium of fiction and literary and cultural essays as much as through philosophical discourse. Similarly Friedman's existentialism derives as much from his studies of existential literature and his own personal experience of Jewish religious culture as from philosophy.

In the conclusion to his *Existentialism* reader Friedman discussed the relation between existentialism as philosophy and existentialism as literature. He argued that "if existentialism means a turning toward the particular and the concrete, we cannot help comparing the abstractness and abstruseness of a great many existentialist philosophies with the relatively greater concreteness and particularity of existentialist literature."[16] He pointed to the works of Kafka, Sartre and Camus as examples. "When a writer is aware of anxiety and of the emptiness of existence," he said, "he does not need to hypostasize that awareness into a negative metaphysics." Kafka stays close to the concrete and does not go outside the actual situation and experience of his characters, even when they are set in relation to a reality that transcends them. In fact Friedman judged that as compared to writers like Kafka all existentialist philosophy seems essentialist by virtue of the fact that it deals with abstract concepts like *Dasein,* for-itself, I-Thou rather than with the truly unique. In saying this Friedman is not denying the validity of existential philosophy, but simply warning us that "the philosophers themselves do not seem to be aware that there is a limit to their claim and that speaking about existence is a long way from dealing with existence itself."[17]

CONCLUSION

Today neither the universe as a whole nor human history as a whole inspires confidence in total or objective meaning. Consequently people go about their lives pursuing a form of meaning that is increasingly privatized. This private pursuit of meaning is often irreligious, and people increasingly lack confidence in any grand design. They seek to find meaning in little things, in personal relationships and in their life stories

16. Ibid., 544.

17. Friedman, *Worlds,* 544–45.

themselves. For all too many, however, as T. S. Eliot said, they have "had the experience but missed the meaning."

To some existentialism may see just "a leap from the inconceivable to the absolutely unthinkable." To others, however, despite the abstruseness of the language, existentialism offers a range of meaningful ways in which human existence is being illuminated in our day. It offers those who are open to exploring it methods and subjects of 'existential illumination' noticeably absent from most schools of modern philosophy which have excluded from the outset existential knowledge and the wholeness of man from their concern.

For Friedman philosophy means bearing witness. In his assessment of the significance of existential philosophy in the conclusion to his reader he wrote: "The issue that must be placed before all existentialist thought [is that of] the relation of existentialist thought to life itself, the question of whether one can authenticate one's truth in one's everyday world." Buber said more or less the same thing when he cautioned Rollo May: "everything else may be discussed purely speculatively, but not our existence. The genuine existentialist must himself 'exist.' An existentialism that contents itself with theory is a contradiction; existence is not one philosophical theme among others. Here witness is made."

We have seen that according to Friedman, beyond a few common points, Existentialism is not a single philosophical school but rather a way of thinking and being that offers a plurality of perspectives and approaches to the meaning of life. Its essence he argued, was its concreteness and its recognition of the uniqueness of each individual life situation.

Perhaps Friedman's most significant contribution to the understanding of Existentialism as a cultural movement was precisely this: to demonstrate its great richness and variety. With his anthology, *Worlds of Existentialism,* he showed us that it must be seen as a contested terrain rather than as a harmoniously integrated intellectual movement. Reading through his writings on existentialism with this in mind we can see exhibited a variety of intellectual subcultures and traditions any or all of which we can use as stepping off points for our own dialogue with the absurd and our own reflections on the meaning of life and death, specifically of our lives and our own moral responsibilities.[18]

18. For example, Thierry Pauchant and his colleagues at the University of Montreal Business School have sought to apply existential concepts to the field of administrative

BIBLIOGRAPHY

Cahoone, Lawrence E. *The Dilemma of Modernity: Philosophy, Culture and Anti-Culture.* Albany: SUNY Press, 1988.

Douglas, Jack, and John Johnson. *Existential Sociology.* Cambridge: Cambridge University Press, 1977.

Friedman, Maurice. *The Hidden Human Image.* New York: Delacorte Press, Delta Books, 1974.

————. *Problematic Rebel: An Image of Modern Man.* New York: Random House, 1963.

————. *To Deny Our Nothingness: Contemporary Images of Man.* New York: Delacorte, 1967.

————, editor. *The Worlds of Existentialism: A Critical Reader.* New York: Random House, 1964.

Jasper, David, and Colin Crowder, editors. *European Literature and Theology in the Twentieth Century.* London: Macmillan, 1990.

Judt, Tony. *Past Imperfect: French Intellectuals 1944–1956.* Berkeley: University of California Press, 1992.

Kermode, Frank. *The Sense of an Ending: Studies in the Theory of Fiction.* Oxford: Oxford University Press, 1966.

Kundera, Milan. "Dialogue on the Art of Composition." In *The Art of the Novel.* New York: Grove, 1987.

Merleau-Ponty. "La Guerre a eu lieu." *Les temps modernes* 1 (October 1945) 64.

Pauchant, Thierry C., and Associates. *In Search of Meaning: Managing for the Health of Our Organizations, Our Communities, and the Natural World.* San Francisco: Jossey-Bass, 1994.

---

and management sciences elaborating the principles of what Pauchant calls a holistic "organizational existentialism" to understand the richness and potential of organizational life. Coincidentally, I found a copy of this book in Maurice's library, with a dedication from the authors, acknowledging his influence on their work. See Pauchant and Associates, *In Search of Meaning.*

PART ONE: AFTERWORD

Dialogical Knowing

UNDERLYING BOTH THE IMAGE of the human and touchstones of reality, as Friedman uses these terms, is a dialogical approach to knowledge that holds that it is in the immediacy of contact that we know and that our objective I-It knowledge is derived from this I-Thou knowing. This means that in our approach to the human sciences as a whole we must be concerned with the dialectical alternation between I-Thou knowing and I-It knowledge or, to put it another way, between dialogue and dialectic.

A dialogical pedagogy, Friedman writes, is that approach to becoming authentically human which is founded on the ontology of the between—the recognition that we become the unique persons we are called to be only in dialogue with other selves. The psychological, that which happens within the soul of each person, is only the secret accompaniment to the dialogue. The meaning of this dialogue is found in neither one nor the other of the partners, nor in both added together, but in their interchange. Dialogical knowing begins in the I-Thou relationship of mutuality, presence, openness, and directness and only then goes over to the categories and structures of the I-It, or subject-object knowledge.

This is particularly true of "non-statistical" research—theoretical, philosophical, historical, phenomenological, existentialist, humanistic, or case study. Of central importance to such qualitative research is that in every case the proper methodology is developed only *after* the tasks of discovering the larger area of interest, delimiting the parameters of this area, and focusing on issues and problems within this delimited area is completed. The researcher begins with some general methodological approach, but the specific methodology that the researcher uses should develop in dialectic with the research itself, particularly as it moves into depth studies of individual cases. There is no single right methodology for all cases but only the methodology that best helps one investigate the problem that one has chosen. At the same time, the basic tool of qualitative research is an open-ended dialogue among those methods that are employed.

Many people set out to do research as if the other (person, place, thing, or text) were just an object and as if there were just one method. But in true research you have to have genuine dialogic participation. To stimulate dialogues with and about ideas presented in Part One you may wish to consider the following questions (whether general or chapter-specific) about the central concepts of each chapter.

To stimulate dialogues with and about ideas presented in Part One you may wish to consider the following questions (whether general or chapter-specific) about the central concepts of each chapter. How would you respond to these questions if, for example, you were speaking to the author of that chapter? How, for instance, do the concerns raised by these questions implicate your life-situation? How would you, assuming you were writing an essay about a similar concern, construct it differently? What materials, which authors, what stories would you select to clarify and deepen your stand? Moreover, if you were personally addressing the authors of these chapters, what question would you ask of them?

Friedman (chapter 1): How do I find the calling through which I become myself responsible to the world's call? Building on Friedman's understanding of experiencing the other side, pick one object/person/place which you see/visit/come into contact with on a daily basis, but something that you take for granted. Now, re-imagine your life but seen through the eyes of this object/person/place. Imagine that you are a periphery on the edges of their life, the same way they are a periphery on yours. Are you more aware of others afterwards?

Stanton (chapter 2): discusses how the dialogue between Maurice Friedman and Martin Buber generated a great deal of Friedman's important work and thought. Imagine having a dialogue with one of the important formative people in your life—what would you like to generate, or what do you think would be generated, from such a dialogue?

Staude (chapter 3): In relation to Staude's discussion of Friedman's view of authenticity, what makes your life authentic? What is your central concern—that thing without which, you wouldn't be you? Why?

Another way to encourage dialogue with the ideas and concerns presented here would be to imagine yourself as a student in one of Professor Friedman's classes. The purpose of education, for Friedman, is to establish a "learning community," one in which there is genuine concern for the otherness of the others. The true teacher has always been aware that, above all, he or she is confronting students with images of the human and that it is precisely through this confrontation that the student is educated. The unique response of every student to the image of the human is that which draws forth the potentialities of becoming and transforms students into "educated" persons who are able to embody and express tradition and thereby become more uniquely human.

In order to understand the values, reasoning, and points of view of his students, Friedman assigned personal academic journals with four steps.

- **Step one** is for the student to select from the reading something that strikes him or her and to write it down in the journal.

- **Step two** is to try then to put it in one's own words, not by translating the quotation into familiar categories or constructs, but by swinging imaginatively over to where the other person is speaking from.

- **Step three** is coming back to one's own side and entering into dialogue with the author's words—both intellectually and emotionally—from where one is.

- **Step four** is to relate what one is commenting on to ongoing issues of the course and of one's life.

How would you apply this journal strategy, either by thinking through a theme or motif from one of the essays or writing about a specific passage that really engages you? To arrive at a more integrated understanding of Friedman's interdisciplinary humanism, you may wish to compare your response to his essay in this part with your response to his other chapters in Parts 2, 3, and 4.

PART TWO

Literature as Dialogue

"LITERATURE IS THE REAL homeland of the image of the human, for it retains the concrete uniqueness of individual persons. At the same time, it allows us a relationship with these persons sufficiently close for them to speak to us as bearers of the human."

—Maurice Friedman

4

The Poetics of Dialogue

The Human Image

MAURICE FRIEDMAN

FTER THE ERAS IN literary theory stretching from the New Criticism and Structuralism to Deconstructionism and post-Deconstructionism, the present situation of literary criticism is necessarily a pluralistic one. I know of no better approach to that situation than to take seriously literature as dialogue and to enter in all seriousness into dialogue with literature. The present pluralistic situation calls for a nonhierarchical egalitarian model for the relationship between the reader and the text and between different interpretations, even though, as Martin Buber, the philosopher of dialogue, stresses, the struggle for a "common logos" is not a team hitched to a wagon but a strenuous tug of war.

The most fruitful approach to literature, in my opinion, is to take seriously the full address of literature to the reader as a whole human person and to discover in our meeting with it that image of authentic human existence that is implicit in the very style of most great literature. In its very particularity, the image of the human in literature gives us the wholeness of the human as more abstract disciplines cannot. Next to the lives of actual persons, literature comes closest to retaining the concrete uniqueness of individual human beings while at the same time enabling us to enter into a sufficiently close relationship with these human beings that they can speak to us as bearers of the human—as exemplifications of what it does and can mean to be a human being.

POINTS OF VIEW

Literature as dialogue implies the meeting between the image of the human, or basic attitude, of the reader and that of the author. This means the combination of faithfulness to literature in its concrete uniqueness and otherness, including the whole fullness of style and form, with response to that literature from the ground of one's own uniqueness, one's life, and one's situation. It is not the symbol, myth, or metaphor, still less the theological concept or metaphysical idea, but the tension of points of view that discloses the true dimension of a novel or a play. A really faithful listening will make it impossible to reduce the work to a single, directly expressed point of view.

All of this applies also to what we call the literature of ideas. So far from lying in one person's isolated consciousness, the idea begins to live and human thought becomes genuine when it enters into genuine dialogical relationship with the ideas of others embodied in someone else's voice. The idea does not reside in a person's head but in dialogic communion between consciousnesses. It is a live event, played out at the point of dialogic meeting and, like the word with which it is dialogically united, wants to be heard, understood, and "answered" by other voices. Even in the so-called "novel of ideas," the author does not think up ideas the way the philosopher does. He "hears" them as they enter reality itself, including the "latent, unuttered future word." Not only is the idea inseparable from the person; but also the voice of the person is inseparable from the dialogue between I and Thou, The person departs, having spoken his word, but the word itself remains in the open-ended dialogue. The authentic sphere where language lives is dialogic interaction. "The mystery of the coming-to-be of language and that of the coming-to-be of man are one," writes Martin Buber.

COMMUNAL LOGOS

It is the communal nature of the logos as at once "word" and "meaning" that makes a person human. The dialogic self stands in faithful dialogue with the word and the voice of the author, and it is just through this dialogue with the other readers and interpreters of literature that they build together the common logos of literature as speech with meaning.

The image of the human and touchstones of reality are two basic metaphors and methodological approaches to human existence and meaning that I have developed independently of each other and at different times. Each grew out of my concern for communicating the interdisciplinary and intercultural significance of dialogue. Though not synonyms, they are reciprocal and reciprocating ways of pointing to the concrete, lived reality of becoming authentically human. Both metaphors emphasize an open dialogue with what we meet, both emphasize discontinuity, both emphasize events. But the image of the human speaks of a gradual building up of our human attitude, as much unconscious as conscious, whereas touchstones of reality come to us in sequence like a rock path across a lake, such as one sees at a Zen Buddhist temple in Kyoto.

DIALOGICAL KNOWING

The dialogical is that approach to human existence which is founded on the ontology of the between—the recognition that we become the unique persons we are called to be only in dialogue with other selves. Dialogical knowing begins in the I-Thou relationship of mutuality, presence, openness, and directness and only then goes over to the categories and structures of the I-It, or subject-object relation. The dialogical enters into the image of the human through the fact that the "image" that we are talking about is not the eighteenth-century notion of a picture of an already existing sense object, but the twentieth-century understanding of a person as the meeting between the human person and the "X" that cannot be unknown as it is in itself. Thus if all people should have Gandhi as their image of the human, nonetheless each would have the unique image that arose from their unique dialogue with Gandhi.

The image of the human involves our becoming—the tension of the "is" and the "ought" in our personal, communal, and social existence. Human's come to awareness of themselves not just through individuality or difference from others but in dialogue with other selves—in their response and in the way they call the other into being. Because one lives as a separate self, yet in relation to other persons and to society, present, past and future, one needs an image of the human to ground one's finding a meaningful way of living. In choosing between conflicting sets of values, in reaching one's own unique potentialities, the image of the human is an embodiment of an attitude and a response. Whether it is an image shared by only one person or by a society as a whole, the individual stands in unique personal relation to it. One's image of the human is not an objective, universal St. Francis, but the St. Francis who emerges from one's own meeting with this historical and legendary figure.

DIRECT MUTUAL RELATIONSHIP

It is only in a direct, mutual relationship that I grasp completely the unique value of the other, experience her side of the relationship and know what can help her. Yet I do not necessarily cease to deal lovingly or at least respectfully, even when she is no longer Thou for me in any but a formal, or potential, sense. I carry the other with me, as it were, as one for whom I am responsible and one to whom I am ready to respond when I meet her again. But when I meet her again, she will not be the same as she was before, and very often I must meet someone with whom I have had no previous real relationship. It is the image of the human and not my universal precept that enables me to say, "nothing human is alien to me." The image of the human enters into and forms that attitude which makes me ready to meet and respond to any persons whatever as a human being with human dignity, someone I stand open to know, to respect, perhaps even to love. Thus the image of the human plays an essential role in linking one moment of realized dialogue with another. It is often, the very form in which dialogue remains potential, awaiting its actualization.

The image of the human can be traced back to 1951 when I first started teaching at Sarah Lawrence College. It has been connected for me with the search for a meaningful and direction-giving image of personal and social existence and as such has figured centrally in six of my books: *Problematic Rebel* (1963 and expanded and reorganized 1970). *To Deny Our Nothingness: Contemporary Images of Man* (1967), *The Hidden Human Image* (1974), *Contemporary Psychology: Revealing and Concealing the Human* (1984), *Dialogue and the Human Image: Beyond Humanistic Psychology* (1992); and *Intercultural Dialogue and the Human Image: Maurice Friedman at the Indira Gandhi Centre for the Arts* [New Delhi] (1995).

A WAY OF RESPONDING

First, if we wish to make a decisive break with the universal and essential "human nature" of earlier philosophy and attain a picture of the human in its uniqueness and wholeness, we must move from *concepts* about the human, no matter how profound, to the *image* of the human. The human image, as I use the term, is not only an image of what we are but also an image of authentic personal and social existence that helps us discover, in each age anew, what we may and can become, an image that helps us rediscover our humanity. "Image" in this context means not a static picture, but a meaningful, personal direction, a response from within to what one meets in the new situation, standing one's ground and meeting the world with the attitude that is rooted in this ground.

The human image embodies a way of responding. Because it is faithful response and not objective content that is central to the human image, each individual stands in a unique personal relation to his or her image of the human, even when it happens to be shared by a society as a whole. One becomes one's self in dialogue with other selves and in response to one's image, one's images of the human. Yet, the more genuine the dialogue, the more unique the relationship and the more truly is the one who is becoming, becoming one's self. The fruit of such response is not that bolstering of the ego that comes from comparing one's self favorably with another or modeling one's self on an ideal, but the confirmation of one's unique personal existence, of the ground upon which one stands.

WHAT OUGHT WE TO DO?

My concern with the human image grew out of my intensive dialogue with literature as well as out of my interest in moral philosophy, the central question of which for me was always, "What ought I, or what ought we to do?" As such it has meant a tension between the "is" and the "ought"—something that is neither merely descriptive nor merely normative. The ethical can be defined, at its simplest, as the tension between "is" and "ought"—between the given of a situation and the direction of movement which we choose in response to a moral demand. A moral problem cannot be grasped adequately without; it must be seen from within the situation of the person confronted with the necessity of moral decision and moral action. It is best expressed in a paragraph from the concluding chapter where I indicate that the image of human is neither "is" nor "ought," nor the combination of the two, it is our becoming in the truest sense of the word, i.e., our becoming as a person and as a human being. In this becoming, what we call the "is" is not a static given. It is a dynamic, constantly changing material that is continually being shaped and given form—not merely by inner and outer conditioning but by the directions that one takes as a person. What we call the "ought," similarly, is not some abstract ideal but a constantly changing, flowing direction of movement that is at one and the same time a response to the present, a choice between possibilities in a given situation, and a line of advance into the future.

MORAL DECISIONS

Moral philosophy is invariably grounded in a concept of human nature; yet this concept usually remains an empty abstraction, and the conclusions of moral philosophy all too often consist of ideas or values so general as to offer little guidance in any specific moral dilemma. What is more, ethics all too often remains on the level of rational thought and conscious moral choice, rather than reaching those inner springs which enable one to decide and to act as a whole person. Moral decision does not take place through the application of already existing universal values or of the conclusions of a dialectic, but through the response of the whole person in particular situations. Into this response enter attitudes that one may not be aware of yet, yet ones that shape one's decision even in new and unique situations. One does not go directly from a conscious precept to a moral action, for no action in which a person involves herself merely on a conscious level could really be moral in a meaningful sense of the term. Rather, one goes from deep-seeded attitudes themselves a product of one's meetings with past situations, to the response to the present situation which produces the moral action. Our image of the human—our images of the human—enter into this response more deeply and fully than any general principle ever could. What is more, one cannot really apply a general principle except by way of an image of the human. Moral terms and precepts, such as humility, considerateness, generosity, loving one's neighbor, take on meaning only when embodied in concrete individuals.

SELF-REALIZATION OR PERSONAL DIRECTION

The image of the human also grew out of my dissatisfaction with the emphasis upon potentialism in the human potential movement and in the shibboleths of self-realization and self-actualization that have played so large a role in humanistic psychology. Even talking about being one's real self has no meaning. Either one is the self that one is totally conditioned to be or, if we are not totally conditioned, one can only become one's "real self" if one has an image of the human to guide one in one's choices. The image of the human distinguishes between a person's potentiality and the direction that person gives to it. Such terms as self-fulfillment, self-expression, and self-realization are comforting to many in our age who vaguely feel that they are living without expressing themselves; yet they offer little real help toward an image of human, for they leave unanswered the question of what direction one must take in order to "realize" or meaningfully "express" the self.

If we had only one set of potentialities, then the question could be simplified to one of realizing them or not realizing them. But our potentialities are, in fact, legion, and until we bring them under the guidance of a personal direction, they are likely to conduct themselves as the demons who named themselves thus before Jesus, rather than as the angelic bearers of abundant life. To give our potentialities direction means to decide—not consciously, but again and again through the response of one's whole being—what is the more and what is the less authentic attitude and response, what way is *ours* because it is true for us and we have committed ourselves to be true to it. Actually, we cannot know our real potentialities in the abstract at all. All we can know are generalizations about ourselves from past situations in which we had different resources. Our actual resources are inseparably bound up with what we are as *persons,* with our direction as persons, and with what calls us out in the concrete situation. We cannot foresee these. Potentiality is not in us as an already existing objective reality. We know it only as it becomes actuality in response to each new situation.

WHOLENESS AND RESPONSIBILITY

Our image of the human and our personal wholeness are integrally related not only because each person's image of the human is unique, but also because our wholeness as persons is inseparable from the unique direction that we take, the attitude and life-stance that we bring to our response to the demand placed on us by the persons and world with which we stand in dialogue. Thus our individuation and our integration cannot be an end in itself, divorced from the unique direction that our image of the human and our touchstones of reality embody. These images and touchstones are our way of going out to meet what comes to meet us.

Particularly important for the link between the image of the human and touchstones of reality is still another passage in the concluding chapter of *To Deny Our Nothingness* where I write that it is essential for an ethic of personal relations that there be a continuity of being responsible *for* a Thou as well as responding to her. Otherwise continuing, committed relationships, such as friendship, love and marriage, would be unthinkable, not to mention the helping relationships of teacher and student, therapist and patient, pastor and congregant. It is only in a direct, mutual relationship that I grasp concretely the unique value of the other, experience her side of the relationship, and know what can help her.

Yet I do not necessarily cease to deal lovingly, or at least respectfully, with her even when she is no longer Thou for me in any but a formal, or potential sense. I carry from one moment of meeting to another the form of relationship. I carry the other with me, as it were, as one for whom I am responsible, one to whom I am ready to respond when I meet her again. But when I meet her again she will not be the same as she was before, and very often I must meet someone with whom I have had no previous real relationship. It is the image of the human and not any universal precept that enables me to say, "Nothing human is alien to me." The image of the human enters into and forms that attitude which makes me ready to meet and respond to any person whatever as a human being with human dignity, someone I stand open to know, to respect, perhaps even to love. Thus, the image of the human plays an essential role in linking one moment of realized dialogue with another. It is, often, the very form in which dialogue remains potential, awaiting its actualization.

OUR BECOMING HUMAN

The reciprocal and reciprocating link, for me, between the human image and my use of "touchstones of reality" is the emphasis upon basic attitudes, or life-stances, that we carry with us from one meeting or situation to the next. Thus touchstones of reality, like images of the human, is a dialogical approach to concrete life events. Another significant mode of comparison involves how each of these approaches comes to be in our actual existence. In *To Deny Our Nothingness,* I indicate that the image of the human does not mean some fully formed, conscious model of what one should become-certainly not anything simply imposed on us by the culture, or any mere conformity with society through identification with its goals. For each one of us, it is made up of many images and half-formed images, and *it* is itself constantly changing and evolving. It proceeds and develops through every type of personal encounter we have: a friend stands by us in a crisis, a poet speaks to us through his poems, a great historical figure affects us through the impact he had on those among whom he lived; the characters of novels and plays seize our imagination and enter into our lives through a dialogue we carry on with them in the wordless depths of our being.

The human image is our becoming in the truest sense of the word, that is, our becoming as a person and as a human being. In this becoming, what we call the "is" is not a static given. It is a dynamic, constantly changing material that continually is being shaped and given form not merely by inner and outer conditioning but by the direction one takes as a person. Similarly, what we call the "ought" is not some abstract ideal but a constantly changing, flowing direction of movement that is at one at the same time a response to the present, a choice between possibilities in a given situation, and a line of advance into the future.

REVEALING WHAT'S HIDDEN

In *The Hidden Human Image* (1974), and in *Intercultural Dialogue and the Human Image* (1995), I pointed to the human image as the hidden ground underlying many disciplines that are usually seen as quite separate—philosophy, education, literature, religious studies, psychology, social sciences, intellectual and culture history. I also pointed to the fact that the human image stands in continual need of being revealed— in each new situation—but like a face or a myth, can never be revealed fully. It is like a river of eternity running beneath the depths of time; in addition, I pointed to the truly terrible way in which the human image has been obscured and all but eclipsed in our day by the Holocaust, atomic bombings, mass starvation, and a thousand gross and subtle ways in which we deny our common humanity and demonstrate "man's inhumanity to man." I pointed, too, to the tragic irony that many who, in our day, seek to bring the human image out of its hiddenness only deepen its eclipse.

The revelation of the human image—its coming forth from its hiding—is a revelation that takes place *between* persons (i.e., therapists and client) or *among* the members of the group. It cannot be equated to the image of the human that each holds or comes to hold separately. The coming into the light of the hidden human image is inseparable from the dialogue itself—a dialogue of mutual contact, trust, and shared humanity. In this sense, "healing through meeting" is identical to the revelation of the hidden human image. This revelation is more than an individual finding an image of the human. It is a *becoming* of the human in relationship—becoming human with such resources as the relationship affords, including the possibility of tragedy when such resources are lacking. It is not the diploma on the wall that assures clients that they have the right therapist. The "rightness" of the relationship depends upon mutual existential trust—and upon an existential grace that is not *in* one person or another but moves *between* the two. When these are not present, or not sufficiently so, then the ground of tragedy has been reached. This touching of the tragic itself unfolds the hidden possibility of the human, as well as shows the real limitations in which we stand.

Dialogue means real meeting with otherness in contrast to dialectic, which usually takes place as the unfolding of a single consciousness through contrasting differing "points of view." In judging great literature, in contrast, we are ourselves judged in our fundamental convictions. In what I call the "dialogue of touchstones," we bring not only ourselves but our own touchstones of reality to the meeting with literature and let the touchstones of reality of the author speak to us at such a depth that new touchstones of reality may emerge for us.

T. S. ELIOT'S *FOUR QUARTETS*

A recent example of this dialogical approach to literature, in which the reader as a whole human person enters into an authentic meeting with that image of human existence implicit in the literature, is found in Kenneth Kramer's *Redeeming Time: T. S. Eliot's Four Quartets* (2007). In a rare instance of ecumenism, Kramer, a former Catholic, has written a book on T. S. Eliot, an Anglican, the main thrust of which is the philosophy of Martin Buber—a great Jewish figure of the twentieth century. The book itself is ecumenism at its finest, since it has a fully open spirit that does not in any way sacrifice one tradition in favor of another. Nor does he draw from Buber's philosophy minus its religious component but makes full use of Buber's central philosophical-religious text and even of Buber's writing on Hasidism—the popular communal Jewish mysticism of the eighteenth and nineteenth centuries—in putting forward his thesis of Eliot's closeness to the spirit of Buber's dialogical thought.

Kramer begins *Redeeming Time* by indicating that *"Four Quartets* contemplates, through idea and word, how timeless moments—of redeeming reciprocity, of graced consciousness—shine through physical landscapes and release the poet from temporal enchantments." Aficionados of Eliot's poetry and new readers alike will find in this dialogical reading an invaluable disclosure of Eliot's new life in the spirit—a "new and shocking / Valuation of all we have been." This book on Eliot's *Quartets* (with references throughout to Eliot's poems, plays, and essays) was the product of a lifetime's effort on Kramer's part of reading, pondering, teaching, and discussing the poetry. The whole book is actually Eliot seen through a Buberian lens—in particular that of Buber's *I and Thou*, but by no means exclusively that, since Kramer has immersed himself deeply in the whole of Buber's writings. Kramer's Buberian reading of *Four Quartets* is thoroughly convincing. Kramer has, in fact, accomplished a remarkable feat in presenting such an apt Buberian lens on *Four Quartets*, but in no way does it neglect all the other voices—and they are many—that have essayed to interpret *Four Quartets*.

Claiming that the words of Eliot's poetry bring us, as philosophy cannot, directly to the door of spiritual reciprocity, Kramer again lays great emphasis on the new intersubjectivity that arises from Eliot's *Quartets*:

> a common *logos*, a communal speaking with meaning—in which true subjectivity (interhuman personhood) arises from the midst of a genuine reciprocity between poet and what meets him in his life. This new attitude of choosing to be chosen, of being willing to surrender one's individuality into ever-deepening reciprocal relationship with the world, gives rise—in self-less and thereby time-less moments—to a liberating freedom that releases him, temporarily at least, from self-imposed limitations.[1]

Kramer follows Buber's understanding of spirit as emerging from the *between*, including, for Eliot, the between of "timeless moments and their recovery in . . . memory." As a result, "[r]edeeming time in the *Quartets* . . . generates a new life—both the 'inner freedom' from suffering and desires along with a renewed relationship to the natural world."[2]

1. Kramer, *Redeeming Time*, 180.
2. Ibid.

Kramer describes "[f]our seemingly different yet mutually transforma-tive paths"[3] that have been laid out in the third and centering move-ments of each of the quartets in turn: the way of darkness, the way of stillness, the way of yogic action, and the way of purification. These descending/ascending interspiritual practices—echoing the second epigram of Heraclitus, "The way up and the way down are one and the same"—indwell one another

After rehearsing each of these spiritual paths (darkness, stillness, actionless action, and purification), Kramer asserts "that the reciprocal immediacies [of each path] are equally timeless. By bringing our voice into dialogue with Eliot's *Quartets*, the common *logos* of which Heraclitus wrote, [Buber's] communal speaking that shapes and is shaped by our common world unfolds." This results in "a 'deeper communion' between the sacred presence and the world, . . . [creating] a fresh universe, a new intelligence."[4]

Despite the effectiveness of Kramer's interpretation of *Four Quartets* through a Buberian lens, we must not conflate Eliot and Buber. Apart from the uniqueness of each of the men and the difference in the spheres of their greatness—Eliot's in poetry and Buber's in philosophy and reli-gious thought—there are several important divergences between Eliot and Buber. In most of Eliot's poetry (Apeneck Sweeney, the "Hollow Men," most of the persons depicted in *The Waste Land,* and even includ-ing Eliot's portrait in *Four Quartets* of people "distracted from distrac-tion by distraction") there is scant respect for the ordinary person. This scant respect was not true of Buber, as shown by his attempts—in his writings and in person—to bring people of the most diverse types into dialogue. "I do not think you are thinking of the common man," Buber once wrote me. "I am thinking of him more and more." Though Eliot was not unconcerned with genuine relations between persons, most of his emphasis, if we follow Kramer's *Redeeming Time*, is on the relationship of the person to God, not on the "interhuman" relationships between person and person that greatly occupied Buber. Buber felt, indeed, that his major contribution was his insistence on holding our relationship to the "eternal Thou" and to one another together.

Finally, even if we accept Kramer's shift from inner illumination to finding timeless moments through dialogue with persons and the world,

3. Ibid., 181.
4. Ibid., 195.

Eliot remained immersed in mysticism as Buber did not. As a young man, Buber was indeed a mystic, and in 1909 he published what I believe was the first anthology of ecstatic confessions drawn from many different cultures and religions.[5] In 1914, however, Buber turned decisively away from his early mysticism, particularly as a result of a failed meeting with a young man at the outset of World War I.

In his original Foreword to *Pointing the Way: Collected Essays*, Buber claimed that the book included only essays that he could stand behind in the present. Since I was its translator from German into English, I pointed out to Buber that he could not really stand behind "The Teaching of the Tao" because of its emphasis upon the "perfected man" in whom Tao attains unity. "The spirit wanders through things until it blooms to eternity in the perfected man."[6] Accepting my criticism, Buber revised his Foreword to state that he retained "The Teaching of the Tao" because it belonged to a stage that he had to pass through before he could enter into an independent relationship with being. He then added an important statement on his new attitude toward mysticism. Instead of bringing into unity his whole existence as he lives it day by day, from the hours of blissful exaltation to those of hardship and of sickness, the person who has experienced mystic ecstasy constantly flees from ordinary life into the detached feeling of unity—of being elevated above life. Eliot, as Kramer portrays him in *Redeeming Time*, does not seek a state in which there is nothing over against him, but he does perhaps seek to deny the self and turn to "the still point" in ways that injure the interhuman dialogue between "I" and "Thou."[7]

BIBLIOGRAPHY

Buber, Martin. *Collected Essays.*
———. *Ekstatische Konfessionen*. Jena: Diedrich, 1909.
———. *Pointing the Way: Collected Essays*. Translated and edited by Maurice Friedman. London: Routledge & Kegan Paul, 1957.
Friedman, Maurice. "Kramer's Buberian Lens on Eliot's *Four Quartets*." *Journal of Ecumenical Studies* 43 (2008) 423–35.
Kramer, Kenneth. *Redeeming Time: T.S. Eliot's Four Quartets*. Lanham, MD: Cowley, 2007.

5. Martin Buber, *Ekstatische Konfessionen* (Jena: Eugen Diedrichs Verlag, 1909).

6. Buber, *Collected Essays*, 50.

7. I have taken the final section of this essay from a much longer review of Kramer's book "Kramer's Buberian Lens on Eliot's *Four Quartets*," used with permission.

5

Maurice Friedman's Dialogue
with Religion and Literature

PAT BONI

INTRODUCTION

T HE FIRST TIME I ever observed the two disciplines—Religion and Literature—taught together was as a guest in a graduate course Maury gave on Martin Buber in the spring of 1967 at Temple University. The topic for the evening was Buber's chronicle *For the Sake of Heaven*, and my then husband, a graduate student in the class, had suggested I read the book so that I would better understand the discussion of that evening. I did so—was thoroughly taken with Buber's ideas, and although I knew there was so much I didn't "get" in that first reading, many things "spoke to my condition," as Maury and the Quakers would say. I remember Maury asking questions of his class regarding the reading assignment that evening, and when none of the students responded to one of the questions, I turned to my husband and whispered, "Should I raise my hand?" Maury saw this and called upon me to respond—and so I did. He apparently was satisfied with my answer and called on me again throughout the evening when no other responses were forthcoming. For me, it was a thoroughly enjoyable evening. I felt confirmed and the confirmation contributed to my going "back to school." In September, I enrolled in Temple University as a full-time undergraduate student. I was 34-years-old, a wife, and mother of two young boys.

In my freshman year I took my first course in Religion and Literature with Maury. "Religion and Literature," he rightly believed, did not describe in any way what he hoped to impart in such a class. What does Religion and Literature mean anyway? Religious literature? Bible? Koran? *Upanishads*? Sermons? Proverbs? Are we speaking of two different disciplines and comparing them? He preferred to call the course "Religious Attitudes in Literature" believing that this more clearly and specifically connoted what was important. I no longer have a copy of the original syllabus but I remember that we were required to read seventeen or eighteen books that semester. Our "text" was *To Deny Our Nothingness* (the title troubled our youngest son Denny who believed in some way it had to do with him!). The first reading assignment was Fyodor Dostoevsky's *The Brothers Karamazov*. That's right—all 922 pages of it! We had, if I remember correctly, two weeks in which to complete the novel.

Franz Kafka's *The Trial* and *The Castle*, Camus' *The Stranger* and *The Plague*, Georges Bernanos' *The Diary of a Country Priest*, Hermann Hesse's *Siddhartha*, Aldous Huxley's *The Devils of Loudon*, and Jean-Paul Sartre's *No Exit* as well as *The Devil and the Good Lord* were also some of the books we were assigned to read. In addition there were Graham Greene's *The Power and the Glory*, Samuel Beckett's *Waiting for Godot*, T. S. Eliot's *Four Quartets*, Ignazio Silone's *Bread and Wine*, and one or two of Elie Wiesel's novels. I think that's it! I assiduously read every one of the works assigned (except, I confess, all of *The Castle*) even though I was taking four other courses that semester.

At the end of my sophomore year I was told that I had to declare a major. A span of about two city blocks separated the Religion Department offices from those of the English Department. I could not make up my mind as to whether I should be a religion major or an English major. I went to the Religion Department and felt that I didn't belong with the "religious" types whom I saw in the student lounge. I then walked over to the English department but suspected that their majors would not have the "existential" questions I was beginning to ask at that time and that the English Department would not be able to answer these questions and that the Religion Department surely would be able to! If only there had been an interdisciplinary program—if only I could have declared I will be a Religion and Literature major! It took two more trips back and forth between the two departments before I ultimately chose to get my BA in

English. But I took almost as many courses in religion as in English as an undergraduate so that by the time I was ready in 1971 to graduate, I knew I would enter the Religion Department and join the Graduate program in Religion and Literature that Maury had instituted in 1967 at Temple University.

In every class in which I was a student of Maury's, whether it was Comparative Mysticism, Existentialism and Phenomenology, Religion and Psychology, Contemporary Jewish Thought, to name only some, Maury's method of teaching was not to lecture but to discuss issues found in our readings, not to cite abstractions but to illustrate ideas—mystical, psychological, philosophical, religious—through poetry, drama, novels, and myths. I was awed by the names of poets, playwrights, novelists that Maury would casually mention in class, showing familiarity with the writer's work, citing a sentence or more of theirs to elaborate on a point he or one of the students had just made. If I did not know the author (and more often than not I didn't) I would promise myself to go to the library and look at some of his or her books. I did not learn about Zen solely from academic studies on the subject—it was through the Zen tales Maury chose for our Comparative Mysticism class that the Zen masters and their teaching came alive. I learned more about Taoism from Lao Tzu's *Tao Te Ching* than any treatise on the subject would have taught me. Similarly with Islam—Sufi tales was my introduction to that religion. And it was *The Bhagavad Gita* that spoke to me about the "psychology" and "spirituality" of the human being as few works by Freud or Jung had ever done. Buber's *Ten Rungs, The Tales of the Hasidim, The Way of Man According to the Hasidim,* and his chronicle *For the Sake of Heaven* gave me a greater understanding of Jewish mysticism than any work about the subject could have done. Meister Eckhart was, for me, a "literary" genius as well as great Christian mystic, and I am still awed by the poetry (if not the poet) of Eliot's *Four Quartets* which, having read first in Maury's Religious Attitudes in Literature, I was re-reading—in light of the mystical—for the class in Comparative Mysticism

In 1982 I received my doctorate. My thesis is entitled *King Lear and the Real* and is an interdisciplinary study on the subject of authenticity as found in the philosophies of Martin Heidegger and Martin Buber and as illustrated by Shakespeare in his play. It is a genuine product of "religious attitudes" in literature (as well as philosophy and the variety of genres found in Martin Buber's writings), and though Maury was not on my committee, having left for San Diego in 1973, I would not have written such a dissertation had he not, through his presence and his wisdom, inspired me and taught me about the meeting of religion and literature in the many courses I took with him over the 6-year period he and I were at Temple University together.

In April 1950, Martin Buber, after receiving a letter from Maury delivered to him in person by Maury's mother when she visited Israel, wrote Maury requesting that he send him his dissertation (on Buber's thought) and that Maury write down his "life experience" and send that too. Buber requested "not thoughts on life, but the tale itself." This was to be done "in utter frankness, but without any self-analysis." In July, Maury sent his 23-page single-spaced autobiography to Buber, and in August, Buber responded with a letter that Maury says "illustrated concretely the important distinction his philosophy of dialogue makes between 'acceptance' and 'confirmation.'"[1] What is important for this discussion of the dialogue with religion and literature is what Buber said Maury had not yet sufficiently developed: "the power of seeing the others instead of feeling their relationship to you." Buber, addressing Maury as "you," but which I hear addressed as well to me and to all, went on to say that "As long as [we] do not see them more really [we] will not be able to describe them, to make [our readers] see them."

In the more than forty years since Buber's observation was received by Maury, he has come to "see" the others—the authors, poets, characters, as well as the events portrayed in the literary works—"really," and his capacity to describe them brings them to life for those readers who themselves would "see" and "hear" the subjects of Maury's writing.

His range of literary knowledge is enormous. Poetry, drama, Hasidic, Zen, and Sufi tales, biographies, novels, short stories, legends, myths, psalms, and sagas—he has read and discussed works of every genre. His is a global vision, encompassing not only literature of America and England, but of India, Japan, Israel, Russia, Africa, France, Germany, Italy, Rumania, Spain, and Native American writers. At the risk of getting carried away by such epic listing, I must cite Maury's dialogue with the poetry of Yeats, Dickinson, Blake, Roethke, Francis Thompson, Hopkins, Auden, Eliot, Levertov, Berry, Dylan Thomas, Whitman, Traherne, and know that I am stopping before the list can be called complete. Huxley, Kafka, Hesse, Wiesel, Melville, Kazantzakis, Koestler, Steinbeck,

1. Quoted in *Genuine Community*.

Toni Morrison, are only a few of the names of the novelists with whom he has had a dialogue. The plays of Miller, O'Neill, Beckett, Sartre, Eliot are just some of those about which Maury has written. And he has had a dialogue with every one of the Hasidic zaddikim whose tales are told by Buber in *Tales of the Hasidim: Early Masters and Late Masters!*

Maury's latest book on the subject of religion and literature is *The Affirming Flame: Poetics of Meaning* (1999). It is, as he says, "the continuation of an old and long-standing love"—his dialogue with modern literature. His master's thesis for his MA in English at Ohio State University in 1947 was devoted to ten European (excluding American and English) novels. His earliest book on the subject, *Problematic Rebel*, and his subsequent one, *To Deny Our Nothingness: Contemporary Images of Man*, are, unfortunately, no longer in print. In 1969 his translation of Buber's religious "mystery play" *Elijah* was published in *Martin Buber and the Theater* (New York: Funk & Wagnalls), which Maury edited and for which he wrote the first three chapters. All three of these books have been of inestimable value to me in my own learning and teaching courses in Religious Attitudes in Literature.

In every one of Maury's books, be they his *Religion and Psychology; The Hidden Human Image; A Heart of Wisdom; The Human Way: A Dialogical Approach to Religion and Human Experience,* to name just a few, or his biographies of Buber: *Martin Buber's Life and Work* (3 vols.), or *Encounter on the Narrow Ridge,* literary allusions abound. His "Critical Reader," *The Worlds of Existentialism,* includes excerpts from the Bible, Camus, Sartre's plays, Rilke, and Kafka, in addition to every important "existentialist" philosopher, theologian, and psychologist. Even in his book devoted entirely to Hasidism, *A Dialogue with Hasidic Tales,* Maury cites ideas from the works of T. S. Eliot, Camus, Kafka, Denise Levertov, Irwin Shaw, and Elie Wiesel.

If we include the genre of biography under the rubric "literature" (most contemporary biographies, I dare say, cannot be considered such), then Maury's concern with what constitutes as authentic a picture of the subject as is possible is vital to his dialogue with religion and literature. Maury believes that most contemporary biography is "really fiction, a deliberately novelized version of a life to lend connections and meanings where none may be."[2] "We do not need to ask that a biography be true to the 'facts' for life itself is something more than a collection of facts.

2. Friedman, *Heart of Wisdom*, 128.

Yet we may fairly ask for an honest faithfulness that tries to bring before us a unique human reality which otherwise we might not be able to enter into dialogue with."[3]

His own genuine dialogue with Martin Buber led, of course, to Maury's beautifully expressed three-volume biography (dialography?) *Martin Buber's Life and Work* and the lovingly written, concise, and comprehensive testimony to Buber's life: *Encounter on the Narrow Ridge*. Among the many accolades the 3-volume biography of Buber received were Emil Fackenheim's belief that it was "a masterpiece" which would "surely be the most authoritative work on Buber in the foreseeable future," and Martin Marty's comment that "All subsequent work on Martin Buber must build on Maurice Friedman's foundation." The editor's comment on the jacket cover of *Encounter on the Narrow Ridge* informs us that throughout this book "Friedman delivers the essential spontaneity of a great man who saw in every encounter a focal point for human growth." I might have chosen a word other than "delivers" but the message is clear. Maury's faithfulness to Buber has given us the unique human reality that no other biography of the man has set forth.

For Maury, literature is art, not life, but it is art which is bound more closely with life than most philosophies about life or forms of knowledge about the human condition. He does not see the real artist as one who defies society in order to express his or her individualism. Camus, as Maury cites and with whom he agrees, said in *Resistance, Rebellion, and Death*, "Art cannot be a monologue."[4]

One can speak of "Buberian attitudes" informing Maury's writing. But he never imposes, nor do I believe he merely "applies," Buber's philosophy to either his books on literature and religion or to his works on psychology. Having authenticated Buber's ideas in his own life—at least to the extent that he remembers, as we all forget and remember, to do so—Maury's words ring true. His ideas are his own in spite of as well as because of his acknowledged debt to Buber's ideas.

What is important is that we authenticate in our reading of great literature the basis of genuine dialogue. This means to maintain the tension between holding to those ideas we have wrested from our past contending with life and with literature, ideas of which we have become fond, and giving ourselves over to the possibility that even in reading

3. Ibid.

4. Friedman, *Nothingness*, 287.

old friends we may hear something new in the meeting. To come to the reading "holding our own ground" without opening ourselves to a genuine meeting with the other is monological.

The meeting of religion and literature, Maury believes, is not to be found by setting forth on one's reading armed with fixed "religious" or "psychological" or "philosophical" ideas and then fitting the literature into those ideas or using the literature to illustrate them.

We must, rather, dig deeper into both religion and literature in order that we may recover and discover for ourselves the ground where they are one: those basic human attitudes which arise in our response to ultimate life realities and to the daily life-situations that confront us. The notion that so many people have today that meaning in literature is to be found most directly in the novel of ideas or the drama of ideas is exactly backward. On the contrary, we only reach the level of abstraction and timeless ideas after hundreds of thousands of years of dealing with the more concrete in legend and in myth.[5] If our meeting with literature is not to be a "mismeeting," then we must be open to meanings at all levels, and the danger involved here is that we may be changed by our encounter with the poem, the drama, the novel, myth, or legend. But this is what genuine dialogue is all about.

Those of us who wish to be in faithful dialogue with the material may still run the risk, as Maury says, of:

> attempting to preserve the separateness of theology and literature as disciplines, language, or modes of consciousness while searching for a metatheory that underlies them or a formal meeting after each has attained a reflective distance from the literature itself. Whether this metatheory takes the form of a philosophy of symbolism, a phenomenology of linguistic comprehensions, a psychology of unconscious archetypes, or an ontology of the disclosure of the meaning of being, it has the same effect of relating religion and literature in terms of concepts and world views rather than in terms of the work itself.[6]

Maury speaks of "theology as event—the way that we walk in the concrete situations of our existence."

To speak thus means an inversion of traditional theology, which rests upon a set of traditional beliefs or a traditional interpretation of

---

5. Friedman, *Human Image*, 99.

6. Friedman, *Heart of Wisdom*, 122.

"sacred history" and biblical events. "Rather it is the event itself that again and again gives rise to religious meaning, and only out of that meaning, apprehended in our own history and the history of past generations that we have made present to ourselves, do religious symbols and theological interpretations arise." Such theology as event makes the staggering claim that "it is in our lives that we apprehend the divine—not through sacred times and places and rituals alone but in the everyday happening, 'the days of our years.'"[7]

It is for this reason that Maury believes that legend, myth, and tale are themselves closer to religious reality than creed, doctrine, and theology—"if one understands such tales not as illustrations of preexisting abstract ideas but as the concrete preservation of the dramatic, dialogical reality of the event." We go to the masters, to paraphrase a Hasidic tale, not because they wax forth eloquently on Torah or Dharma, not to hear them expound upon profundities, but to watch them lace and unlace their shoes.

It is his faithfulness to the particular that pervades Maury's dialogue with religion and literature again and again. In our Hasidic Tales community that meets once a month for a pot-luck supper and a discussion on the life and visions of the zaddikim about whom Buber has written in *Tales of the Hasidim: The Early Masters and Later Masters*, Maury is insistent that members of the group not stray off into a universal never-never land, that we do not get too carried away with our own "theological," "philosophical," or "psychological" concepts, but that we address ourselves to the particular situation of each individual rebbe and then bring ourselves to the discussion with our own touchstones of reality. Buber's "lived concrete" is, for Maury, not an "idea" to be merely expounded on in ponderous academic terminology. He insists on the concrete as opposed to the vague, theoretical, and universal pronouncements we are, most of us, too apt to make. And it is through literature, it bears repeating, that the lived concrete is most authentically illustrated.

Maury's chapter on "Poets of the Here and Now" in his book *The Affirming Flame* "establishes a link between the mystic's direct intuition of meaning in the meeting with the particular and that meaning that is found in 'the Dialogue with the Absurd' . . ."

---

7. Friedman, *Hasidic Tales*, 29.

> I coin the phrase "mystics of the particular" for those who find meaning in their direct meeting with the particular without recourse to any world view or overall philosophy, theology, or metaphysics. To do this is to forgo the comfort of the general and the universal when the meeting with the particular no longer seems to yield meaning. This is perhaps the philosophical equivalent of St. John of the Cross' "dark night of the soul" or Ferdinand Céline's *Voyage au Bout de la Nuit*.[8]

In the same chapter, Maury discusses a diverse group of poets and thinkers who are also mystics. What holds together these figures from varied cultures and religions "is not only that they have discovered meaning in the particular but also that through their very language, whether used in poem, poetic prose, devotional literature, or philosophy, they have enabled us to attain an awareness of the ineffable—a sense of the presence in which we live and move and have our being."[9]

Real communication, Maury has learned in the years since Buber's letter to him, "means that each of us has some real contact with the otherness of the other." A woman once asked Maury after a lecture in response to a point he had just made: "Isn't this just a matter of semantics?" "Lady," Maury retorted, "I make my living by words!" What he meant was that he takes words seriously, struggles with them and his audience and himself until "the word that is spoken," to use Buber's phrase, becomes a meaningful dialogue between him and his reader or listener. The "how" of what Maury says in his books is far less important than the "what" and the "why" he says what he says.

To best describe Maury's own "methodology" in his books that are concerned with religion and literature is to quote the words he writes in *The Affirming Flame* as "an invitation to a dialogue with literature itself." On the frontispiece of that book, Maury's dialogue with religion and literature is again perfectly expressed: "Poetry is the soul's announcement that even when it is alone with itself on the narrowest ridge it is thinking not of itself but of the Being which is not itself, and that this Being which is not itself is visiting it there, perplexing and blessing it (Buber, *Between Man and Man*)."

---

8. Friedman, *Affirming Flame*, iv–v.

9. Ibid., 24.

THE IMAGE OF THE HUMAN

Of Maury's first published book on the dialogue between religion and literature Martin Buber wrote:

> *Problematic Rebel* is . . . especially important because its theme is not expounded through the discussion of concepts but through representative figures of the narrative literature of two genera- tions—that of Melville and Dostoievsky and that of Kafka and Camus. The theme is the revolt of man against an existence emp- tied of meaning, the existence after the so called "death of God." This emptying of meaning is not to be overcome through the il- lusionary program of a free "creation of values" as we know it in Nietzsche and Sartre. One must withstand this meaninglessness, must suffer it to the end, must do battle with it undaunted until out of the contradiction experienced in conflict and suffering, meaning shines forth anew. That Maurice Friedman assigns these figures to two basic types, "Rebel" and "Exile," and brings them into relationship with Prometheus and Job, makes his book of still greater value."

In the preface to the first edition of *Problematic Rebel,* Maury wrote that this book "grows out of years of concern with the problem of the modern image of man . . ." and tells us that that image which grows out of this book is "above all, a product of the meeting of philosophy and litera- ture." It is a philosophy of literature and philosophy through literature.

More precisely, it is the product of approaching literature in terms of the "image of man" that emerges when a character is portrayed in suf- ficient depth that he speaks to us, through his very uniqueness, not only of the man of a certain period but of man as such.

In the years that have passed since Maury wrote that, I believe the only thing he would change (and has done so) is "image of man" to im- age of the "human." It is the human image that is of paramount impor- tance to Maury in any study of religious attitudes in literature. In the first chapter of *To Deny Our Nothingness*, Maury says:

> The image of man . . . is an integral part of man's search to un- derstand himself in order to become himself, of his search for an image of authentic personal existence. "Authentic personal existence" does not mean some standard imposed from without, or some universal "ought" that need only be applied. It implies a meaningful, personal direction, a response from within to what

one meets in each new situation, standing one's ground and meeting the world with the attitude that is rooted in this ground.[10]

Inasmuch as there is no such thing as human existence in general,
it is the concrete uniqueness of the persons we meet in a great work of
literature whose situation and response to his or her particular situation can speak to us and point the way to our becoming more aware of
authentic rather than inauthentic modes of response.

In its very particularity, the image of [the human] in literature gives
us the wholeness of [the person] as more abstract disciplines cannot.
Next to the lives of actual [persons], literature comes closest to retaining
the concrete uniqueness of individual [men and women] while at the
same time enabling us to enter into a sufficiently close relationship with
these [persons] so that they can speak to us as bearers of the human—as
exemplifications of what it does and can mean to be a [person].[11]

Maury believes that when we reduce a literary work to specific
categories, we have an instance of "mismeeting." We have come to the
work armed with particular ideas in advance and fail to hear the real
voice therein. Whether we apply Jungian or Freudian, theological or
philosophical categories to the work or set about to "find" the symbols,
we are destroying the concreteness of our particular encounter with the
literature. To approach the meeting of religion and literature in terms
of the image of the human, on the other hand, is to understand literary
interpretation as essentially dialogical. As Buber has taught, the life of
dialogue teaches us to "meet others and to hold [our] ground when [we]
meet them." To apply this to the dialogue with literature, Maury says:

> means the combination of faithfulness to literature in its concrete
> uniqueness and otherness, including the whole fullness of style
> and form, with response to that literature from the ground of
> one's own uniqueness. Reversing the emphasis, we can say that
> approaching the meeting of religion and literature in terms of the
> image of [the human] implies not only bringing ourselves to the
> dialogue but the most faithful possible listening to the implicit
> intention, the underlying attitude, the point of view of the work
> of literature. Since every work of literature, even a poem, is frozen
> speaking in which the voice must be liberated from the objective
> form, a really faithful listening will make it impossible to reduce

10. Friedman, *Nothingness*, 17.

11. Friedman, *Human Image*, 98.

the work to a single, directly expressed point of view. From this it follows that it is not the symbol, myth, or metaphor, still less the theological concept or metaphysical idea, but the tension of points of view that discloses the truly religious depth-dimension of a novel, play, or poem.[12]

In a work of literature a character's ethical conflict, his or her wrestling with the particular issues, the ultimate decision that is made can offer us an image—positive or negative—of the human as no moral dictates, creeds, or pronouncement can. As Maury has said: "Moral values are not verified by abstract knowledge: they are authenticated in our lives—by our withstanding and being true in the situations that confront us." "The image of man cannot offer the precision of linguistic analysis or the inspiration of idealism. But it can set us once more on the road toward a moral philosophy that is both honest and genuine—one that does not reduce the 'ought' to the 'is' nor displace the 'ought' from the actual to the ideal."[13] Maury has also said:

> Insofar as religion may be described at its deepest level as a basic attitude or relationship arising in the encounter with the whole reality directly given in one's existence, one can say that the life attitude which underlies any ethics must ultimately be of a religious depth. But one need not say so; for the reality to which the image of [the human] points lies deeper than the articulations of belief and nonbelief. It does not have to do with metaphysical essences or theological creeds, but with that existential trust which enables one to stand one's ground before what confronts one and to meet it in a way faithful to its otherness and one's own uniqueness.[14]

It is in literature that Maury finds the "real homeland of the image of [the human]."[15]

DIALOGUE WITH THE ABSURD

An image I use again and again in teaching not only Religious Attitudes in Literature but in all my classes is that of the "Modern Job," as Maury calls the one "who trusts and contends within the Dialogue with the

12. Ibid., 103.

13. Friedman, *Nothingness*, 373.

14. Ibid., 372.

15. Ibid., 27.

Absurd." Maury does not discuss this subject in *Problematic Rebel* in as much detail as he does in his later books (see especially his section "Dialogue with the Absurd" in *The Affirming Flame*), though the seeds of that idea are certainly present in his early work and elaborated on in *To Deny Our Nothingness*. He speaks of his metaphor in discussing *The Castle*, for example, "to speak of a dialogue in which ultimate reality addresses K. only through absurd social reality, rather than to decipher the Castle into God and the village into the community."

> In *The Plague* too there is a reality that speaks through the absurd, and Rieux is an illustration of the one attitude which remains open to this reality. Father Paneloux, by accepting suffering and evil as objective divine order, runs aground on the rock of the absurd. Tarrou, by recognizing the absurd and rejecting it, excludes any meaning other than that of his own saintliness. Rieux, by remaining in dialogue with the absurd—neither accepting it nor cutting off from it but fighting with it and receiving from it—attains the meaning that the absurd has to give us.[16]

Dialogical meaning, for Maury, is "never that of a comfortable faith or a harmonic *Weltanschauung*. It is tragic at best and more often grotesque." In the *Shoah*, which he calls the ultimate Dialogue with the Absurd, this meaning "goes beyond anything with which we are familiar from our ordinary lives. It is, nonetheless, a meaning reached in dialogue, as opposed to that subjective affirmation of meaning in spite of the absurd affirmed by the Camus of *The Myth of Sisyphus* or the invention of values championed by Sartre.[17]

The words Maury wrote in *Problematic Rebel* hold as much truth today as they did when he first wrote them—the dialogue with the absurd is a stance that must be embraced if we are to find a way to go forward—contending and trusting at the same time. "Today meaning can be found, if at all, only through the attitude of the [person] who is willing to live with the absurd, to remain open to the mystery which he can never hope to pin down."[18] In *To Deny Our Nothingness* he adds to this: "This dialogue means an open-minded and courageous standing one's ground before the absurdity of a world that one cannot image, of

16. Friedman, *Problematic Rebel*, 485–6.

17. Ibid.

18. Ibid., 468.

an otherness that one cannot grasp—not even in the meeting with one's fellowman—and of the self within that one cannot fathom."[19]

Maury tells of his first coming to teach at Sarah Lawrence College and being struck by the fact that because *The Book of Job* was in the Bible his students regarded it as blind faith and failed to understand the actual text. They read it through the eyes "of what their ministers called 'faith' but what was actually no more than a mind-set, toward which their elders were positive and they negative." [20]I teach Hebrew Scriptures and have also taught courses on the Bible as Literature and I try to convey to my students, as Maury points out, that "*The Book of Job* was not 'the Bible as Living Literature'; it was living literature that was later taken into the Bible." There are, in almost every class, two or more students who fail to enter into real dialogue with the Bible because they want it to be the fixed word of God—engraved in stone by the Hand (?) of the Almighty and not a jot or tittle to be altered by the human hand. Hence, the existential situation of Job is not anything that these students will be able to enter into relationship with; there is no "inclusion," no "imagining the real," for they have come to the Bible encased in their fundamental ideas and not to an encounter with religion and literature. There is no readiness on the part of these students to "confront ultimate questions," there is no "shattering of security" because they will not risk losing the solid ground of their own "theology." "Job speaks for [the human being]," Maury says, "because he speaks for himself."

Maury's dialogue with the Bible is, with the possible exception of his writings on the Psalms with which he has been in dialogue, nowhere manifested as profoundly as in his dialogue with *The Book of Job*.

> [Job] penetrates so deeply into the uniqueness of his own situation that his protest becomes a protest against the suffering of all [persons], his witness for himself a witness for man [and woman] as such. Job is the true existentialist. He does not begin with any theories on the nature of God or of the nature of man. He holds fast to his trust in the real God whom he meets in the dreadful fate that has befallen him, and he holds fast to the facts of his innocence and his suffering. At the heart of the Book of Job stands neither "blind faith" nor denial of God, but trusting and contend-

---

19. Friedman, *Nothingness*, 354.
20. Friedman, *Human Image*, 99.

ing, recognizing his dependence on God and standing firm on the ground of his created freedom.[21]

The Modern Job in his dialogue with the absurd does not accept evil or cut himself off from history to avoid it. He "faithfully affirms what confronts him as the 'given' of his own existence, and at the same time contends with, as the Biblical Job contends in his dialogue with God. The Dialogue with the Absurd does not mean either denial or affirmation on principle, but standing one's ground and meeting what comes with clear-sighted trust—in each new situation that confronts one affirming where one can affirm and withstanding where one must withstand."[22] The religious person meets God, says Maury, "not in the aseity of the philosophers, but in the events and meetings of concrete life, in the Dialogue with the Absurd."[23] Our dialogue with the absurd, Maury says, "implies a trust that though the absurd will never be anything but absurd, meaning may emerge from our meeting with it."[24]

CONCLUSION

In my dialogue with Maury's dialogue with those prose writers and poets whose own dialogue with the eternal Thou reverberates in their writing, I am constantly moved to read the works of the subjects of Maury's books and essays. This has extended—in the 35 years I have known Maurice Friedman—to the philosophers, sociologists, and psychologists with whom he has also been in dialogue. I have met so many people—almost all of those writers whose names I cited previously—through Maury's books and essays. The authors and their characters come alive for me in the pages filled with his perceptions, quotations from their works, and deep insights into the situations portrayed, and infuse in me a desire to read, and meet, those writers whom Maury has met and whose writing he is discussing. What comes through Maury's writing is his enthusiasm for the material, his intellectual and spiritual vitality, his profound understanding not only of the words and meaning of those about whom he writes but of existence in all its fullness, contradictions, joys, and tragedies.

21. Friedman, *Problematic Rebel*, 18.
22. Friedman, *Nothingness*, 347.
23. Friedman, *Heart of Wisdom*, 228.
24. Friedman, *Hasidic Tales*, 153.

Maury's dialogue with the authors of the many works on which he has written extends to the critics of these authors as well. It is not only his dialogue with the individual writer that informs his books on religion and literature, but with those critics of the particular author whose studies he has prodigiously read. In his dialogue with the secondary sources, Maury's insights of the critic's understanding often prove, at least to my way of thinking, invaluable. His disagreement with their understanding as well as his agreement is deeply thought through, and though he may criticize them, having come to them with his own way of thinking, he "hears" what they have to say and does not approach his secondary (or primary) sources prepared with an agenda—which of course could not and would not be dialogue.

One of Maury's original contributions to understanding the life of dialogue is what he calls "touchstones of reality." In chapter 1 of his book *Touchstones of Reality* (1972) he first used the term. What he is concerned with "is glimpses of a way at once uniquely personal and broadly human." I think when one discovers the real in a work of literature—that is, one sees the events and choices of a particular character and can bring that situation into dialogue with one's own life—not taking away the uniqueness of the situation as described in the life of the author's creation, but recognizing the particular conflict or choices or situations as those of one's own life—then one understands the importance of what Maury means by "touchstones of reality." Our contact with the touchstones of the authors and their characters is still, as Maury says, "our contact."

We must have the courage to let the "frozen sea that surrounds our hearts," as Kafka said, be broken up by the "axe" of great literature. Beckett wanted his plays "to claw," and Buber believed that one must labor with a living book "hours at a time as with a headstrong horse, until covered with sweat" we stand before it and read this book that we have tamed. "It is a dangerous book," to be fastened with a heavy lock and hung on a chain which is attached to the strongest beam—a beam that is warped. But one who has subdued the living book:

> knows the secret names of the demons and knows how to summon them.
> He does not walk like all the world. He hesitates at every step, for he fears to tread on a soul. He has experienced something.
> I think that every real book is Ar Vif.

> The real reader knows this, but far better still the real writer—
> for only the writing of a real book is actually danger, battle, and
> overpowering. Many a one loses his courage midway, and the
> work that he began in the reading of the signs of the mystery he
> completes in the vain letters of his arbitrariness. There exists only
> a little reality of the spirit in this book-rich world.[25]

"Great literature," Maury has said, "simply because it is great, is deeply threatening."[26]

The image of the human as one finds it in great literature may be Maury's greatest contribution to the meeting of religion and literature. For the human being, as Maury knows, is the one who can wrest meaning from the particular situation in which he or she finds herself, and if the words written by the poet or author reflect an awareness of his or her conflicts, joys, transgressions, and triumphs and are heard by the reader, something of the eternal manifests itself. Still, we must be able to risk—great literature, is indeed dangerous. So is real living. But when the poets sing their praises and laments, when the dramatist gives us an Oedipus, a Lear, or Willie Loman, and the novelist creates a Rieux, a Zossima, or one who confronts holocausts, loss of faith, suffering, separation from and death of loved ones, we get a glimpse of what it means to be and what choices are available to a human being. When a writer creates a character who stands before the "cruel antitheticalness of existence itself," or experiences the "eclipse of God," yet who contends with and withstands the tempests through his or her own dialogue with the absurd, and thus becomes for us, the reader, a genuine image of what it means to be human in a world not of our own making, we have the meeting of religion and literature.

Maury's own life of dialogue is beautifully demonstrated in his prayer that the spirit be relevant to our life "and that life be open to the demand of the spirit. We meet God not in the structures of the theologians and the concepts of the philosophers, but the events and meetings of the concrete life."[27] It is through the lives of the great poets and novelists as discerned in their works, that, as Maury has taught us, images of the human way of life may be discovered; in their literature the reader

---

25. Buber, *Believing Humanism*, 46.

26. Friedman, *Human Image*, 103.

27. Friedman, *Hasidic Tales*, 71.

can come to the "real homeland of the image of [the human]" and even discover the eternal voice of the Thou.

The next-to-last words of this chapter are Maury's words of wisdom; he grants to Rabbi Pinhas of Koretz the last.

> Only we can remove from our eyes that one small hand that shuts off from us the enormous sights and mysteries which fill the world. Only we can bring to light the hidden human image—the image of the imageless God. Whoever says that the words of the Torah are one thing and the words of the world another must be regarded as a person who denies God.[28]

BIBLIOGRAPHY

Buber, Martin. *A Believing Humanism: Gleanings*. Translated by Maurice Friedman. New York: Simon & Schuster, 1967.

Friedman, Maurice. *The Affirming Flame: A Poetics of Meaning*. Amherst, NY: Prometheus, 1999.

———. *A Dialogue with Hasidic Tales: Hallowing the Everyday*. New York: Human Sciences Press, 1988.

———. *A Heart of Wisdom: Religion and Human Wholeness*. Albany, NY: SUNY Press, 1992.

———. *The Hidden Human Image*. New York: Delacorte, Delta, 1974.

———. *Problematic Rebel: an Image of Modern Man*. New York: Random House, 1963.

———. "The Road to Genuine Community: Dialogue, Confirmation, and Trust." 1997.

———. *To Deny Our Nothingness: Contemporary Images of Man*. New York: Delacorte, 1967.

28. Friedman, *Heart of Wisdom*, 229.

6

Interior Dialogue and the Human Image

KENNETH P. KRAMER

"'You call something dialogue which I cannot call so,' Buber remarked to
Carl Rogers; 'I would want another term between dialogue and monologue for this.'"

—Martin Buber[1]

IT WAS THROUGH THE PhD program in "Religion and Literature" that
he founded and directed at Temple University in the late 60s and early
70s, and through the influence of *To Deny Our Nothingness* that I first
came to meet Maurice Friedman. My earliest significant memory of
Friedman, in fact, was learning in his seminars to avoid the temptation
to reduce literature to "contents," or "themes," or "symbols," and at the
same time to develop a dialogical approach to religion and human experience. "I have always felt," I recall Friedman saying in one of his graduate seminars, "that the two central statements in Buber's *I and Thou* were,
first, 'all real living is meaning,' and second, what he says of the I-Thou
relationship: 'by the graciousness of its comings and the solemn sadness
of its goings, it teaches you to meet others and to hold your ground when
you meet them.'"

Indeed, one of the most indelible memories that remains with me
from Friedman's graduate seminars was the way he illustrated the back
and forth movement between "I-Thou" relationships and "I-It" relations.
"Buber distinguishes between an I-Thou knowing and an I-It knowledge.

1. Buber, *Knowledge of Man*, 178.

The I-It knowledge comes again and again from the I-Thou knowing. It is not, as we imagine, some objective reality in itself. Rather, it is a swinging back and forth between I-It and I-Thou." Extending his right hand, fingers down, he would trace an invisible infinity sign with his hand, his fingers turning upside-down as they traced their way back up the curve and then turning facedown upon reaching the top of the other curve. How powerfully life-changing Buber's words, along with Friedman's clarifications and applications, have become in my life. By focusing on the central significance of Buber's dialogical philosophy, Friedman's words have encouraged me to enter into real engagement with literature that addressed me personally and which again and again draws me into dialogue with its speaking.

When I first arrived at Temple in 1968, having just taught for the first time at St. Andrew's Presbyterian College (courses in "Christianity and Culture" and "Modern British and American Poetry"), I lacked any specific direction toward a dissertation topic. I remember mentioning, in a conversation with Friedman, who was my dissertation advisor, that other graduate students in the English department, where I was also taking courses, had encouraged me to write my dissertation on some obscure figure in order to avoid duplicating existing studies. Friedman, however, encouraged me in a different direction. "You ought to do something that is really meaningful to you, to write about someone who really addresses your humanness." This sage advice led me to write my dissertation on T. S. Eliot's *Four Quartets* as meditative poetry, which, more than thirty years later, led to the publication of *Redeeming Time: T.S. Eliot's Four Quartets* (2007).

However I did not *really* meet Maury until more than twenty years after I graduated. My second meeting began when in 1993 I visited him in his home in San Diego, ostensibly to record an interview about his views on death and dying. "If you were bedridden with no chance of recovery," I remember asking him, "would you ever consider physician-assisted suicide as a way to end your suffering?" "This is a question," he responded, "that I cannot answer ahead of time." And then he said something that I often quote in similar conversations: "It depends on what resources would be available to me at that time." This response is a telling example of how Friedman has appropriated Buber's dialogical philosophy into his life. This essay, and to an extent the book itself, turns upon the interhuman consequences of "second meetings" with Friedman. Here, I will first speak of his methodological approach to human existence and meaning, the "human image" metaphor (prior to 1964, he called it "the image of man") by comparing its earlier and later adumbrations. I will then briefly address two questions: one aimed at clarifying his thought (who/what most significantly shapes Friedman's own human image?) and the other aimed at deepening and expanding it by addressing the question: what about "interior dialogue"?

BECOMING UNIQUELY HUMAN

Under what conditions and by what reasoning does Friedman articulate what it means to be fully human? As I grow older, he has said, it is Buber's philosophical anthropology that speaks more and more to me. To be a philosophical anthropologist, one has to be able to bear solitude and to become a question to one's self. This is because philosophical anthropology goes beyond cultural anthropology in that it asks questions not just about human beings, but also about the human itself—about 1) our wholeness, and 2) our uniqueness. Rather than focusing on human "essences," to grasp human beings in their wholeness Friedman focuses on the unique particularity and complexity of interrelationships between freedom and personal direction. For this reason, Friedman writes: "the human image is our becoming in the truest sense of the word, that is, our becoming as a person and as a human being."[2] Friedman writes: In the dialogical view we become persons in what Martin Buber calls the "I-Thou" relationship—the direct, reciprocal, present relation between the person and what comes to meet him or her as opposed to the indirect, nonmutual relation of "I-It."[3]

Of course, it is impossible to completely study the corpus of a living person. Yet, looking back over the body of Friedman's work, it is possible to say that six of his "human image" books co-implicate one another: *Problematic Rebel: Melville, Dostoievsky, Kafka, Camus* (1963); *To Deny Our Nothingness: Contemporary Images of Man* (1967); *The Hidden Human Image* (1974); *Dialogue and the Human Image: Beyond Humanistic Psychology* (1992); *Intercultural Dialogue and the Human Image* (1995); and *The Affirming Flame: A Poetics of Meaning* (1999). In these texts, the "human image" is described as 1) an underlying dialogi-

---

2. Friedman, *Contemporary Psychology*, 17.
3. Ibid., 23.

cal attitude that calls us into being by pointing us towards meaningful choices between conflicting sets of values, and 2) as an ever-recurring unique response of our whole person to particular demands placed upon us.

More concretely and closer to human lives, the "human image" metaphor emerged from Friedman's intense dialogue with literature. Because it retains the concrete interactions between unique persons, literature for Friedman is the real homeland of the "human image," as it brings us into more intimate relationship with "bearers of the human." During his extensive work on Buber's philosophy of dialogue as a mean-ing-oriented metaphor, the "human image' was developed in response to Friedman's response to literature. Accordingly, the emphasis of litera-ture for Friedman is not as susceptible to generalizations or universal-izations as more abstract disciplines are. Through a reader's dialogical engagement with text, author, characters, and language, an "image of the human" arises which cannot be either objectified on the one hand, or reduced to a subjective interpretation on the other. That is, we do not imitate the behavior of a character, or allow a visual impression to affect us, but rather we enter into a living dialogue with the character which forms into a reciprocal relationship that in turn enters into our response to concrete situations. Exactly, and uniquely, in this way images of the human influence our thinking, insights, intuitions in ways that shape and reshape our behavior.

In *Problematic Rebel,* for instance, Friedman situates his intensive study of Melville, Dostoievsky, Kafka, and Camus in the context of the death of God and human alienation and estrangement. Emerging from this study, for Friedman, was a depth image of modern human existence that gathers together and holds points of tension between personal free-dom and psychological compulsion, especially as embedded in the sto-ries of Prometheus and Job. If Prometheus embodies and reflects finite power, and is aware both of the limitations of this power, and of the abil-ity to see beyond the limits of his finitude, Job represents the figure who maintains the tensions between trusting and contending. If Prometheus affirms the subjective rebellion against all order and values, leading to an "either-or" thinking, Job stands his ground in order to meet whatever comes in each new situation and, rather than trying to deny it or retreat from it maintains an "existential trust" in life.[4]

4. Friedman, *Problematic Rebel,* 491.

A subtle, yet crucial, shift in emphasis occurs between *Problematic Rebel* and *To Deny Our Nothingness*, where his starting point becomes the absence of contemporary human images which provide meaningful social direction. While his understanding of the "human image" as his central methodological approach does not change, it becomes self-consciously interdisciplinary. In this work, Friedman creates a typology of responses to the absence of meaning-giving human images: the modern socialist (Malraux, Steinbeck, and Silone), the modern vitalist (Bergson and Kazantzakis), the modern mystic (Huxley, T. S. Eliot, and Martin Buber), the modern saint (Bernanos, and Greene), the modern Gnostic (Weil, Jung, and Hesse), the psychological person (Freud), the modern pragmatist (James, Dewy, and Sullivan), the existentialist (Nietzsche, Sartre, Kierkegaard, and Camus), and the absurdist (Beckett and Kafka). Each "type" or "image" becomes like raw material needing to be shaped, if possible, into what William James termed a "live option" for authentic human existence.

Reading through *Problematic Rebel* and *To Deny our Nothingness*, it soon becomes clear that the "image of the human" directs us to its most recurring dynamic: holding tensions between polarities (e.g., between descriptive and normative, unique and universal, personal and social, potentiality and direction) in ongoing exchanges. In *The Hidden Human Image*, Friedman shifts his attention to the unique quality of the "human image"—at the same time hidden and revealed. On the one hand, it is hidden by brutal and inhumane episodes in history and personal life (whether mass destruction, or personal suicide) calling into question the very ground of the human. And on the other hand, ironically the "image of the human" may be obscured in the very attempt to reveal it. For example, the behaviorist's reduction of human knowledge to what is empirically verifiable and human values to mere emotional assertions of preference illustrates how an effort to reveal the human can further fixate it. That is, what is revealed can become configured in such a way as to obscure the human dynamic beneath abstract categories that are taken as reality.

In *The Affirming Flame* (1999), Friedman figures his own dialogue with literature into a culminating image of "affirming and withstanding." His thought follows a progression from discovering meaning in the particulars of the "lived concrete", to threats of meaninglessness, evil, and the absurd, to the necessity of holding a tension between affirming and withstanding. What gives the "affirming and withstanding" image its disclosive power is its life-stance implications, at once *universal* (here everyone can stand without being limited by analytic categories), and *unique* (here I can stand without ignoring the concrete expressions of evil that I encounter). By holding the tension between "affirming and withstanding," for Friedman a dialogical person becomes the tension. Otherwise, affirming and withstanding would not point to the always-in-the-process-of-becoming "way" one enters each moment. This life-stance, trusting and contending, affirming even in the midst of withstanding, is a "stance in which meaning is found in immediacy without any pretense to an overall, comprehensive meaning that would make the absurd any less absurd."[5]

FRIENDSHIP WITH BUBER

Yet, where does Friedman himself stand? Who shapes and demonstrates the "image of the human" for him? Clearly, Martin Buber became the most meaningful and creative presence in Friedman's life. Indeed, Friedman continues to be in dialogue with, be shaped by, and bring Buber's highly dialogical response into each new situation. Although Friedman never studied formally with Buber, through Buber Friedman came to a deep concern with Hasidism, biblical Judaism (the Hebrew Bible), psychotherapy, education, social philosophy and social problems, existentialism, and the life of dialogue—all of which he has expressed in his writing and teaching over the years. What Friedman especially inherited from Buber was a profound caring about responding to each person's unique address with a wholeness of his being. This interhuman response includes genuine decision, what the Hasidim call *kavana* (deep inner intention). Buber's life gave Friedman a magnificent expression of authentic dialogue, which is "a part of our birthright as human beings, for only through it can we attain authentic human existence."[6] How significant, then, Friedman's closing words in his one-volume life of Martin Buber, *Encounter on the Narrow Ridge*: "In a time when we are in danger of losing our birthright as human beings, Martin Buber has given us again an image of the human." [7]

---

5. Ibid., 202.

6. Friedman, *Buber: Life of Dialogue*, 97.

7. Friedman, *Narrow Ridge*, 460.

Although Friedman did not meet Buber until after six years of immersion in his work, their first encounter was both memorable and instructive. It was on October 31, 1951, at the Hotel Marcy on 96th Street in New York, that he first met Buber. Buber was staying there while teaching at the Jewish Theological Seminary. Buber welcomed him by looking deeply into his eyes while taking his hand. Friedman's initial response was to feel how totally "other" Buber seemed. His eyes were of a depth, gentleness, and directness that Friedman had never before, or since, encountered. Indeed, in 1961, a year after Friedman had spent four months in Jerusalem with Buber, he asked himself, "What did I experience when I looked into Buber's eyes?"[8] Upon reflection, Friedman realized that when he looked into Buber's eyes, he experienced that Buber really included him and thereby placed a demand on him to be fully present. This was not an easy demand since, as Friedman notes, like many people he is sometimes present and sometimes "distracted from distraction by distraction" as T. S. Eliot puts it in *Four Quartets*.

As they talked, Buber told Friedman of his meeting several days before with Eliot in London. They had been brought together by Ronald Gregor Smith, translator of *I and Thou* and *Between Man and Man*. When Friedman asked Buber whether he did not find his own opinions different from those of Eliot, Buber replied: "When I meet a person I am not concerned with opinions but with the person."[9] Friedman took this response as a reproach because, as he later realized, he had turned Buber and Eliot into positions in a dialectic within his own mind and lost their reality as dialogical persons.

Fortunately, we have an indication of what Buber thought about Friedman. In the Summer of 1955 Friedman taught a course in Contemporary Religious Thought for the Department of Religion at Columbia University. Due to the success of this course, in 1956 Friedman was considered as a possible regular faculty member in the department. Buber agreed to write a letter recommending Friedman for the position. "I am going to tell you what I think of Maurice Friedman," Buber wrote to the department. "I do so at his request, but I rather like doing it," Buber added, continuing:

8. Friedman, *Intercultural Dialogue*, 14.
9. Friedman, *Narrow Ridge*, 334.

I have learned to know what a kind of man he is, just by seeing, in the course of about five years, how he works. The work I am alluding to interested me first because my own thought was its subject, but soon I was attracted by his way of working. He began by having a clear-cut idea of what he wanted to make, and then he devoted himself to it. He concentrated on the matter the power of his mind, a brave lot of powers, and he went on without flinching. Now I must tell you, it was not an easy job. He had to gather a mass of stuff, to coordinate it, and to build up something like a system out of what was never intended to become such a thing. This he could do only by true understanding, his best quality indeed. He understands the ideas he meets, and he understands even the persons who thought them, as persons who thought just these ideas and not different ones. I am sorry to say that he had to do in this case with a somewhat resisting subject, but he succeeded to grasp it adequately. His best faculty is to express and to explain what he has understood . . . I have the impression that I have told you what perhaps no other could tell you about the man. It is because for all these years I have been a witness and now I have come to give evidence.[10]

Buber affirmed here two of Friedman's pedagogical qualities—understanding ideas and the person who thought them; and expressing and explaining what he has understood. These interrelated characteristics continue to deem Friedman's work of the highest value.

INTRALOGUE

Since dialogue and the "human image" are inseparable from Friedman's viewpoint, it is impossible for me not to ask a question about inner dialogue. Does it impact Friedman's dialogical presentation of the human image? Is it possible that interior dialogue, when combined with external dialogue, could deepen and expand Friedman's approach to human existence and meaning? A personal story Friedman tells about his chief dissertation advisor—Professor Arnold Bergstraesser—suggests how interior dialogue implicates the "human image." When Friedman had finished his dissertation on all of Buber's work then in print, Bergstraesser asked: "What will keep you from reading this dissertation in ten years and asking yourself, 'Did I know that then!'?" What he meant, Friedman

---

10. Martin Buber's letter is taken from Maurice Friedman's unpublished manuscript, *My Friendship with Martin Buber.*

has come to realize ever more deeply over the years through interior interactions with that question, is that his insights gleaned from the study of Buber's thought might become lost if he failed "to authenticate them, and make them real by bringing them into my life."[11]

Yet I can hear Friedman, in response, referring to a 1957 dialogue between Martin Buber and Carl Rogers at the University of Michigan. At one point Rogers shifted the topic of discussion from dialogue between two persons (e.g. therapist and client) to another type of meeting—"the person's relationship to himself." Rogers remarked that in his practice he noticed that some clients reported "very vivid moments in which the individual is meeting some aspect of himself . . ."[12]

Buber, however, was skeptical. A significant difference exists, for Buber (and for Friedman), between interpersonal dialogue with a unique other and intrapersonal dialogue with an aspect of one's self. Missing in the latter is the possibility of "the moment of surprise." Being surprised by an aspect of one's self remains phenomenologically and existentially different from being surprised by the uniqueness of the other. In the former case, the possibility of surprise is conditioned and limited to one's own understanding and awareness; in the latter, surprise is not restricted to my experience and embodies what can be known in no other way. [13] But Rogers persisted. He expressed a desire to play recordings of interviews for Buber in which "surprise" does, in fact, occur for some of his clients. "A person can be expressing something and then suddenly be hit by the meaning of that which has come from someplace in himself which he doesn't recognize. He really is surprised by himself."[14] This segment of their dialogue ended with each agreeing that meeting "otherness" within oneself deserved a different designation. "You call something dialogue which I cannot call so," Buber remarked; "I would want another term between dialogue and monologue for this."[15]

---

11. Friedman, *Hasidic Tales*, 71.

12. Buber, *Knowledge of Man*, 178.

13. Buber, however, writes that the "basic presupposition of conversation is missing from [dialogue with myself], otherness, or more concretely, the moment of surprise." He added that the "human person is not in his own mind unpredictable to himself as he is to anyone of his partners . . ." (*Knowledge of Man*, 113.) That is, because we are not unpredictable to ourselves we cannot be a genuine—questioning and answering—partner to ourself.

14. Ibid.

15. Ibid. For a discussion on this passage see Anderson and Cissna, *The Martin Buber—Carl Rogers Dialogue*, especially 67–76.

But isn't there another kind of dialogue, an interior dialogue with another person (especially, though not necessarily, someone with whom you have shared in public conversation), which expresses a degree of otherness through recollected words spoken/written by this dialogical partner? Perhaps the term "intralogue" can be helpful. Neither "genuine dialogue" nor "monologue," intralogic exchange, as I use the term here, is not just ordinary stream-of-consciousness thinking, or what Richard Hycner (co-founder of the Institute of Dialogical Psychotherapy along with Friedman) calls "intrapsychic dialectic," referring to the "interaction between two polarities within the single person."[16] Nor is it merely an interior soliloquy or dramatic monologue. However awkward the neologism, intralogic exchanges, or dialogized thinking, involve a remembered and/or imagined interaction between myself and a recollected other.[17] Anthropologist Vincent Krapanzano uses the term "shadow dialogue." Krapanzano writes that by this term he refers to those dialogues in which one partner to the primary dialogue that one has with an interlocutor, real or imaginary, is not present. "Such dialogues are 'silent', 'mental', 'quasi-articulate', 'beneath consciousness', though capable, at least in part, of becoming conscious."[18] While initially silent, the key to such interior dialogized thinking is not only that it becomes conscious but as well influences and enters into future exterior dialogues.[19]

But how does intralogic interaction differ from intrapsychic dialectic? Surprisingly, a persuasive insight for responding to this question is found in Buber's 1957 "Postscript" to *I and Thou*. Responding to thoughtful questions asked over three decades about the meaning of his dialogi-

16. Hycner, *Person and Person*, 70.

17. Buber hints at the possibility of having an internal conversation with an aspect of myself (what Socrates called an "internal scribe"), or what Buber called "the Thou-I," the "genius, the spirit I am intended to become" (*Between Man and Man*, 26–27). Paul Tillich, in an unpublished introduction to his *Systematic Theology*, wrote that "the dialogue with myself was far from being a form of monologue . . . the fights with the living 'Thou' were more important for the development of my thought than the academic discussions from book to book" (84).

18. Krapanzano, "On Dialogue," 289.

19. In response to Friedman's closing remark as moderator of the Buber-Rogers exchange—that it was "a *real* dialogue, taking place in front of an audience . . ."—Buber changed his mind about the efficacy of public dialogue. He later instructed Friedman to delete the last paragraph in "Elements of the Interhuman" in which he stated that public dialogue cannot be spontaneous, or immediate, or unreserved.

cal philosophy, at one point he wrote about the possibility of genuinely questioning a person who was no longer living.

> Let the questioner make present to himself one of the traditional sayings of a master who died thousands of years ago; and let him attempt as well as he can, to take and receive the saying with his ears, that is, as though spoken by the speaker in his presence, even spoken to him. To do this, he must turn with his whole being to the speaker (who is not to hand) of the saying (which is to hand). This means that he must adopt towards him who is both dead and living the attitude [life-stance] which I call the saying of *Thou*. If he succeeds . . . he will hear a voice, perhaps only indistinctly at first, which is identical with the voice he hears coming to him from other genuine sayings of the same master. [20]

Here Buber hints at an inner-worldly dimension to the dialogical process. Between dialogue and monologue, interior conversations can occur between recollected others and myself when I am able to turn toward them with my whole being and make them present by imagining the other's thoughts, feelings, and experiences in a way that provides a context for hearing the other's voice as if spoken directly to the listener. "Hearing" the other's voice prevents us from following a one-track course of ideas by demanding that we respond personally and uniquely to what we hear.

Unlike ordinary interactions, intralogic recollections include interior exchanges with what others have said or written, or even with what one imagines the other would say. Becoming uniquely human, I believe, involves exterior dialogues and intralogues. In our humanness, we necessarily move back and forth between outer and inner exchanges whose interpenetration sets new intuitions, new associations, and new interhuman-divine/human dialogues in motion. The whole person thus expresses and embodies cross-fertilizing implications of these two types of "dialogue," whose outer-inner correlations animate and extend the human image by inspiring, challenging, and pointing to ways of becoming fully present.

But how does intralogic interaction function without devolving into intra-psychic dialectic? Recall for a moment the second movement of T. S. Eliot's "Little Gidding," in which the poet walks the streets of London as an "air warden" during World War II, at dawn after a blitz-

---

20. Buber, *I and Thou*, 128.

krieg bombing. Suddenly, he "meets" a shadowy figure, someone from his past, a "compound ghost" (one and many) who is both there and not there. The ghost, who is finally unidentifiable, has been likened to one of Eliot's great literary teachers like Dante, Shakespeare, Mallarmé, and Yeats, among others. The poet says:

> So I assumed a double part, and cried
> And heard another's voice cry: "What! Are *you* here?"
> Although we were not. I was still the same
> Knowing myself yet being someone other—
> And he a face still forming: yet the words sufficed
> To compel the recognition they proceeded.[21]

Then, after directing the poet to an agonizing self-assessment upon the effort of a lifetime through the eyes of old age, the ghost ends by indicating that "his exasperated spirit" will continue to proceed "from wrong to wrong" "unless restored by that refining fire/ Where you move in measure like a dancer." Could these lines also suggest reciprocal interaction between interior and exterior dialogue in which these forms of dialogue move together like dancers?

The speaker's encounter with the "compound ghost" is made explicit in the paradoxical dialogue between them. While the speaker perceives himself in the ghost, and thus is talking to an aspect of himself, the ghost is at the same time separate and capable of speaking independently. The main protagonist of the poem—the poet himself—takes us into his interior dialogue, assuming, in London's dawn, a double part comprised of his old self (who "met one walking") and a new self (who is blown toward him and compels recognition). There is a necessary paradox in this "internal" dialogue: words are spoken by the other, yet there is no other person actually speaking them. At the same time, the poet does not make them up entirely. They arise, as it were, from past encounters, from prior speakings and listenings. Voices emerge from multiple shared discourses associated with persons or ideas.

Intralogic voices, analogously, though spoken in me (for no one else is speaking them), are not just my voice speaking. For this reason, intralogic exchanges are not simply random thoughts, or idle ruminations, but a type of "inward commerce" (with, or in the presence of, an interiorized other) that does not stand by itself but leads back into public dialogue.

21. Eliot, "Little Gidding," 141.

I am proposing for this reason that these two forms of dialogue—one primary, direct, spoken back-and-forth: the other secondary, indirect, silently recollected—can become reciprocally concurrent, or as Buber put it, "an imperative interchange [between] the systole and diastole of the soul . . ."[22]

Because intralogic exchanges influence further conversation, I wonder if Friedman would not agree that at times these two forms of dialogue—spatial and interior (even if the latter is viewed as subordinate to the former) flow into each other and can thus supplement, even trans-figure, one another. Indeed, what I am writing now (not to mention the thought and work behind this book) results, partially, at least, from in-tralogic relations with-and-against Friedman. In these silent exchanges, questions about his relationship with Buber often arise: "Recalling your meetings with Buber, what dimensions in his practice of dialogue stood out the most and/or most influenced you?" and "In your own ongoing dialogue with Buber's thought, is there one thing, more than others, that you feel needs augmentation?" As if in response, I hear Friedman say: "Buber always responded genuinely in the moment in a way that invited you to do the same."

To mention just one example, let me end with an intra/extra-di-alogic embodiment of my main point. In my inward commerce with Friedman, I once heard myself silently asking: "As you look back now from the place of having been so significantly influenced by Martin Buber's thought, have you at moments experienced reservations or doubts about his words in ways that set you off in a different direction?" This led to a subsequent phone conversation with Friedman, in which I asked him if he could recall an encounter with Buber that challenged him, or helped shape the human image for him, and then I added, "an anecdote not published elsewhere?" He agreed to give this question some thought. His email, several days later, seems to me an altogether appropriate conclusion for this essay.

> I liked jokingly to say that for me Buber was the prophet of the "It" rather than of the "Thou."
>
> *Martin Buber:* "How old are you?"
>
> *Maurice Friedman:* "Thirty-five."

---

22. Buber, *Knowledge of Man*, 54–55.

Buber: "If you don't get your life in order, you will be a really unhappy man by the time you are fifty."

Maurice: "I am unhappy now."

Buber: "You don't know the meaning of the term."

People often ask me if Buber really lived his philosophy. To this
I can and will testify. He "walked his talk," as people like to say
today. He really lived the life of dialogue, and to him it was really
"the only life worth living," as I. F. Stone said of Buber's friend
Albert Camus. That this has included, on my part, some distancing from and contending with Buber has never dimmed my
gratitude and love for him in the years when he was alive and in
the years since. [23]

23. When Friedman sent Buber a baccalaureate speech he gave at the University
of Vermont in 1961, where he referred to Camus as an atheist, Buber wrote back and
said, "Don't call him an atheist. He is one of those people I speak of in religion and philosophy who destroy the images that no longer do justice to God" (*Buber and Human
Sciences,* 11).

BIBLIOGRAPHY

Anderson, Rob, and Kenneth Cissna. *The Martin Buber—Carl Rogers Dialogue: A New Transcript with Commentary*. New York: SUNY Press, 1997.

Buber, Martin. *Between Man and Man*. New York: Macmillan, 1965.

———. *I and Thou*. Translated by Ronald Gregor Smith. 2nd ed. New York: Scribner, 1958.

———. *The Knowledge of Man*. Edited by Maurice Friedman. New York: Harper Torchbooks, 1965.

Eliot, T. S. "Little Gidding." In *Complete Poems and Plays*. New York: Harcourt, Brace & World, 1952.

Friedman, Maurice. *Contemporary Psychology: Revealing and Obscuring the Human*. Pittsburgh: University of Duquesne Press, 1984.

———. *A Dialogue with Hasidic Tales: Hallowing the Everyday*. New York: Human Science, 1988.

———. *Encounter on the Narrow Ridge: A Life of Martin Buber*. New York: Paragon, 1991.

———. *Intercultural Dialogue and the Human Image*. New Delhi: Indira Gandhi National Center for the Arts, 1995.

———. *Martin Buber: The Life of Dialogue*. Chicago: The University of Chicago Press, 1955.

———. *Problematic Rebel*. Rev. ed. Chicago: University of Chicago Press, 1963.

Hycner, Richard. *Between Person and Person: Toward a Dialogical Psychotherapy*. New York: Gestalt Press, 1991.

Krapanzano, Vincent. "On Dialogue." In *The Interpretation of Dialogue*. Edited by Tullio Maranhao. Chicago: University of Chicago Press, 1990.

Tillich, Paul. "Personal Introduction to My Systematic Theology." *Modern Theology* 1.2 (1985) 84.

PART TWO: AFTERWORD

Dialogical Knowing

◯◯

To stimulate dialogues with and about ideas presented in Part 2 you may wish to consider the following questions (whether general or chapter-specific) about the central concepts of each chapter. How would you respond to these questions if, for example, you were speaking to the author of that chapter? How, for instance, do the concerns raised by these questions influence your life-situation? How would you, assuming you were writing an essay about a similar concern, construct it differently? What materials, which authors, what stories would you select to clarify and deepen your stand? Moreover, if you were personally addressing the authors of these chapters, what question would you ask of them?

Friedman (chapter 4): If the text of literature exists in the dialogical sphere between the writer and the reader, then what is the significance of the difference between them? Does one play a larger part than the other—i.e., in being shaped or shaping the novel, poem, or play? In what ways does the dialogue go back and forth, to prevent it from becoming static?

Boni (chapter 5): Think of a literary text that you have read that has influenced your life in a meaningful way. How did it change you? Do the circumstances you would bring to it now change your reading?

Kramer (chapter 6): Kramer's chapter brings forth the idea of "interior dialogue," which he calls "intralogue." Do you believe that it is possible to engage in interior dialogue—a dialogue with a recollected other as if in the other's presence? If so, with whom do you enter an interior dialogue and about what?

Another way to engage in dialogue with the ideas and concerns presented here would be to imagine yourself as a student in one of Professor Friedman's classes. The purpose of education, for Friedman, is to establish a "learning community," one in which there is genuine concern for the otherness of the others. The true teacher has always been aware that, above all, he or she is confronting students with images of the human and that it is precisely through this confrontation that the student is educated. The unique response of every student to the image of the human is that which draws forth the potentialities of becoming and transforms students into "educated" persons who are able to embody and express tradition and thereby become more uniquely human.

In order to understand the values, reasoning, and points of view of his students, Friedman assigned personal academic journals with four steps.

- **Step one** is for the student to select from the reading something that strikes him or her and to write it down in the journal.

- **Step two** is to try then to put it in one's own words, not by translating the quotation into familiar categories or constructs, but by swinging imaginatively over to where the other person is speaking from.

- **Step three** is coming back to one's own side and entering into dialogue with the author's words—both intellectually and emotionally—from where one is.

- **Step four** is to relate what one is commenting on to ongoing issues of the course and of one's life.

How would you apply this journal strategy, either by thinking through or writing about a specific passage that really engages you? To arrive at a more integrated understanding of Friedman's interdisciplinary humanism, you may wish to compare your response with his essay in this part to your response to his other chapters.

PART THREE

Religion as Dialogue

"RELIGION FOR ME IS neither an objective philosophy nor a subjective experience. It is a lived reality that is ontologically prior to its expression in creed, ritual, and group. At the same time, it is inseparable from these expressions, from what I call 'touchstones of reality.'"

—Maurice Friedman

7

Religion and the Religions

Touchstones of Reality

MAURICE FRIEDMAN

ONE OF THE MOST important double pulls experienced in Western spiritual cultures is that between the exploration of "inner space" through mystic meditation and the call to make real the space *between* person and person in the life of dialogue. This is not a question of "inner" versus "outer," since the interhuman, when it is genuine, demands that the inwardness and uniqueness of each partner be brought into the meeting. We are so used to thinking of the spiritual life as a goal that we set out directly to attain mystic self-realization, enlightenment, even saintliness. Instead of allowing our becoming to take place naturally and spontaneously as a byproduct of the way we meet life, we make ourselves an end in ourselves and thus distort and pervert the very means that we use.

The search for enlightened consciousness raises the question of whether the essence of the true person is to be found in consciousness or in the whole person. Is it found by leaving the world that is given to us—the social world, the world of nature, the world of the senses? Or is it found by remaining in relation to the life of the senses and to other people? Is the goal of life enlightened awareness and individual spiritual salvation or is it a way of life that does not attain individual perfection yet affirms and redeems the human world?

ULTIMATE REALITY

My great teacher, Joachim Wach, defined religion as a total response of the total being to what is experienced as ultimate reality. "Total response" because in religion, as distinct from scientific inquiry and aesthetic emotion, the whole being is responding and the whole being is involved in the response. Religion as we know it has always expressed itself in doctrinal forms as myth, creed, theology, metaphysics. It has expressed itself in practical forms as rituals, masses, and prayer—communal and individual. It has expressed itself in social forms as brotherhoods, churches, and sects. It is impossible, indeed, to understand any religion except in terms of these three expressions and their interrelations.

But for all that, one cannot reduce religion merely to these expressions and interrelations, for their matrix is the religious reality that is expressed, and what is expressed is not in itself directly expressible. One of the great errors in the approach of many people to religion is to see it as a form of philosophy or metaphysics that is going to prove that God exists or describe his nature and attributes. This is to reduce God to an object, a part of the universe, to make him subservient to our logic, and in any case has to do with the detached observer rather than the involvement of one's total being. Religion is a way that one walks. Religion is a commitment. Religion is one's basic response *whether* or not one calls oneself religious and *whether* or not one affirms the existence of God. Some of our "labyrinthine ways," whether we are fleeing "the Hound of Heaven" or not, are so far underground that we ourselves are not aware of them when we come up again.

Religion for me, accordingly, is neither an objective philosophy nor a subjective experience. It is a lived reality that is ontologically prior to its expression in creed, ritual, and group. At the same time, it is inseparable from these expressions and cannot be distilled out and objectified. The *religious* at this deepest level might be described as a basic *attitude* or relationship arising in the encounter with the whole reality directly given to one in one's existence.

DIALOGICAL METHODOLOGY

For this reason, we shall not be satisfied with approaching religion through a double negative—*not* objective and *not* subjective—or even by defining religion as a dialogical reality in which the objective expressions and subjective experiences are merely the byproducts of and accompaniment to dialogue. We shall want, instead, to speak of this dialogical reality itself and in its own terms as an event of meeting that comes to light before our abstractions into external and internal objective and subjective thought and feeling.

Our approach to religion is therefore a dialogical one. I use the word *dialogue* here not just in the sense of two people speaking, but in the sense of openness, directness, mutuality, and presentness. Dialogue means in this context a mutual knowing, a knowing in direct contact in contrast to a detached subject's knowledge of an object. In genuine dialogue the experiencing of senses and imagining the other's situation work together to make the other person wholly and uniquely present. For this dialogue to be real, one must not only mean the other, but also bring oneself fully into the encounter, and that means saying at times what one really thinks about the matter in question. But dialogue may also arise in our meeting with a nonhuman reality, the sunset over the ocean, a ghost pine on Point Lobos, the cry of the loon, the grandeur of the mountains, and the aggravations of everyday toil. It may also come in that indirect dialogue we know as art—paintings, sculpture, poetry, dance, and orchestral and chamber music.

This is particularly true of "non-statistical" research—theoretical, philosophical, historical, phenomenological, existentialist, humanistic, or case-study. Of central importance to such qualitative research is that in every case the proper methodology is developed only *after* the tasks of discovering the larger area of interest, delimiting the parameters of this area, and focusing on issues and problems within this delimited area is completed. The researcher begins with some general methodological approach, but the specific methodology that the researcher uses should develop in dialectic with the research itself, particularly as it moves into depth studies of individual cases. There is no single right methodology for all cases but only the methodology that best helps one investigate the problem that one has chosen. At the same time, the basic tool of qualitative research is an open-ended dialogue among whichever methods are employed.

HAVING RELIGIOUS EXPERIENCES

Not all religion is dialogue, of course, and neither is all knowing or, for that matter, all human experience. In one sense, human experience includes just everything in a person's life, inner and outer, conscious and unconscious, waking reality, fantasy, or dream. In another, it may be limited to what is singled out from among the stream of happenings, that which has an impact and stands out for itself. When we say, "I had an experience," we mean just that: something surfaces from the general flux as an event in itself and does so precisely because it impinges on us in some way, whether through the feelings it arouses—pleasure, pain, joy, misery—or through the significance we attach to it, or through the wonder it evokes. Although we certainly are not consciously aware of all the experiences that happen to us, we can, nonetheless, say that experience is that which we become aware of.

If there are difficulties that attend any study of human experience, there are still greater difficulties that attend a study of religious experience. When William James wrote his great classic, *The Varieties of Religious Experience,* he presented with admirable openness a whole range of "religious experiences" from mysticism and drugs to saintliness and conversion. Though his conclusion was pragmatic ("Religion is real because it has real effects"), it was not yet subjective in the way that religious experience has since tended to become. Today a religious experience is less something that seizes one on one's way than it is an experience that one "has," often by willfully setting out to have it. This is so much the case that I am often inclined to jettison the term *religious experience* entirely in favor of *religious reality* or *religious event* or any other term that might help liberate us from the bondage of the new subjectivism.

From this it should be clear that we cannot understand experience either as merely external or internal or even as a sum of the two, with some part of each experience the one and some part the other. Experience in the truest sense is itself an event of the "between." It is our meeting with whatever accosts us in the situation in which we find ourselves, dragon, damsel, or dream. One of the things that makes it difficult to understand this, as we have said, is our habit of regarding experience as something that takes place inside ourselves.

It is important therefore to recognize that *religion* is often treated as being the external forms that seem to the observer to make up religion—ritual, organization, creed—and experience is often seen as the subjective aspect of our existence—our feelings, our consciousness, or even our unique participation in an event common to ourselves. Looked at in this way, we could then speak of the meeting of religion and experience as a way of pointing to the reality of the between that cannot be caught in the objective forms of religion or the subjective forms of experience. Only in this way, perhaps, can we point ourselves back-and-forward to that "ultimate response to what is encountered as ultimate" which we have tentatively defined as religion.

SERMON ON THE MOUNT

To speak of religion as event in no way means to reduce religion to ethics. It means only that our total existence is involved in religion, that it is *not* some sacred upper story that has nothing to do with the rest of our lives. The Sermon on the Mount is no doubt a compilation from different traditional texts, but it is also without doubt built from teachings that Jesus gave or was reported to give to the people to whom he spoke as he walked about in Palestine. That some people have regarded this teaching as unrealistic or too idealistic in no wise detracts from its concern with the whole of human existence. "If the salt hath lost its savor, wherewith shall it be salted?" If the human being has lost that which makes him or her truly human, there is no way to replace this with something else such as power or success or prestige. Even if it is, as Reinhold Niebuhr claimed, "an impossible ideal," it is still relevant. It still brings us into judgment because it sets a direction for our movement.

One of my students was once profoundly troubled because, in teaching the Sermon on the Mount, I raised the question of whether the students thought Jesus' injunction to turn the other cheek and walk the second mile was in accordance with human nature as we are coming to understand it from modern psychology. She was not troubled because this is a troublesome question, as it is indeed, but because she had never thought of the Sermon on the Mount as a teaching that *she* might follow. For her it was only a part of the image of Christ's perfection! When Jesus ceases to be an image of the human and becomes instead an image of the divine, the *way* in which our existence is involved, if we are Christians, is likely radically to change, though not the fact of that involvement.

EIGHT-FOLD PATH

A similar development actually takes place in Buddhism. Whether or not Gautama actually went through the noble Eightfold Path himself before attaining enlightenment, it seems certain that he or some of his disciples devised the Eightfold Path—right views, right resolution, right speech, right action, right livelihood, right will, right mindfulness, and right meditation—as a mnemonic guide to others who are following the path to enlightenment and Nirvana. It is unthinkable that this Path was taught simply as an adornment to the image of the Buddha's perfection. Later when the Buddha came to be worshipped, the marks of perfection were quite other, physical ones, or they were stories of his sacrifice of himself in previous births, as in the Jatatka Tales. But even when Mahayana Buddhism developed the concepts of Buddhahood, Transcendent Wisdom, and salvation through the grace of the Bodhisattva, none of these implied a moving of religion from the ground of existence to that of a timeless ideal or spiritual upper story. The whole existence was still claimed, though in a radically different way.

This is equally evident in Taoism and Confucianism. Whether the *Tao Te-Ching* be translated as "The Canon of Reason and Virtue" or as "The Way of Life," it is still manifestly a way that a person walks. It is not an isolated ethic; for its central concern is with the tao that rounds the way of heaven and earth and is the way of the person. At first glance the analects of Confucius might appear more as pure ethics, or even etiquette, yet its link with the heaven that "knew" Confucius when no one else knew him, is as unmistakable as its concern with the whole of human life. In Hinduism the ethical occasionally appears like a stage one must attain or go through to reach higher spiritual paths. Yet the four yogas, or *margas*, of discrimination, action, devotion, and meditation themselves constitute a total way of life.

A WAY THAT WE WALK

Whatever may be the case with religion, the religious person has always been aware of the central importance of our images of true human existence. This is because the religious life is not in the first instance affirmation of a creed nor is it philosophy or gnosis—an attempt to know about the world or God—but a way that the human person walks *with God*, a flowing with the Tao, a discovery of "the action that is in inaction, the inaction that is in action." For the religious person, it is not enough to have a philosophy of life: one must live one's philosophy. "Not to say Torah but to be Torah"—this is the existential demand that all religion ultimately places on us.

Philosophies of religion are ultimately meaningless abstractions if we divorce them from the living Buddha, Lao-tzu, Confucius, Jesus, Mohammed, Moses, St. Francis, and the Baal-Shem-Tov. Swami Prabhavananda and Christopher Isherwood claim in their introduction to the *Bhagavad-Gita*, the Hindu "Song of God," that it does not matter whether Christ or Krishna really lived because we have their teachings and they are universal. In so doing they miss the central reality from which all religious teachings spring and to which they again and again point back: the image of the human. The historical Krishna is not so important to Hinduism as the historical Jesus is to Christianity. But even so a one-time historical human image stands behind the avatar.

If religion accordingly is a way that we walk, then the whole of human life is included in it. Yet that life comes to wholeness not additively or by abstraction but only in the up surging of events in which all the moments of the past are caught up into the present and given new reality by it. Such an event could be an hour of prayer at a time of great need—when we are facing death or are facing the death of loved ones. Or it could be a moment of breathtaking awe before a waterfall or in the midst of a raging storm at sea. Or it could be an action in which we gather together all the past means of our life in one great hour of devotion or sacrifice. In all cases, it is an event in which we attain selflessness not by giving up the self, as the ascetics suggest that we do, but by the totality of our response. In such a totality, we are taken out of ourselves, called out by something to which we respond so fully and spontaneously that our self is neither our aim nor our concern but only the self-understood and self-evident ground of our responding.

Whatever may be the case with religion, the spiritual person has always been aware of the central importance of our images of true human existence. This is because the spiritual life is not in the first instance affirmation of a creed nor is it philosophy or gnosis—an attempt to know *about* the world or God—but a way that the human person walks *with* God, a flowing with the Tao, a discovery of the action that is in inaction and the inaction that is in action. For the spiritual person, it is not enough to have a philosophy of life; one must live one's philosophy. "Not to say Torah, but to be Torah"—this is the existential demand that all spiritualities ultimately place on us.

VIA HUMANA

I coin the term the *via humana* to situate my view in contrast with the two traditional approaches—the *via positiva*, which describes the attributes of God, and the *via negativa*, which emphasizes the utter unknowability of God and speaks only of what God is not. For this reason, the importance of touchstones of reality as an approach is that it does not claim to be the absolute truth, but it also does not abandon us to come completely subjective relativism. It witnesses to as much reality as we can witness to at that moment. In opposition to both the *via negativa* and the *via positiva*, therefore, I would make bold to call touchstones of reality the *via humana*. Only through it can we keep close to the concrete reality, without pursuing theology at the expense of the fully human or humanism at the expense of closing man off from the nameless reality that he meets in his meeting with everyday life.

In viewing religion as dialogue, I am taking "religion" out of the context of theology and religious symbolism and giving it the broader meaning of the dialogical approach to religion and human experience—the way that we walk in the concrete situations of our existence. If we wish to put this in a theological context, we might speak of theology as biography or religion as event. But to do so already changes radically the traditional beliefs and presuppositions nor even upon a traditional interpretation of "sacred history" and biblical events.

Rather it is the event itself that again and again gives rise to religious meaning, and only out of that meaning, apprehended in our own history, and the history of past generations that we have made present to ourselves, do religious symbols and theological interpretations arise. For this reason, I have found it difficult to go along with those of my friends who call for a return to theology as an antidote to the excessive naturalism and restrictive "humanism" of the recent past. I believe in a larger humanism that is defined not by negation of transcendent reality but precisely by the fact that it negates nothing and is open to the concrete and unique, even if it should manifest itself, as William James puts it, "in the very dirt of private fact."

To understand the *via humana* in greater depth it is important then to grasp the interrelationship of the *human image*, and that of *touchstones of reality*. They are not synonymous, yet both are ways of "meeting the nameless Meeter," both claim that "meaning is accessible in the lived concrete." As such, both are ways of speaking of the central biblical paradox that we are created in the image of an imageless God whom we cannot define or describe, imitate, or model ourselves after yet can relate to, meet, "know" in the direct, unmediated knowing of mutual contact in the events of our lives. To plumb this paradox is not an excursus in biblical theology, for essentially the same claim stands behind all religion.

A MIDDLE WAY

Along with the "human image" metaphor, unlike scientific generalizations, touchstones of reality provide valid insights confirmable in some situations but not all. Touchstones of reality are closer to events than insights. They provide no secure purchase above the stream of living. We are left with the problem of when to move in the direction of insight and abstraction and when to move back into the living waters. The approach of touchstones of reality is nowhere more fruitful than in trying to understand religion.

This approach arose not out of a moral searching, as did images of the human, but as a way to tell my own story and a way to speak of religious reality. I particularly wanted to avoid the absolutist and universalist claims made for religious reality, on the one hand, and the various subjectivist attempts to discredit and explain away that reality, on the other. To achieve this I had to find a metaphor that avoided all universalist abstractions that attempted to take us out of time. But I wished to wed touchstones to the two-sided reality of events rather than to the mere passage of time as such. For this reason I put forward "touchstones of reality" as closer to events than insights and yet that which we carry away with us from central events of our lives and that affects the way in which we enter into and respond to new events.

My coinage of touchstones of reality also grew out of my concern for communicating as concretely as possible what I mean by religious reality and for the autobiographical events of my life that I use to illustrate that reality. Touchstones of reality are like insights, except that they are closer to events. An insight arises from a concrete encounter, but we tend to remove it too quickly and completely into a plane of abstractions. Any existential truth remains true only insofar as it is again and again tested in the stream of living. However true our touchstones, it will cease to be true if we do not make it real again by testing it in each new situation. This testing is nothing more or less than bringing our life-stance into the moment of present reality. In contrast to the scientist who is only interested in particulars insofar as they yield generalizations, we can derive valid insights from the unique situations in which we find ourselves without having to claim that they apply to all situations. We take these insights with us into other situations and test the limits of their validity.

Like images of the human, touchstones of reality offer a way in the present and into the future as objective metaphysics and subjective inspiration or emotion do not. But it is not a fixed way that frees us from the task of renewing past touchstones of reality in the present. However true our touchstone, it will cease to be true if we do not make it real again by testing it in each new situation. This testing is nothing more nor less than bringing our life-stance into the moment of present reality. Any existential truth remains true only insofar as it is again and again tested in the stream of living. We have no secure purchase on truth above this stream.

A DIALOGUE WITH HASIDIC TALES

Of the religions with which I have been in dialogue over the years—especially Hinduism, early Buddhism, Taoism, Zen, and Christian mysticism—Hasidism has spoken most strongly to me. Hasidism is the popular mystical movement of East European Jewry in the eighteenth and nineteenth centuries. The Hebrew word *hasid* means "pious" and is derived from the noun *hesed*, meaning loving-kindness, mercy, or grace. The Hasidic movement arose in Poland in the eighteenth century, and, despite bitter persecution at the hands of traditional rabbinism, spread rapidly among the Jews of Eastern Europe until it included almost half of them in its ranks. Hasidism is really a continuation in many senses of biblical and rabbinical Judaism.

The Hasidim founded real communities, each with its own rebbe, who was the leader of the community and who was also called the zaddik, the righteous or justified person. Each one of these zaddikim had his own unique teaching that he gave to his community. Originally as it was passed down from generation to generation, the leadership devolved not so much on those who receive a doctrine but on those who could embody a way of life. Thus the first effect of the zaddik was to bring the people to immediacy in relationship to God.

Hasidism has spoken most strongly to me through *Tales of the Hasidim*—the "legendary anecdotes" that bear true witness in stammering tongue to the life of the Hasidim as Martin Buber has presented it to us. If I am asked about the uniqueness of Hasidic mysticism, I do not give a definition: I tell a tale. I can best witness, I believe, to the way in which Hasidism speaks to my condition through the tales themselves. One can find motifs in Hasidism that add up to a teaching—a way of life. But these motifs are very closely interrelated, and they are not so much parts of a system as they are wisdom. Hasidism emphasizes the uniqueness of each person without stressing self-realization. For instance, "When I get to heaven," said Rabbi Zusya, "they will not ask me: 'Why were you not Moses?' but 'Why were you not Zusya?'"[1]

HALLOWING THE EVERYDAY

In Hasidism I found an image of an active love and fervent devotion no longer coupled with self-denial or metaphysical theorizing—namely, hallowing the everyday. This teaching of hallowing the everyday has been given concentrated expression by Martin Buber in his little classic *The Way of Man according to the Teachings of Hasidism*:

> By no means . . . can it be our true task, in the world into which we have been set, to turn away from the things and beings that we meet on our way and that attract our hearts; our task is precisely to get in touch, by hallowing our relationship with them, with what manifests itself in them as beauty, pleasure, enjoyment. Hasidism teaches that rejoicing in the world, if we hallow it with our whole being, leads to rejoicing in God . . . Any natural act, if hallowed, leads to God, and nature needs man for what no angel can perform on it, namely its hallowing.[2]

We human beings have been placed in the world that we may raise the dust to the spirit. Our task, as long as we live, is to "struggle with the extraneous and uplift and fit it into the divine Name." All sacraments have at their core a natural activity taken from the natural course of life that is consecrated in them. But the heart of the sacrament is equally that it does not level the event down to a symbolic gesture or mystically exalt it to "an exuberantly heartfelt point," but that it "includes an elementary, life-claiming, and life-determining experience of the *other*, the otherness, as of something coming to meet one and acting toward one." Therefore, it is not merely "celebrated" or "experienced." It seizes and claims the

---

1. Buber, *Hasidim: Early Masters*, 251.
2. Buber, *Hasidism and Modern Man*, 142.

human being in the core of his wholeness and needs nothing less than his wholeness in order to endure it. This otherness with which one comes into contact is a material or corporeal one; for "there is no rung of human life on which we cannot find the holiness of God everywhere and at all times."[3]

Once the Kotzker rebbi surprised a group of learned men by asking, "Where is the dwelling of God?" "What a thing to ask!"[4] they laughed at him. "Is not the whole world full of his glory!" But the Kotzker said, "God dwells wherever man lets him in." Buber's comment on this tale at the end of his classic little work *The Way of Man According to the Teachings of the Hasidim*, is too relevant to hallowing the everyday to leave unquoted here: "This is the ultimate purpose: to let God in. But we can let him in only where we really stand, where we live, where we live a true life. If we maintain holy intercourse with the little world entrusted to us, if we help the holy spiritual substance to accomplish itself in that section of Creation in which we are living, then we are establishing, in this our place, a dwelling for the Divine Presence."[5] "The hallowing of the world will be this letting-in," Buber comments. This is a task that not only Jews but Christians and indeed people of any religion and culture may and must shoulder.

HERE WHERE ONE STANDS

In the sixth chapter of *The Way of Man*, Martin Buber retells Rabbi Bunam's story of Reb Eisik, son of Reb Yekel, who lived in Krakow, but who dreamt three times that there was a treasure buried beneath a bridge in Prague, and finally set out and walked the whole enormous distance to Prague. He found the bridge, but was afraid to approach it because of the soldiers who guarded it, until the captain of the guard noticed him and asked him kindly what it was he wanted. When he had told the captain his dream, the latter exclaimed, "And so to please the dream, you, poor fellow, wore out your shoes to come here!" If he had had faith in dreams, continued the captain, he would have had to go to Krakow when once a dream told him to go there and dig for treasure under the stove in the room of a Jew—Eisik, son of Yekel. When Rabbi Eisik heard this,

3. Buber, *Ten Rungs*, 37; *Hasidim: Early Masters*, 66; *Origin and Meaning*, 166; *Hasidim: Later Masters*, 17.

4. Buber, *Hasidim: Later Masters*, 277.

5. Buber, *Hasidism and Modern Man*, 176.

he bowed, traveled home, dug up the treasure from under the stove, and built with it a house of prayer.

The moral of this story, says Buber, is that the fulfillment of existence is only possible "here where one stands," in the environment which I feel to be natural, in the situation which has been assigned me as my fate, in the things that happen to me and claim me day after day. If we had power over the ends of the world and knew the secrets of the upper world, they would not give us that fulfillment of existence that a quiet, devoted relationship to nearby life can give us.

There is another aspect to this tale which Buber does not bring out, but which his life and my own and that of most moderns show to be essential. Perhaps if we had not gone to "Prague," we should not have discovered that the treasure was hidden beneath our own hearth. There is meaning in our searching, even when it takes us far afield, if it enables us to come back home to the unique task that awaits us. A young person raised in Judaism or Christianity is often barred from any genuine relationship to these religions by the fact that they are associated in his mind with the parents against whom he must rebel; with a social system the injustice of which is manifest; and often, in addition, with a shoddy way of presenting the religion that seems more concerned with group belonging or social snobbery than with anything genuinely religious. Such a person might find liberation in the teachings of Hinduism, Buddhism, or Zen Buddhism that he encounters unencumbered by relatives and institutions. After these have liberated him, he may be able to go back to find the treasure under his own hearth. When one does come back, it is with a new relationship such as only the fact of distancing makes possible.

This was my own experience in relation to Judaism. Brought up in a liberal Judaism of a very thin variety, I could never have returned to Judaism and established a new and deeper relationship with it had I not gone through Hinduism, Buddhism, Zen, Taoism, and Christian mysticism. Nor have I lost these other touchstones. They are part of the way in which I came to Hasidism and relate to it. Even if young people do not find their way back—and my own way to Hasidism was far more a way forward than a way back—they are still those who set out from Cracow. Whatever treasure they really find, however far it may be from home, is still bound to those original roots. These roots are embedded in the ground on which they stand and from which they respond to the new touchstones that call to them.

THE RENEWAL OF TRUST

Two basic metaphors and methodological approaches to human existence and meaning—images of the human and touchstones of reality—together, point us to the deeper understanding that all religion is founded on the basic trust that the world is not a place in which we are hopelessly lost. About five years after the original publication of *Martin Buber: The Life of Dialogue*, I wrote to Buber saying that if I were to write it again, I would write a conclusion showing "existential trust" to be the real heart of Buber's teaching. Buber replied that I was right, that existential trust was indeed the heart of the attitude underlying his life and thought. Since then, I have expounded my own understanding of "basic trust" growing out of the "partnership of existence" and enabling us to live without the intellectual and creedal securities of theological systems, and philosophical world views. The existential trust that stands at the center of the life of dialogue is the "holy insecurity" which is willing to go out to meet the unique present even without knowing one's way ahead of time. The person of existential trust is able to accept the unique which is present in each new situation, despite all resemblance to the past.

The question for those on a spiritual journey therefore is this: can we discern a way in which we can move to quench the burning of our souls, to overcome the eclipse of God with a renewed and deepened trust? The crisis of human kind today is, as Buber indicated in an essay "Genuine Dialogue and the Possibilities of Peace," a crisis of trust. Bound up with this loss of trust in the closest possible fashion is the crisis of speech, for I can only speak to someone in the true sense of the term if I expect him or her to accept my word as genuine. The fact that it is so difficult for present-day persons to pray goes together with the fact that it is so difficult to carry on a genuine conversation. This lack of trust in Being, this incapacity for unreserved intercourse with the other, points to an innermost sickness of the sense of existence.

Evil or illusory as the world may be, sinful or ignorant as we are, religions point to a way, a path, that leads from darkness to light, from lostness to salvation, from evil to redemption. Genuine trust means trust in this present which I am never going to grasp fully with my mind since there are always at least two points of view, two realities which can never be included in any single perspective—my own existence and what is over against me. It also means trust in the future—trust that we may meet the Thou again in a new form and a new situation. These two trusts supplement each other. Ultimate trust—trust in existence itself—is trust in the present and the future at once. It is trust in the God who will be there even as he will be there, who will be with us even when we walk, as we will, in the valley of the shadow of death.

Trust accepts the fact that a genuine relationship is two-sided and therefore beyond the control of our will. What can be known in this situation can be known only by taking the risk of entering into the relationship. This is a real risk, without guarantees of any sort, for we may find a response and we may not. Therefore, trust must never be understood as trust that in this particular occasion we know there will be a response. Genuine trust is a readiness to go forth on this occasion with such resources as we have and, if we do not receive any response, to be ready another time to go out to the meeting.

The trust in existence that enables us to live from moment to moment and to go out to meet what the new moment brings is the trust that makes it possible that in new meeting we again become whole, alive, present. If I trust in a person, a relationship, this means that despite what may and will happen, I shall enter into relationship again and bring all the past moments of meeting into the present meeting. The particular person who is my partner may die, become sick, disturbed; he or she may betray me, rupture the relationship, or simply turn away and fail to respond. Sooner or later something of this happens for most of us. When it does, it is trust which enables us to remain open and respond to the new address of the new situation. If we lose our trust in existence, conversely, we are no longer able to enter anew into real dialogue. A new conscience, a dialogical spirituality, must arise in and between human beings which will summon them. As Buber writes in *Eclipse of God*, we need to penetrate again and again into false absolutes "with an incorruptible, probing glance" until one can "glimpse the never-vanishing appearance of the Absolute."[6] It is this God who is *recognized* in each genuine meeting with the utterly new, the utterly unique.

6. Buber, *Eclipse*, 120.

BIBLIOGRAPHY

Buber, Martin. *Eclipse of God: Studies in the Relation between Religion and Philosophy.* Translated by Maurice Friedman et al. New York: Harper Torchbook, 1952.

———. *Hasidism and Modern Man.* Translated by Maurice Friedman. New Jersey: Humanities Press, 1988.

———. *The Origin and Meaning of Hasidism.* Translated by Maurice Friedman. New York: Horizon, 1960.

———. *Tales of the Hasidim: The Early Masters.* Translated by Olga Marx. New York: Schocken, 1961.

———. *Tales of the Hasidim: The Later Masters.* Translated by Olga Marx. New York: Schocken, 1961.

———. *Ten Rungs: Hasidic Sayings.* Translated by Olga Marx. New York: Schocken, 1947.

———. *The Way of Man According to the Teachings of Hasidism.* New York: Citadel, 1964.

Friedman, Maurice. *Martin Buber: The Life of Dialogue.* Chicago: University of Chicago Press, 1955.

James, William. *The Varieties of Religious Experience.* New York: Random House, 1902.

8

Encountering the Ineffable

Maurice Friedman's Dialogue with God

DONALD MOORE

LTHOUGH MAURY FRIEDMAN HAS been in dialogue with many of the world's religions, I choose to limit my remarks on his dialogue with God to the tradition of the Hebrew Bible. This is where he himself seems finally to have taken his stand. In the conclusion of *You Are My Witnesses* he points to three proponents of the biblical tradition, Martin Buber, Abraham Heschel, and Elie Wiesel, as the types of witnesses God needs in our contemporary era.[1] I will place Maury in that same category and examine three key areas of religious significance in his writings: faith (or existential trust), revelation, and prayer.

FAITH

Faith for Maury, as for Buber, is primarily *emunah* as opposed to *pistis*, wholehearted trust rather than knowledge/content. He tells us that at the beginning of his doctoral studies he decided to make faith, defined as "a basic trust in life", the central theme of his study plans. By this he meant a study of those "original sources of religious faith—of trust in life—from which theology and metaphysics are usually derived—the Psalms, the Prophets, the life of Jesus, the 'Way of Life' of Lao-tzu . . ."[2] For over fifty years Maury has adhered to this plan. This also was the motivating factor

---

1. Friedman, *You Are My Witnesses*, 278.
2. Friedman, *Touchstones of Reality*, 81.

behind so much of Martin Buber's retelling of the Hasidic tales. Buber wanted to recapture the power and vitality of Hasidic faith as found in the moment of the lived encounter, and to preserve therein its dialogic character.

Maury finds this faith-as-trust at the very core of the Hebrew Bible, especially in the Psalms and the prophets. He points in a special way to Psalm 23: "Though I walk through the valley of the shadow of death, I shall fear no evil, for Thou art with me." It is a question here of faith in God's abiding presence and concern, a trust in the God who is with us as we walk in the shadow of death. This is the God who is recognized in each encounter, though the encounter be utterly new and unique. We go forth to each encounter with trust, a trust which is ultimately a recognition of the powerlessness and poverty of the human condition. *Emunah* does not provide us with an escape from the valley of death. Each of us must walk alone through that valley; each must live *in* that valley.

Trust in God does not imply that we know who or what God is. We have no concept or definition that would remove from us the imagelessness of the biblical God. Nor is it a trust that God will do this or that for us. Rather it is simply "that unconditional trust that enables one, as long as one has the strength to do so, to go forth and meet what comes." It is a trust in the very meaning of existence. "Trust in God and existential trust are identical."[3] Such trust does not rest upon belief in the existence of God, for such a belief, in Maury's view, would rest on proofs of God's existence. A God whose existence could be proven would not be the Creator and Lord of history. As Buber had earlier written, for the authentic Jew "the idea of the non-existence of God lies outside the realm of that which was conceivable by him."[4] The person of biblical faith centers on the fidelity of God. God is so present to us that we may trust ourselves to God completely. This is a Presence which constantly makes demands upon our lives. What is important is not so much a faith in God's existence but the actualization of this faith through the attitudes and decisions of one's life.

Emunah calls one to partnership with God in holy insecurity, guided only by God's presence. This presence serves as guidance, but it is a guidance that provides no answers, no solutions. Persons of faith still have to direct their own steps. They are not absolved from the responsibility

3. Ibid., 328–9.
4. Buber, *Two Types of Faith*, 38.

of deciding for themselves what is demanded in a particular situation. Yet what God demands of them at *this* moment they can only learn here and now and not beforehand. They must realize that they are responsible before God for this *their* hour and that they carry out their responsibility for this hour before God in so far as they are able. What confronts them is a sign, a word from God, a word that stands in no dictionary and yet demands an answer. This responsibility in certain respects belongs to each and every person. One cannot yield that responsibility to some other individual or group or institution. To yield that responsibility to another is to pervert the meaning of faith, one's relationship of absolute trust in God. One owes this responsibility to God alone. One's response for this hour is made with the awareness of God's abiding presence, a presence which is indeed counsel, for one approaches this hour, aware that one is living one's life before the face of God.

This Jewish agnosticism expressed by Maury, Buber, and many others over the last century has its counterpart in what is often referred to as Christian agnosticism. John Courtney Murray, perhaps the most renowned of American theologians of the last century, reminded us that one of the constant concerns of Thomas Aquinas "was to protect the mystery of the divine transcendence from prying scrutiny." Aquinas put this in quite forceful terms: "One thing about God remains completely unknown in this life, namely, what God is." Aquinas stated this truth so often and so uncompromisingly that, as Murray points out, "his commentators have become a bit alarmed at the patent poverty of the knowledge of God" that he would permit us. We can in no way crowd God into a concept. God's transcendence will always escape our conceptualizations. But Murray issues a caution: despite all of Aquinas's agnosticism concerning our understanding of God, he demonstrated that our confession of ignorance "is not to be made effortlessly, at the outset of inquiry," otherwise our ignorance is simply "absence of knowledge and not itself a mode of knowing." Ignorance of God becomes true knowledge of God when it results from an inquiry "that is firmly and flexibly disciplined at every step." Christian theology holds for a true knowledge of God as well as a valid language about God. Our way to such knowledge is to follow all the "scattered scintillae that the logos has strewn throughout history and across the face of the heavens." We follow them "until they all fuse in the darkness that is the unapproachable Light." Along this way all the resources of language and of thought "must be exploited until they are exhausted." Only at this point should we confess our ignorance and lapse into silence. But now "this ignorance is knowledge, as this silence is itself a language—the language of adoration."[5]

Perhaps Maury could not accept these arguments of Christian agnosticism, but they clearly support Buber's insistence that the eternal Thou can never validly become an object in the world of It. We might even consider Christian agnosticism as a possible bridge linking *emunah* and *pistis*, or more appropriately, authentic Judaism and authentic Christianity.

Maury's strong defense of human freedom resonates closely with Catholic theology, especially since the Second Vatican Council (1962–1965). Human existence for Maury betokens "genuine historical destiny," not a divine blueprint that "we merely act out." It is a destiny that implies "real freedom with which to act, real resources to praise, bless, thank, but also to contend with God . . ." Maury is convinced that we are "the partners of God in existence, the co-creators who work together in completing creation . . . helping it toward redemption."[6] Such language could have been lifted directly from Vatican II's *Gaudium et Spes,* its Constitution on the Church in the Modern World.

One final aspect of faith as *emunah* should be mentioned. Maury sees this life of unconditional trust in God as the basis for that "holy insecurity" that he recognizes as so central to Martin Buber's understanding of the human person. It implies life lived on the "narrow ridge." In this lived relationship one does not have the certainty of metaphysical truth, but only the experience of mutual knowing which springs from genuine meeting, from wholehearted presence to the other, and ultimately from wholehearted presence to the One who is eternally Other, eternally Thou. Maury cites a 1954 letter from Buber which gave him greater insight into this "narrow ridge", into the uniqueness of each "touchstone of reality":

> I open my heart to the Law to such an extent that if I feel a commandment being addressed to me I feel myself bound to do it as far as I am addressed . . . In certain moments, some of them rather regular, I pray, alone of course, and say what I want to say, sometimes without words at all, and sometimes a remembered verse helps me in an extraordinary situation; but there have been

5. Murray, *Problem of God,* 70–73.

6. Friedman, *You Are My Witnesses,* 278–79.

days when I felt myself to enter into the prayer of a community, and so I did it. This is my way of life, and one may call it religious anarchy if he likes . . . I cannot say anything but: put yourself in relation as you can and when you can, do your best to persevere in relation, and do not be afraid.[7]

Here there are no guarantees, no absolutes, no certainties, but only the risk of going forth to meeting, trusting in existence, taking one's stand in relation, confronting the other with the whole of one's being, and thus living in "holy insecurity."

REVELATION

In *Martin Buber and the Eternal Thou* Maury is in agreement with Buber's assertion that the one teaching that fills the Hebrew Bible and which has become a basic teaching of Judaism is that our life is a dialogue between the above and the below, with God addressing humankind and in turn being addressed by humankind. God speaks to each person, and each is invited to respond by doing or not doing. This address or encounter belongs to the essence of biblical revelation. From the biblical perspective the fundamental reality is speech, a dialogical relationship.

Buber reminds us in *I and Thou* that in the beginning stands relation. Each lived moment carries on this dialogue so that all that happens, all that befalls us, is taken as a sign of address. What one tries to do or fails to do is taken as a stammering attempt to respond as best as one can, or there is simply a failure to respond. The Bible should be understood as having a primordial oral character. The meaning of the address cannot be grasped objectively, but only dialogically. It does not offer itself to an objective understanding. Ideally, the Bible should always be read in living presence; which means one must be present and listen faithfully to the Voice behind the written word. It is primarily through history that God addresses humankind, and this implies "the concrete significance of this time, this place, this situation. Revelation does not imply some universal truth always there for one to apprehend at each moment. Rather revelation consists of "the Eternal entering into time" and ones meeting the Eternal "in a moment of time, in a moment of

---

7. Ibid., xvi.

history, whether it is the personal history of the individual or the history of a group of people."[8]

In Maury's understanding of biblical revelation, God is in no way reducible to the world or to humankind. Rather God remains in relation with all reality, creating anew at every moment and sustaining at every moment. Maury's historical view of revelation means that God has a stake in creation and in history. History here is no longer cyclical or repetitive like the seasons of the year, but linear, moving from creation to redemption, the ultimate goal of history.

While the Bible must be considered a privileged locus for revelation, everything in life has the possibility of becoming a sign or vehicle of revelation. Revelation is rooted in "openness to the wonder of the everyday." Anywhere that one takes one's stand should be considered holy ground. The rabbi of Kobryn insists "there is no rung of human life on which we cannot find the holiness of god everywhere and at all times." One's dialogue with God takes place in the heart of the everyday. It means one hears and responds to God's guidance and direction, to God's "Torah", at each hour, a unique response for each unique situation, and not "a fixed, objective, universal law" demanding obedience always and everywhere. By no means can God's address be limited to the Scriptures; rather "the word of the Creator speaks forth from the creation and the creatures each day anew," from an environment that may appear to be strange, unusual, even hostile.

Maury uses the lovely story, retold by Buber, of Rabbi Eisik, son of Yekel, who travels from Krakow to Prague in search of treasure because of a dream, only to realize the treasure he has been seeking is hidden under the hearth of his own home. There are many who must "travel to Prague," embracing perhaps a strange country or culture or religion, before they can recognize the treasure that was always there, hidden under the hearth of their own home. "There is meaning in our searching, even when it takes us far afield." Maury points to his own pilgrimage from Judaism through Hinduism, Buddhism, Zen, Taoism, and Christian mysticism, back to Judaism via Hasidism. Each of these touchstones remains with him and enriches his understanding of Judaism. Should someone not find the way back, whatever treasure they find remains "bound to those original roots . . . [which] are embedded in the ground

---

8. Friedman, *Touchstones of Reality*, 130.

on which they stand and from which they respond to the new touchstones that call to them."[9]

However it comes to humankind, God's revelation has for its purpose the formation of a people who will work on the redemption of all creation. Revelation is a call to the service and hallowing of creation, and it is through such service that one achieves one's own fulfillment. God wants to come to the world, to make this truly God's world and God's kingdom, but God wills this goal to be accomplished by human deed. Humankind becomes the "completer" of God's creation and the "initiator" of God's redemption. There are no rules for achieving this task. There is no set method for bringing it about. One must enter into the task with one's whole being and bring every aspect of one's existence into it. One must not allow any sphere of life "to remain separate from God." God claims the whole of one's personal existence, one's social, political, cultural life, one's "inner intentions" as well as one's "outer acts." Nothing is excluded. "The Holy is not a separate and secluded sphere of being. It is open to all spheres of being and it is that through which they find fulfillment." Maury would urge one to give oneself wholeheartedly to that which encounters one here and now in this unforeseen moment.

All hallowing begins, from the human side, within the depths of the individual person and implies the hallowing of the human within that person. Maury insinuates through his *via humana*, as does Buber throughout so much of his writings, that one can approach God only through becoming human. One is created in order to become human, and one becomes human through relation, through presence to the world and to other human beings. The one who is authentically human becomes both symbol and sacrament. As Maury expressed it: "The highest manifestation of the religious symbol is a human life lived in relation to the Absolute."[10]

As one becomes human, one draws oneself and one's world into the sphere of the holy. Or to put it in other Hasidic terms, through living a truly human life, one lets God into the world. Maury insists repeatedly that what is really important is not so much *what* one believes but rather *how* one *lives*. Is one living a life that is authentically human? Does one's belief system bring one to a deeper understanding of the human person?

9. Friedman, *You Are My Witnesses*, 167–70.

10. Friedman, *Buber and Eternal*, 19, 139.

As Maury says of the Hasidim, "It is not the doctrine that is important but the way of life, the image of the human."[11]

From a biblical and Christian perspective I would strongly endorse Maury's approach to religion. One cannot be authentically human without in some way being a religious person. Karl Rahner used the term "anonymous Christian" to describe persons whose lives reflected the demand to be authentically human. Perhaps it would be more judicious to use the term "anonymous believer," referring to all those who in one way or another in their human struggles "call upon the Nameless out of the night and yearning" of their garret window.[12] Persons of genuine faith, those who are open to and responsive to God's revelation, are recognized far more by the lives they live, by who they are, rather than by the beliefs they profess.

PRAYER

Although there are many deserving aspects of Maury's dialogue with God that might be considered, I limit myself finally and briefly to just this one. So much of what Maury has written about faith and revelation, as well as about religion and God, underscores an aspect of his thought about which he writes very little. I think it appropriate to say *of* Maury what Professor Arnold Bergstraesser said about Buber *to* Maury as he was finishing his doctoral dissertation at the University of Chicago: "Do you know Buber's secret? It was prayer." Maury mentions that he was "amazed" by this remark. Bergstraesser, of course, was not referring to long hours of formal prayer. But rather that Buber "brought himself into presentness every hour of his life in a real openness."[13] Maury himself could not have carried on his own life of dialogue and shared so many of his own touchstones of reality unless he too lived with that sense of presentness and openness which he ascribes to Buber.

If I might add a personal note: I too was amazed when I read of Professor Bergstraesser's remark as I was preparing this paper. For independently of Bergstraesser and Maury, I had come to a similar conclusion as I was preparing a second edition of my own work on Buber's religious thought. So much of what Buber has come to say about the

---

11. Friedman, *Heart of Wisdom*, 64.

12. Buber, *I and Thou*, 66.

13. Friedman, *Heart of Wisdom*, 218; cf. *Touchstones of Reality*, 341.

tragedy of religion, the obstacles that religion presents to us in our life of faith, the dangers of codification and centralization within religion, has as its source not religion-as-such but religion-without-prayer. Buber's repeated censures of the law imply a law "emptied of the spirit" where the living Voice has been stifled. The law, as well as all the other forms and images and teachings of religion, must be immersed in "the truth of the encounter." They must be brought into the presence of the Other; they must be accompanied by a life of prayer. So many of the goals toward which humankind is called to strive, especially that of community, cannot be achieved, in my reading of Buber, without a deep sense of prayer, without a sense of being present and open to that which confronts one here and now.[14]

Maury too writes of the various expressions of religion, by which he means, I presume, the various "forms" of religion—images, symbols, rites—as inevitably coming loose from their mooring, becoming detached and independent. Hence there is the need to reestablish the original meeting "that creed, ritual and social form no longer lead us back to."[15] The original meeting in Buber's terms, and I am sure also in Maury's, implies that moment of absolute or pure relation, the moment of encounter with the eternal Thou, that wholehearted presence to Presence which is the essence of prayer. God is near the forms of religion as long as they are not removed from God. What removes these religious forms from God is the lack of prayer in religion. As long as prayer is an intimate part of religion, God remains near these forms of religion. Religions live as long as prayer lives within them. Degeneration of the religions presumes the degeneration of prayer within them.[16]

Thus when Maury speaks of the need to "reestablish" the original meeting, I believe he is speaking of that moment of pure or absolute relation from which the forms of religion have their derivation. The creeds, rites, doctrines and symbols of religion, in so far as they are rooted in the moment of encounter, retain the capacity to lead us back to this revelatory moment, not to explain or capture or unveil the moment, but to bring us once again to the encounter. Unfortunately, such religious "forms" again and again surface to become more than what they are; the adherents of a religion tend to substitute them for that reality to which

14. Moore, *Buber: Prophet*, 252–60.

15. Friedman, *Heart of Wisdom*, 215.

16. Cf. Buber, *I and Thou*, 118.

they merely point. That is hardly the fault of the symbols and doctrines and creeds as such, but rather of those who make these religious forms so much more than what they are meant to be. This occurs when the adherents of a religion abandon prayer.

Maury tells us that the life of prayer can be sustained only "if we bring ourselves to each situation with all that we know and have been." These words convey so much of Maury's professional life. He cites the words of the Baal Shem Tov: "Alas the world is full of enormous lights and mysteries, but man hides them from him with one small hand." Maury then adds the insightful comment: "Prayer is the removal of that hand."[17]

Maury concludes his *Touchstones of Reality* in this manner:

> The kingdom of God cannot be localized in the immanent or the transcendent, within us or beyond us. It is both the personal—the quality of individual living—and the social—the realization of justice, righteousness, and loving kindness in lived community. It is dialogue, trust, and grace—moving among us. It is the covenant of peace—the task that demands us and the partnership of existence that sustains and comforts us. It is our touchstone of reality—our discovery and confirmation of them in the cruel and gracious happenings of our lives.[18]

These words could only come from one whose life is characterized by a presence and openness to the mystery which confronts us at every moment, from one whose life is rooted in prayer. Thank you, Maury, for your witness to a life of dialogue.

---

17. Friedman, *Heart of Wisdom*, 218–9.

18. Friedman, *Touchstones of Reality*, 341; cf. *Heart of Wisdom*, 219.

BIBLIOGRAPHY

Buber, Martin. *I and Thou.* New York: Scribner, 1957.

———. *Two Types of Faith.* Translated by Norman Goldhawk. New York: Harper Torchbooks, 1961.

Friedman, Maurice. *Abraham Joshua Heschel and Elie Wiesel: You Are My Witnesses.* New York: Farrar, Strauss, Giroux, 1987.

———. *A Heart of Wisdom: Religion and Human Wholeness.* Albany: SUNY Press, 1992.

———. *Martin Buber and the Eternal.* New York: Human Sciences Press, 1986.

———. *Touchstones of Reality.* New York: Dutton, 1972.

Moore, Donald. *Martin Buber: Prophet of Religious Secularism.* 2nd ed. New York: Fordham University Press, 1996.

Murray, John Courtney. *The Problem of God.* New Haven: Yale University Press, 1964.

9

Maurice Friedman's Dialogue with Asian Religions

NATHAN KATZ

MAURY ALWAYS TAUGHT US that *meaning* was neither in the mind of the perceiver nor in the object perceived, but in the meeting between the two. Whether discussing a novel by Kafka, a Zen anecdote, or a Bible story, he would insist on this point: it would be inauthentic to assert claims about a text's meaning independent of the reader. And he would hasten to further admonish us: but the text's meaning is not simply in the mind of the reader. Meaning only emerges, he would conclude, in the dialogical meeting of the reader and the text, in the "in-between."

Therefore, to write about Maury's dialogue with Asian religions, I have to write about my dialogue with Maury. He was my teacher, one of my most significant intellectual influences, and an inspiration towards a career as a professor of religious studies. To be faithful to my teacher, I should not write about him, but about my relationship with him—because that is the way Maury always talks about religion, literature, philosophy, and psychotherapy by indicating the "in-between."

Maury was my teacher at Temple University during the late 1960s, a wonderful/terrible time at universities. It was wonderful because of an open-mindedness, a willingness to experiment, which I have not seen since; a hunger for experience rather than abstraction; and a passion for the social issues of the day. It was terrible because students demanded "relevancy" from their professors, a demand which was little more than arrogance and impatience in fancy dress; because discipline mattered naught; and because we all, faculty and students alike, lived under the burden that a poor grade point average could mean the loss of a student deferment and a one-way ticket to Vietnam.

An undergraduate student majoring in literature, I was buffeted about by the cultural winds of the day: the anti-War movement, hippiedom, a fascination with things Asian, a mystical/mythical quest, and a variety of psychotherapeutic experiences—all tempered by a good-natured hedonism. And it was in this context that I enrolled in Maury's course on Jewish and Comparative Mysticism.

Maury's teaching style and intellectual approach were suited to those times. It was the first course I'd taken which was taught in a circle. Discussion replaced the lecture. "Authority" did not reside behind a lectern, but was to be discovered in an insightful reading of the day's text.

But the course was more than that. It took me some time to realize that Maury's approach to Lao Tzu or the *Bhagavad Gita* or the Ba'al Shem Tov was not so different from his approach to his students. He was able to listen, to hear and to respond, better than any adult I'd yet encountered. I began to understand that Maury listened to a text, rather than fit it into a preconceived framework. But I only realized that after I'd observed him actively listening to his students.

An incident brought this home for me. During those days, I became immersed in student political activism—against the war, the draft, the university, established religion. Against authority. A group of students started up an alternative campus newspaper called the *Temple Free Press*. I fancied myself a writer (as well as a mystic, revolutionary, cultural pioneer, and a host of other self-aggrandizements) and so spewed out a range of articles. Students and faculty, especially Maury, seemed to like what I wrote. Eventually I was asked to become an editor. But I hesitated. If I took up the title, then might I not become locked in to an ideological/intellectual position? Simply by creating an established order, I feared losing the very openness and spontaneity which I uncritically lauded. I was perplexed, and I asked Maury if I might see him outside of class. I remember it all so very clearly. We sat at a counter at Linton's restaurant on Broad Street, near my subway stop. Maury ate a Brown Betty as I poured out my hesitations about assuming the editorship, my views on politics and spirituality, on family and religion. I remember those details so well, but I do not remember a word Maury said. I do remember him listening. And I came away from that conversation knowing my mind much better. I declined the editorship because of that conversation with

Maury, but it is not his words that I remember, but his silence, his listening. I began to understand that by listening, we allow the other to speak for him/herself, and that this was the key to Maury and his approach to the study of religions. Listening.

I took other courses with Maury as well, about Existentialism and about Literature. But that course on Jewish and Comparative Mysticism was the best course of my undergraduate career. I remember the readings very well, because I have used most of them in the courses I teach. We read the Hindu classic, the *Bhagavad Gita*, the font of Taoism, the *Tao Teh Ching*, writings by the German mystic, Meister Eckhart, a collection of Zen stories entitled *Zen Flesh, Zen Bones*, and Buber's *Tales of the Hasidim*.[1]

HINDUISM

We studied the *Bhagavad Gita* in the nondualist (and highly problematic) translation by Swami Prabhavananda and Christopher Isherwood. Maury, like a number of scholars and artists, had been attracted to the Ramakrishna Mission In fact, he was a student of the Philadelphia branch's remarkable resident teacher, Swami Yatiswarananda. Like his mentor, Martin Buber, Maury "was concerned with Hinduism before he became concerned with Hasidism and Jewish mysticism."[2] When then-chairman of Temple's Department of Religion, the Jewish-Sufi Bernard Phillips, wanted to bring in someone to teach a course on Hinduism, Maury was involved in hiring Swami Nikhilananda of the Mission's premier branch in New York. I took my first course about Hinduism with the Swami.

Maury's dialogue with Hinduism was shaped by these swamis as well as by fellow western students such as Isherwood, Aldous Huxley and W. T. Stace. The Ramakrishna Mission, known in some cities as the Vedanta Society, is based on the nondualist, social-activist teaching of Swami Vivekananda, a charismatic, turn-of-the-century Bengali brahmin, one of the leaders of the "Hindu Renaissance." He named his movement for his *guru*, a pious nineteenth-century Calcutta renunciate, Swami Ramakrishna, devotee of the goddess Kali. Unlike his *guru*,

---

1. Isherwood and Swami Prabhavananda, trans., *The Song of God: Bhagavad Gita*; Bynner, trans. *The Way of Life according to Lao Tzu*; Blakney, trans., *Meister Eckhart*; Reps, *Zen Flesh, Zen Bones*; Buber, *Tales of the Hasidim*, 2 vols.

2. Friedman, "Buber and Oriental Religions," 152.

however, Vivekananda was thoroughly nondualist in outlook, a minority tradition in India which is at odds with the majority's worship of a personal deity. Vivekananda's Hinduism emphasized nondualism as well as programs for the uplift of the "backward classes" of India and a renewal of Hinduism in the light of modern science and technology. In America, mystical monism rose to the foreground of the Mission's ethos, while Vivekananda's social concerns found scant expression. Perhaps it was felt that America's Judaic and Christian traditions provided ample religious contexts for the pursuit of social justice, while lacking the spiritual and meditational richness of Hinduism.

Maury's dialogue with Hinduism involved the practice of meditation as much as reading texts. This is characteristic of his approach to religion in general, a study undertaken by the whole person, not only the intellect—an approach which was especially well-suited during that experience-hungry decade. But Maury was not being trendy; he had begun his intensive study of Hinduism while on service as a conscientious objector in the Civilian Public Service Camps near Philadelphia during the Second World War. Maury wrote of this period: "I turned full-force to *advaitin* (nondualist) Hinduism as taught by . . . Swami Yatiswarananda, a disciple of Ramakrishna's whom I saw weekly at the Vedanta Society in Philadelphia. I meditated three hours a day . . ."[3] The role of meditation and religious experience in Maury's apprehension of Indian nondualism, or Advaita, is clear in both his writing and his teaching. This is not to say that Maury eschewed intellectual work. One familiar with Advaita's literature will recognize many traditional metaphors in the passage of Maury's below. But one also hears the immediacy of his own experience and reflection:

> To me the Hindu Upanishads' progress to absolute subjectivity can be understood in terms of our common experience in which the dreamer is more real than the dream, in which the continuity of the self is set in contrast to the flux of the world that the self witnesses, in which we are aware at times of the consciousness as detached from the senses, as when we concentrate so much on a certain matter that although our auditory senses are fully functioning, we do not hear what is going on around us. Though music is playing, we do not hear the music. Someone may even call our name, and we do not hear it. This is true with all the other senses too. One can look and yet not see anything because one is

3. Friedman, *Heart of Wisdom*, 11.

intent on something else. If we can thus withdraw the consciousness from the senses, we can conceive of the mind remaining
within itself without going out to the senses. . . . Thus the very beginning point of the Hindu yoga of meditation is the withdrawal
of consciousness from the senses into the mind, leading to inner
illumination . . .

Finally, according to mystics the world over, we find, by going
within, an intensified consciousness that not only is ineffable and
all-absorbing, including every other sensation, reflection, and
concern, but also is a self-evident and self-validating reality of
existence, compared to which our waking consciousness seems
unreal. When dreaming, we feel that our dreams are real, but
when waking we know that they are only dreams compared to
the waking consciousness. Similarly, when we attain this higher
consciousness, our waking world seems to us, in comparison, a
dream. Thus the world is unreal only in comparison with this
higher reality.

In *Through the Looking Glass* [Maury often referred to what
I thought was just a children's story], the "Wood with no Name"
is one of the eight squares through which Alice must pass before
she can become Queen Alice. Alice comes on a fawn in the wood
and asks it what its name is. The fawn says, "I can't remember,
but I'll tell you when we get to the edge of the wood." Alice puts
her arm around the neck of the fawn, and they walk together to
the edge of the wood. Then the fawn comes to and says, "Why,
I'm a fawn, and *you* are a little girl!" and scampers away in great
fright. Thus the name gets in the way of the basic reality. Only
when we progressively back away from the world of particulars,
are we ready to arrive at that awareness of identity that is at the
root of the mystical experience. The philosophy itself does not
give one the experience, but it may be a necessary preparation for
it—for the final leap—just as in Plato's *Republic* the dialectic of
the philosopher leads him out of the cave up the hill to the top of
the hill when he then makes the leap to the sun, which represents
direct knowledge of the Good, the True, and the Beautiful.

Having arrived at these two separate points, the absolute
subjective essence within the self and the absolute objective essence of reality, then through a combination of direct mystical
experience and philosophical contemplation stimulated by that
experience, the two aspects of absolute subjectivity and absolute
objectivity are identified. In a lightning flash there arises the
central insight of the Upanishads and of the whole nondualistic
Vedanta: *Brahman is Atman, tat tvam asi*—Thou art That.[4]

---

4. Ibid., 12–14.

This was fairly typical of Maury's approach to religion, one that involves at least three interconnected steps. First there is the careful study of a tradition's core texts, preferably at the feet of a master within that tradition. It was in this way that Maury had read the *Upanishads* and the *Bhagavad Gita* with Swami Yatiswarananda. Second, there are constant, apt cross-references to other traditions and literatures, be they drawn from classical Greek philosophy or *Through the Looking Glass*. Third, Maury undertook the spiritual practice associated with the text, in this case the practice of certain forms of Hindu meditation. Finally, his approach was crowned by an immediate dialogical encounter with the text, a mystical experience in which the tradition and the investigator meet.

As Maury led his students through Prabhavananda and Isherwood's *Bhagavad Gita*, it was obvious that he spoke with an authority borne of the experiences indicated in the text, that he knew what the text was about in a most immediate sense. Temple's Religion Department unkindly (and unfairly, I still believe) had been castigated as a "zoo theory" approach to the study of religion, a university which substituted imams, rabbis, priests, swamis, and roshis for dispassionate, objective scholars.[5] I had taken courses with Swami Nikhilananda and with the Korean Son (Zen) monk, Seo Kyung-bo, so it was not so unusual to me that a religion professor taught texts which he had mastered experientially. What was singular about Maury, however, was that he had experienced a text in a tradition that was not his own.

Or was it? Maury liked to use that term, "to make something one's own," to describe the lasting effects of having experienced a text or idea dialogically, openly, non-objectifyingly. Maury wrote of his dialogue, "Hinduism was at one time in my life a 'live option,' in William James's phrase, a road that I could and did not follow. I have taken a different path in the years since. Yet I believe that the options which we choose and later reject are almost as important for us as the options we ultimately choose and make our own. They remain within us, like an obligato to the melody of our lives."[6] What was it that led Maury away from Hinduism? There were two factors, each ironic. The first was a perceived lack of a social dimension, that aspect of Vivekananda's thought which had become attenuated in his American centers. Second, it was a lack of symbolic and emotional richness, which philosophically and temperamentally is

5. Welch, *Graduate Education*.

6. Friedman, *Heart of Wisdom*, 12.

precisely where Vivekananda differed from Ramakrishna and from 99 percent of all Hindus who worship a qualified god (*saguna brahmana*) rather than a transcendent Absolute (*nirguna brahmana*). Maury described his disinfatuation with Hinduism: "I felt [a growing tension] between various pulls: toward active love, the search for the truth, toward meditation and spiritual exercise, and my desire for a way to express my emotions in worship. What troubled me most was the lack of a tradition or symbol to which I could wholly give myself. My attempts to meditate on Sri Ramakrishna, on Christ, and on the Buddha did not resolve my conflict."[7] And what is Hinduism's obligato for Maury? "[I]t gives existence a depth-dimension that is always there for me even when I do not spell it out—a transpersonal consciousness the reality of which I recognize, though not as the only reality."[8]

Maury taught us that "the central statement in the central Hindu scripture the *Bhagavad Gita* is, 'He who sees the action that is in inaction, the inaction that is in action, is wise indeed.'" [9] In fact, when I teach the *Bhagavad Gita* in my introductory Hinduism courses today, one of my examination questions is to explicate just this *shloka* (verse), so Maury's focus is something I have made my own.

Like Mahatma Gandhi, Maury saw the *Gita* as a manual for the practice of *karma-yoga*, the discipline of action, the spiritual principles upon which social activism could be based. Also like Gandhi, Maury was a pacifist who understood the *Gita*'s fabled battlefield of Kurukshetra as an allegory for quotidian life (*dharmakshetra*). Maury explained:

> Karma yoga—the yoga of action—is action without attachment to the fruits of action. You live in the world and act, but you are not acting for the sake of the result. If you want to help others, you can only do so out of your spiritual state of being. You cannot cultivate that state of being in order to help others. If you do so, you will be thinking of the fruit of action, and therefore your state of being will not be that out of which effective action can proceed. This is a paradox. But this is the only true, the only effective action, according to the Gita.[10]

---

7. Friedman, *Touchstones of Reality*, 52.

8. Friedman, *Heart of Wisdom*, 12.

9. Ibid., 14.

10. Ibid., 15.

From Maury teaching us about Hindu mysticism, I came to learn a good deal about his approach to religion. The first principle I deduced about his approach is that religions, first and foremost, are not objects. While one may *grasp* or *master* an object, one must *listen to* one's dialogue partner. And if one really listens, then the tradition will not be squeezed into preconceived categories which do not precisely "fit," but one ultimately allows it to speak with its own voice.

The second principle is about what's at stake in the study of religions. It is not primarily a career or a reputation, but one's own spiritual life which is on the table. In a dialogical encounter one may be irrevocably changed, and if this sort of dialogue is the essence of Maury's method, then we are in danger of changing, of growing, as we learn. Maury's approach to religions involved the whole person—body, mind and spirit—and not merely the intellect. "[I]n religion," he wrote, "as distinct from scientific inquiry and aesthetic emotion, the whole being is responding and the whole being is involved in the response."[11] And it is that whole being which is effected by the dialogical encounter, so that when one emerges from the encounter one may "make his own" that text or tradition, after which it becomes a "touchstone of reality" which remains part of oneself, one is thereby altered. As such, Maury's approach is a risky business—indeed, risk and openness, a necessary condition for there to be genuine encounter, are closely allied.

ZEN BUDDHISM

Openness, risk and change are central in Maury's understanding of Zen Buddhism. The Buddha himself taught that all of experience has three characteristics: unsatisfactoriness, impermanence, and absence of an abiding essence—*duhkha*, *anitya*, and *anatman*. "If we try to hold on to any part of existence, we will suffer," Maury explained.

> We will suffer because the attempt to hold on goes against the fact of change. Our very enjoyment of this moment must mean our suffering and sadness in the next moment. It cannot but be so. If we were able to enjoy the moment, relate to it, and then let it go, that would be different. But something else happens. Not only do we have this momentary relationship, but then we fix it; we record the fact that this was a pleasurable sensation or we shrink from it. As a result, we are not able to accept the

11. Friedman, "Touchstones," 5.

simplest and most elementary fact of human existence—that all things change, perish, and pass away. Human life is a vain search for building security. We fruitlessly try to shore it up in every direction, like Kafka's mole who is never done fortifying his hole. Unable to accept her child's death, Kisogatomi went to the Buddha and pleaded, "Bring my child back to life." Eventually she realized that death is a part of human existence, and she was able to put her child aside.[12]

The lesson which Maury most often drew from the Buddha's teaching about impermanence was to remain close to the concrete situation. This is how he understood Mahayana Buddhism's great emphasis on compassion (karuna) and the "second wing" of enlightenment, along with wisdom (prajna). The Buddha was compassionate, Maury taught, because he "always remained close to the concrete situation, to the pragmatic problem at hand."[13]

On one level, in the Buddhism of the Pali Canon, this "remaining close to the concrete situation" was reflected in the Buddha's exclusive concern "with the human, with anthropology, rather than with metaphysics or cosmology."[14] Indeed, in the entire Pali Canon, the one text which most often intrigues western scholars is the Cula-Malunkya Sutta. In this text, the Buddha's disciple, Malunkya, is plagued during his meditations with "metaphysical" questions. Try as he might to still his mind, questions plague him: Is the world eternal or not? Is the self the same as the body or different from it? What happens after death? In other words, Malunkya is obsessed with the sort of questions which occupy most religions. In frustration, he goes to the Buddha and demands definitive answers.

It is the Buddha's answer, or rather his non-answer, which for many interpreters marks off Buddhism from all other religions. The Buddha does not answer Malunkya. Rather, he counter-questions. He asks Malunkya whether a promise of such definite answers was what led him to become a disciple in the first place. Ascertaining there have been no false pretenses, the Buddha told one of his most famous parables, that of the arrow.

12. Friedman, Heart of Wisdom, 15–16.

13. Ibid., 16.

14. Ibid.

Malunkyaputta, it is as if a man were pierced by an arrow that was thickly smeared with poison and his friends and relations, his kith and kin, were to procure a physician and a surgeon. He might speak thus: "I will not draw out this arrow until I know of the man who pierced me whether he is a noble or a brahman or merchant or worker." . . . "I will not draw out this arrow until I know the name and clan of the man who pierced me." . . . "I will not draw out this arrow until I know of the man who pierced me whether he is tall or short or middling in height." . . . "I will not draw out this arrow until I know of the man who pierced me whether he is black or deep brown or golden skinned." . . . "I will not draw out this arrow until I know of the man who pierced me to what village or market town he belongs." . . . "I will not draw out this arrow until I know of the bow from which I was pierced whether it was a spring-bow or a cross-bow." . . . "I will not draw out this arrow until I know of the bow-string from which I was pierced whether it was of swallow-wort or of reed or sinew or hemp or a tree." . . . "I will not draw out this arrow until I know of the shaft by which I was pierced whether it was of reeds of this kind or that." . . . "I will not draw out this arrow until I know of the shaft from which I was pierced what kind of feathers it had—whether those of a vulture or heron or hawk or peacock or some other bird." . . . "I will not draw out this arrow until I know of the shaft from which I was pierced with what kind of sinews it was encased: whether those of a cow or buffalo or deer or monkey." . . . "I will not draw out this arrow until I know of the arrow by which I was pierced whether it was an ordinary arrow or some other kind or arrow." Malunkyaputta, this man might pass away or ever this was known to him. In the same way, Malunkyaputta, whoever should speak thus: "I will not fare the Brahma-faring under the Lord until the Lord explains to me either that the world is eternal or the world is not eternal . . . or that the Tathagata neither is nor is not after dying," this man might pass away, Malunkyaputta, or ever it was explained to him by the Tathagata.[15]

Maury found in Zen a form of Buddhism in which this anti-metaphysical, pragmatic aspect of the Buddha's teachings found fullest expression by remaining close to the concrete situation. And moreover, he found in this closeness to the concrete situation an echo of his own dialogical approach to religion, one which eschews abstraction for immediacy. Of Zen he wrote:

15. Horner, *Middle Length Sayings*, 2:99–100.

Religion is often taken to be a movement away from mundane reality to the spirit floating above it. Zen Buddhism says no such movement is possible: there is only the one spirit-sense reality. It says, secondly, that it is our reason that has created the impression that there are these separate worlds of spirit and sense-intellect . . . we have the remarkable statement that the "one" and the "ten thousand things" are identical, that "nirvana is samsara." It is our minds that bifurcate existence into body and spirit, the one and the many. We cannot overcome our existential dilemma by fleeing from the many to the one; for this very attempt to overcome dualism leads us to another dualism—that of the one as opposed to the many. One must instead go right to the concrete particular that is at the same [time] the Buddha Nature. There is no process of abstracting from the concrete reality, of uncovering the essence and shucking off this world . . . the very particularity of things, their very name and form, is the only means through which one can attain enlightenment.[16]

It is not a great leap to see that this "closeness to the concrete situation," simultaneously the Buddha's compassion and the essence of Zen, would be most cogently expressed in stories, rather than in doctrines, myths or rituals. And this was my personal key to the course, my link between Hasidism and Zen. And I believe Maury was on a similar wave-length, since after all the two texts which were compilations of stories were Buber's *Tales of the Hasidim* and Paul Reps' *Zen Flesh, Zen Bones*. I took up this point in my term paper, which compared the use of the story in these two traditions. Long ago my paper was discarded, but I still remember it, and I remember that Maury liked it very much. My point was not only that there were similarities between the stories told by the Hasidic rebbes and the Zen masters, although I took pains to show these similarities. My larger point was about why these two traditions relied so heavily on stories to transmit their wisdom: because unlike the mystical poem, the epic, the aphorism, or contemplation, stories have such a lively immediacy, that they by their nature remain "close to the concrete situation."

Maury saw in Zen a kind of "culmination" of Buddhism, a view very much in accord with Zen's self-understanding which he gleaned not only from texts and scholarly studies, but from years of dialogue with leading

---

16. Friedman, *Heart of Wisdom*, 16–17.

Zen teachers, includiong D. T. Suzuki, Nishitani Keiji, and Chang-chi Chen.[17] As Maury put it:

> The Vedantists and the early Mahayana Buddhists were on the right track in trying to overcome the idea that things are divided up into myriads of discriminate particles, but from the Zen point of view, they did not go far enough. They turned it into an intellectual conception, and they said, "Reality is the 'not-two'" and fell into a world of intellectual discrimination between spirit and matter, the one and the many, the not-two and the ten thousand things. They could not get to the reality which is so concrete that it baffles all of our attempts to grasp it by any of these forms of mental categories. As a Zen text puts it, "They take the finger pointing to the moon for the moon itself."[18]

This Zen insistence that the name or symbol is not the thing itself was very influential upon Maury's approach to religions. He told a story of his encounter with a southern Christian student, who asked whether Maury had faith in theology, to which Maury replied that he had faith in God, but not in theology. For Maury, it was God's living presence and not our categories and doctrines which matters, which sustains him. And it was just this view which he found reinforced from an unlikely, nontheistic ally—Zen Buddhism. As he put it:

> There is much in both Zen Buddhism and Taoism which raises serious questions about the assumption of most of the intellectual currents of the nineteenth and twentieth centuries that *analysis* is the way to reach reality. If I take a thing apart into its supposed parts, have I thereby grasped this thing? Only if I assume that all things are really reducible to their component parts. That often means, only if I have already found what I believe to be the basic reality—such as a Marxist dialectic or a form of economic determinism or Freud's or Jung's theory of the libido or the analytic categories of the linguistic philosopher.[19]

I was fascinated by Zen, but even more so by Tibetan Tantric Buddhism. At that time, there was very little to read on the subject, but I avidly devoured John Blofeld's *The Tantric Mysticism of Tibet*, the Evans-Wentz edition of *The Tibetan Book of the Dead*, Lama Govinda's spiritual

17. Friedman, "Buber and Oriental Religions," 166.

18. Friedman, *Heart of Wisdom*, 18.

19. Ibid.

pilgrimage journal, *The Way of the White Clouds*, and Mme. Alexandra David-Neel's accounts of her travels in Tibet[20]. I had spent the previous summer in Bouddhanath, a Tibetan sacred complex near Kathmandu, Nepal, and during my journey I had begun to learn Tantric meditational techniques from a nearby lama. I remember also my class presentation for the course, for which I used a wrathful Tibetan meditational painting, a *thang-ka* of "The Ender of Death," Yamantaka. After my talk about Tantric meditation, Maury commented about how I "had made it my own," meaning that my sources were not only the books I had read, but the lama who had taught me and, moreover, my own experiences with the meditation techniques. Later, after I graduated, Maury helped me to continue my studies of Tibetan Buddhism. He wrote to his former student at Sarah Lawrence College, Hope Namgyal née Cook, erstwhile Maharani of Sikkim, and she arranged for me to study Tibetan language and history at Gangtok, and the rest, as they say, is history.

My interest in Tantra at the time coincided with a fascination with the analytical psychology of Carl G. Jung. I had been in Jungian therapy for about a year, which enhanced my appreciation of the mystical and mythical. Since I looked up to Maury as an intellectual mentor, I fantasized dialogues between him and my Jungian therapist. Clearly, I had not yet learned to make important distinctions. I remember the first time I brought up Jung in the seminar, and was aghast to hear Maury dismiss him "as a Modern Gnostic." I was aghast in part because I had no idea what he meant. Weren't the Gnostics mystics, and weren't mystics the "good guys" of religious history? After all, weren't we together learning from their legacy?

In time I came to learn what Maury meant by "Gnostic": one who sought reality by withdrawing from externals and immersing himself in a private, divine, inner world. By such a definition, the Gnostic came to represent all that is self-centered, all that is world-denying, in religion. I later read what Maury wrote about Jung:

> Jung's equation of gnosis with psychic experience is typical of modern man. But in contrast to other modern advocates of "experience," Jung does not value all experiences, but only those found within, and particularly within the unconscious. Like the

---

20. Blofeld, *The Tantric Mysticism of Tibet*; Evans-Wents, ed., *The Tibetan Book of the Dead*; Govinda, *The Way of the White Clouds: A Buddhist Pilgrim in Tibet*; David-Neel and Lama Yongden, *Secret Oral Teachings in Tibetan Buddhist Sects*.

ancient Gnostic, he sees the outer world as evil, and even the inner world that is accessible to man becomes good only when it comes into touch with that hidden deity within the soul—the unconscious . . . This gnosis, so far from leading Jung to abandon himself to the uniqueness and concrete immediacy of any given experience, leads him to seek for the "universal meaning" in it, that is, the meaning which fits his own theories.[21]

I did not give up on one of my heroes, Jung, very easily. Jung, for me, offered an important tool for entering into the recesses of the psyche, and in this sense he remains for me a "touchstone of reality." However, what Maury intimated in his book, *To Deny Our Nothingness*, has turned out to be more correct that perhaps even he had anticipated: Jung's flirtation with Nazism was not aberrant, but a logical consequence of a worldview which prefers an inner retreat to a concrete situation. "If this notion of a 'redeemer personality' who becomes a leader through following his unconscious 'destiny' is disturbing, Jung's association of this leader with the dictator of the totalitarian states—the greatest apparatus of collective conformity known to man—is more disturbing still," Maury warned.[22] I did not immediately reject Jung, but I was surprised to learn from Maury's vehemence that his dialogical, sympathetic approach to religion did not preclude harsh judgments when he found them appropriate. Maury's was not the "yes-to-everything" spirituality of the Sixties, I realized, but something much more nuanced.

TAOISM

Maury's most enthusiastic "yes" during that semester was to Taoism, or so it seemed to me. He later wrote that Taoism, Zen Buddhism and Hasidism "are three mysticisms of the 'particular,' which gives the lie to the Perennial Philosophy that there is some one essence in all of mysticism."[23] Indeed, nowhere does one find a mysticism less encumbered by religion than Taoism. Scholars have long distinguished between the "philosophical Taoism" of Lao Tzu and Chuang Tzu from the "popular Taoism" of rituals and magic which pervaded Chinese folk culture, and it was to Taoism's two greatest teachers that the course turned.

---

21. Friedman, *Nothingness*, 150.
22. Ibid., 158.
23. Friedman, "Buber and Oriental Religions," 153.

Maury found in Taoism a philosophy of action very similar to what he found in the *Bhagavad Gita*, as he explained:

> The center of Taoism is the Tao—the way of life and the human way in which one finds the "natural" course that flows with the stream rather than runs against it. Taoism accepts the opposites of *Yin* and *Yang*—feminine and masculine, dark and light, earth and heaven, receptive and active—without insisting on one or the other. It does not hold them in tension but swings easily from one to the other. Hence its action is *wu-wei*, the action of the whole being that had the appearance of nonaction because it does not intervene or interfere. This action seems most effortless just when it is most effective . . . Lao-tzu's *Way of Life*, in the classic poetic translation of Witter Bynner, has proved to be of a lasting and ever-new significance for me as no other Eastern scripture has. It does not contain the mystic secret of supreme enlightenment or *nirvana* or even *satori*. Rather, like that Confucian wisdom to which it otherwise seems so opposite, it represents a path that is not far from common consciousness, a wisdom that gently informs and gently reproves just where our lives most stray from it. My own life, indeed, like that of most of the overcommitted persons of affairs whom I know, has often seemed to me what I once wrote of K., the hero of Franz Kafka's novel *The Castle*, an illustration of the very opposite of everything that Lao-tzu taught about flowing with the Tao. But this is precisely why, along with its necessary Confucian counterpart of structure, propriety, and reciprocity, Taoism speaks so powerfully to our condition.[24]

Maury was always very interested in openness (which was expressed by his keen ability to listen), about remaining close to the concrete situation which he understood as the compassion of the Buddha, about "sanctifying the everyday" as Hasidism put it. And he was of necessity interested in the barriers to that openness, the barrier of preconceptions and of certain uses of language. He found in Lao Tzu's classic a nuanced understanding of both the barriers which language erects and, paradoxically, of the power of language to point to the concrete. He quoted Lao Tzu and explicated the passage:

> *Existence is beyond the power of words*
> *To define:*
> *Terms may be used*
> *But are none of them absolute.*

24. Friedman, *Heart of Wisdom*, 22.

In the Hindu Vedanta it is only Brahman, the One without Second; in the metaphysics of Plato and Aristotle, it is only the Good or the Unmoved Mover that cannot be defined. The very nature of finite existence to these latter implies that it even be delimited into name and form, same and other, category and class. For Zen Buddhism and Taoism, in contrast, it is existence itself that is illimitable and ineffable. In Taoism both the core and the surface are essentially the same.

If name be needed, wonder names them both:
From wonder into wonder
Existence opens.

Plato said that wonder is the beginning of philosophy, but the philosopher, as Martin Buber has said, neutralizes his wonder in doubt. From Descartes to the present even the beginning of philosophy is doubt and not wonder. Only here and there . . . is any comparable insight found in the Western world. The one "name" that does not falsify existence, dividing it up and closing it off, is wonder. "From wonder to wonder existence opens." Taoism is an existential mysticism which the concrete, precisely in its concreteness, reveals vista upon vista to the eyes of the person who meets it in openness. "The senses" as Heraclitus said, are only "bad witnesses to those who have barbarian souls."

This means no disparagement of words. Only those words that attempt to fix and delimit, to close off and confine, are unreal, not those that point beyond themselves to a concrete reality that no concept can delineate.

Real words are not vain,
Vain words are not real;
And since those who argue prove nothing
A sensible man does not argue.

Words do not control reality, they serve it—for the person who uses them in flowing openness of reciprocity. "The oracle at Delphi neither reveals nor conceals," wrote Heraclitus. "It indicates." The sane person, in consequence, is the one who does not try to capture existence as a whole within the limited, and limitedly useful, categories of analysis, whether scientific, psychoanalytic, or linguistic. Life reveals itself in images if one opens oneself to the image in such depth that one allows it to speak—as every image does—of its source.[25]

---

25. Friedman, *Heart of Wisdom*, 22–23.

Maury also found in Lao Tzu interpersonal wisdom. Drawing upon such verses as "I find good people good / And I find bad people good / If I am good enough." and "A sound man's heart is not shut within itself / But is open to other people's hearts," Maury inferred Lao Tzu's meaning that

> people do not possess fixed character—good or evil, honest or dishonest—but that the way in which I approach them, the way in which I allow the Tao to flow between myself and them frees them to possibilities of goodness, trust, and openness, just as my mistrust and categorizing makes it difficult for them to break out of habitual modes of dishonesty and mistrust. "Bad people" and "liars" are not bad and dishonest in the way a table is a table or a chair is a chair. Approached with openness and trust, they may be able to respond in kind. Approached with hatred and distrust, they will be confirmed in the mold in which their earlier interactions have already fixed them.[26]

Maury's spiritual journey led him on many other paths as well—to Christian mysticism, Sufism, early Buddhism, and eventually to Hasidism. But it was his encounters with Advaita Hinduism, Zen Buddhism, and Taoism, which impressed me the most deeply, perhaps because at that time in my life those were my greatest sources of inspiration.

But as Lao Tzu wrote, we do not possess fixed, unalterable natures. Maury has changed since his days at Temple University in the late 1960s, and my own path has circled back to traditional Judaism. Through all these meanderings, we have remained in contact and have become friends.

After I graduated from Temple, I spent two years working in Afghanistan, during which time I was able to master Dari sufficiently to study with some of the Sufis there. Then I began working on Tibetan, as Maury had helped to arrange, in Sikkim, then a tiny principality in the eastern Himalayas. When I returned to Temple to begin my graduate studies, I was disappointed to learn that Maury had left for California.

After earning my doctorate, I joined the faculty of Williams College in Massachusetts, and there was influenced by my colleagues' interest in postmodernism. I was able to invite Maury for a lecture and a faculty seminar, where there was an uncomfortable exchange between the nihilistic postmodernists and Maury's dialogical approach. I came away from

---

26. Friedman, *Heart of Wisdom*, 25.

that exchange somewhat shaken, and drawn again to Maury's open, life-affirming approach. It was not long after that I left Williams for a warmer climate, spiritually as well as climatically.

After learning and writing about Buddhism for a decade, while on sabbatical leave in Sri Lanka my wife and I visited the Jewish community at Cochin in South India. We were very struck by what we found: wonderful people with whom we had an immediate rapport; a community perhaps 2,000 years old on the verge of extinction; a beautiful synagogue which appealed to me as no synagogue ever before; and the realization that no one was there to write a book, to compose the requiem, for this community. We took the task on ourselves. We returned to the United States, I refreshed my Hebrew and read a great deal, and two years later returned to document Jewish life in Cochin before it was gone forever. We spent a year, living in a Jewish home, praying in the synagogue, getting to know the people of Jew Town. By the time we left, we found that observing traditional Judaism has seeped into our marrow, to borrow the metaphor from the book by Paul Reps to which Maury had introduced me long before. We have since become observant, but my experiences with Buddhism and Hinduism remain very significant touchstones of reality for me. In fact, after writing about the Jews of India, my scholarly attention has turned to the interactions and resonances between Indic (Hindu and Buddhist) and Judaic civilizations.

Perhaps I hadn't realized how much of Maury's approach I had internalized. The first major paper we wrote about the Jews of Cochin described their acculturation into the Hindu society of Kerala, as expressed in their unique Passover observances.[27] I sent a manuscript to Maury, and he read it in a way no one else has. He saw there a lived dialogue between Jews and Hindus, a dialogue which modified both cultures, a dialogue both like and unlike what he had been pursuing. It was different because it was corporate, it was between groups and not individuals. But it had the same characteristics as the sort of dialogues Maury had been pursuing: mutual respect, openness, a focus on the concrete. It was a good paper, but only Maury could have seen it in just that way, and in so doing he made me see it differently. In so seeing it, I recognized some of the debt I owe him. Whether aware of it or not, Maury and his

---

27. Goldberg, Ellen S. and Nathan Katz. "Asceticism and Caste in the Passover Observances of the Cochin Jews." In *Journal of the American Academy of Religion* 57:1 (1989) 53–82.

approach to the study of religions has become a touchstone of reality for me.

BIBLIOGRAPHY

Blakney, Raymond B., translator. *Meister Eckhart*. New York: Harper Torchbooks, 1941.

Blofeld, John. *The Tantric Mysticism of Tibet*. New York: Dutton, 1970.

Buber, Martin. *Tales of the Hasidim*. 2 vols. New York: Schocken, 1947, 1948.

Bynner, Witter, translator. *The Way of Life according to Lao Tzu*. New York: Capricorn, 1962.

David-Neel, Alexandra, and Lama Yongden. *Secret Oral teachings in Tibetan Buddhist Sects*. San Francisco: City Lights, 1967.

Evans-Wents, W. Y., editor. *The Tibetan Book of the Dead*. London: Oxford University Press, 1960.

Friedman, Maurice. *A Heart of Wisdom: Religion and Human Wholeness*. Albany, NY: State University of New York Press, 1992.

———. "Martin Buber and Oriental Religions." In *Buddhist and Western Philosophy*, edited by Nathan Katz. New Delhi: Sterling, 1981.

———. *To Deny Our Nothingness: Contemporary Images of Man*. New York: Delta, 1967.

———. *Touchstones of Reality: Existential Trust and the Community of Peace*. New York: Dutton, 1974.

———. "Touchstones of Reality: Toward a Philosophy and Methodology of Religion." In *Searching in the Syntax of Things: Experiments in the Study of Religion*, by Maurice Friedman et al. Philadelphia: Fortress, 1972.

Govinda, Lama Anagarika. *The Way of the White Clouds: A Buddhist Pilgrim in Tibet*. Berkeley: Shambhala, 1970.

Horner, I. B., translator. *The Collection of The Middle Length Sayings (Majkjhima Nikaya)* London: Pali Text Society / Routledge & Kegan Paul, 1975.

Isherwood, Christopher, and Swami Prabhavananda, translators. *The Song of God: Bhagavad Gita*. New York: New American Library, 1951.

Reps, Paul. *Zen Flesh, Zen Bones*. Harmondsworth, UK: Penguin, 1971

Welch, Claude. *Graduate Education in Religion: A Critical Appraisal*. Missoula: University of Montana Press, 1971.

10

You Are My Witnesses

Maurice Friedman and Abraham Joshua Heschel[1]

HAROLD KASIMOW

A CCORDING TO THE BAAL Shem Tov, the founder of Hasidism, all our encounters with other human beings hold great significance. The truth of this teaching is borne out in my own life by the profound effect that two remarkable men have had on me: Maurice Friedman and Abraham Joshua Heschel. I want to express infinite gratitude to these two witnesses for *Tikkun olam,* literally "the perfecting of the world." *Tikkun olam* is the belief that human beings share a great deal of power with God in bringing about a real transformation in the world that is created and ruled by God. Both Friedman and Heschel are aware of the imperfection of the world, but both refuse to adjust to the falsehood and vulgarity in it. They speak out strongly against the emphasis which contemporary American culture places on success and power. Heschel was and Friedman continues to be passionate and articulate champions of human rights in pursuit of peace and justice for all people.[2]

In this essay I will focus on Friedman's and Heschel's attitudes toward other religions. I am convinced that our perspectives on other religious traditions play a major role in hindering or promoting peace and justice. Interfaith dialogue and peace go together. Interfaith dialogue is

1. The title for this essay is from Maurice Friedman's book *Abraham Joshua Heschel and Elie Wiesel: You Are My Witnesses.*

2. See the contributions of both Heschel and Friedman to the volume *The Challenge of Shalom,* edited by Polner and Goodman.

imperative in our time because it is a path to creating a world of greater understanding, thereby helping to eradicate prejudice and intolerance. I take very seriously the following statement on peace and interfaith dialogue by the Christian theologian Hans Küng: "My thesis, therefore, is: no world peace without peace among religions, no peace among religions without dialogue between the religions, and no dialogue between the religions without accurate knowledge of one another."[3]

This extraordinary statement must be taken as one of the great challenges for our time if we are to preserve our fragile planet. Küng's assertion that there can be "no world peace without peace among the religions" challenges the religious leaders of the world to interpret their respective traditions in such a way as to encourage spiritual strength that would defeat the violence and destruction, the persecution and intolerance often committed in the name of religion. Leaders must recognize that all religions have brought beauty and astonishing enrichment to millions of believers, but they have also been the cause of great suffering and anguish because of their claims of infallibility.

I am convinced that the belief that there is only one valid religious tradition is a major cause for the hostility between people of different faiths and is a main obstacle to authentic interfaith dialogue. If religious people are to eradicate the forces of violence and evil—even among their own people—and help to bring peace, they must first renounce the exclusivist attitude toward other religions and turn to the vision and wisdom of the spiritual giants of the world's religious traditions. I believe that the works and actions of Maurice Friedman and Abraham Joshua Heschel, two extraordinary teachers, can move us in the direction of greater concern for each other, of confirming each other in our uniqueness.

In my study of the religious traditions of the world I have found a great deal of similarity in their attitudes toward other faiths; they all move in the direction of exclusivism and triumphalism. This is the case not only with Judaism, Christianity, and Islam, but also with Hinduism and Buddhism. On the whole, the major thinkers in these five religious traditions do not entertain the possibility that other traditions may be just as valid. They all seem to agree that their way is the only true way and that followers of other traditions are in error. In some cases they see the other religions as earlier stages of development. But in most cases

---

3. Küng, "Christianity and World Religions," 194.

these thinkers did not acknowledge that salvation or liberation could be obtained through other faiths.

We are well aware of the Christian view that outside the church there is no salvation and the Muslim view that there is only one authentic God-ordained religious tradition for humanity: the straight path of Islam.[4] We may read in texts that deal with world religions that Asian religions are far more tolerant of other paths. However, in my judgment, one of the most tolerant forms of Hinduism—the Ramakrishna Vivekananda version—nevertheless teaches the superiority of Hinduism. Even other forms of Hinduism such as Bhakti Yoga are seen as earlier stages of spiritual development. It also seems to me that the central thrust of the Buddhist tradition, in spite of its great stress on compassion and wisdom, is that it is the only true path. The way of the Buddha is the only path that leads to true liberation.

Similarly, in my opinion, the most widely held view among Jews throughout the ages is that Judaism is the only true religion. The following statement by Immanuel Jakobovits, the former chief rabbi of Great Britain, can serve as a good example of the contemporary Orthodox attitudes towards other faiths. He writes: "As a professing Jew, I obviously consider Judaism the only true religion. Judaism, to be true to itself, is bound to reject, for instance, the divinity of Jesus or the prophecy of Mohammed as false claims; otherwise its own claims, such as the supremacy of Moses' prophecy and the finality of Mosaic law . . . could not be true. Two mutually exclusive statements of conflicting fact can never be completely true."[5] Rabbi Jakobovits can find support for his position both in the Talmud and among most medieval Jewish thinkers. In his epistle to Yemen, Moses Maimonides, the most influential Jewish thinker of the Middle Ages, wrote: "The difference between our religion and the other denominations that liken themselves to us is like the difference between the living, rational individual and the statue skillfully molded out of marble, wood, silver, or gold that looks like a man."[6]

A number of contemporary rabbis and Jewish scholars involved in interfaith dialogue have centered their attention on the Talmudic doc-

---

4. For a valuable examination of Christian attitudes toward other religious traditions, see Knitter, *Introducing Theologies of Religions*. For Muslim views of other religious traditions, see the works of Sayyid Abul A'la Mawdudi and Seyyed Hossein Nasr.

5. Jakobovits, in *Jewish Belief*, 112–13.

6. Maimonides, "Epistle," 99.

trine of the Seven Commandments of the Sons of Noah, which state that "the righteous of all nations have a share in the world-to-come." This doctrine is considered a valid basis for granting validity not only to Christianity and Islam but also to other religious traditions. The following statement by Ezra Spicehandler is typical of this view: "Judaism is certainly not the one true religion. Even according to the Talmud, all who observe the Noahide laws have a share in the world to come."[7] Rabbi Ben Zion Bokser argued that "the classic Jewish position that the righteous of all nations and all faiths have a share in the world to come implies the legitimacy of diverse paths to God."[8]

Nevertheless, the fact remains that Jews have accepted the view of Maimonides that it is not enough for the gentile to observe the Noahide laws. He or she must follow these laws because they are commanded by God. I am in full agreement with Paul Van Buren when he states that "Jews are going to have to work out their understanding of the church from their central affirmations of God, Torah, Israel and not out of something as off-to-the-side as the Noahide tradition."[9]

The danger of misusing religion for personal, selfish ends and the danger of claims of infallibility are very troubling to Friedman and Heschel. Both wrestled at length with the issue of religion as a cause of evil in the world. Yet in spite of the evil committed in the name of religion, Friedman and Heschel, true to their tradition, never give up the idea of *tikkun olam*. Their trust in God and love for human beings gives them the strength to continue their work, not for personal salvation, but for the advancement of redemption.[10]

7. Spicehandler, in *Jewish Belief*, 232–33.

8. Bokser, "Bible, Tradition, Judaism," 16.

9. Van Buren, "Reply," 31.

10. In view of the negative image of man that they present to us, one may find their stress on redemption rather surprising. One of Heschel's most important premises is that contemporary human beings live in agony and that "the humanity of man is no longer self-evident" (*Who Is Man* [Stanford: Stanford University Press, 1965], 25). He writes: "The overriding issue of this hour in the world and Western civilization is the humanity of man. Man is losing his true image and shaping his life in the image of anti-man" ("The Jewish Notion of God and Christian Renewal." In *Renewal of Religious Thought*, edited by L. K. Shook [New York: Herder and Herder, 1968], 114). And Heschel warns us that we should not "take lightly man's pronouncements about himself" (*Who Is Man* [Stanford: Stanford University Press, 1965], 24.) This view is strongly supported by Friedman, who says that "We cannot deny . . . that no matter how monstrous, misshapen, irrational, and distorted the images of man presented to us by contemporary

In my judgment, the most promising Jewish view towards a pluralistic world, one that could encourage genuine interfaith relations, is the way of Friedman and Heschel. I speak of the way of Friedman and Heschel because I find a very strong affinity in their views of other religious traditions. I first became aware of this affinity when I was writing my dissertation on Heschel under Friedman's direction.[11] In his unpublished manuscript written in 1986 titled "Abraham Joshua Heschel and Interreligious Dialogue," Friedman confirms his strong affinity for Heschel on this issue: "On rereading Heschel's essay "No Religion Is an Island," I am astonished at how fully what Heschel says about interreligious cooperation corresponds to my own approach to interreligious dialogue via what I call the "dialogue of touchstones." In *The Human Way* I claim that the only realistic modern approach is that of religious pluralism. This is exactly what Heschel says and in the same spirit of dialogue and even of a dialogue of touchstones."

In the first part of his essay, Friedman quotes approvingly from Heschel's article "No Religion Is an Island." I will therefore present Friedman's entire selection from Heschel so that we can understand as fully as possible both Heschel's and Friedman's views of other faiths.[12]

> Parochialism has become untenable . . . Horizons are wider, dangers are greater . . . *No religion is an Island*. We are all involved with one another. Spiritual betrayal on the part of one of us affects the faith of all of us. Views adopted in one community have an impact on other communities. Today religious isolationism is a myth. (345)

> My first task in every encounter is to comprehend the personhood of the human being I face, to sense the kinship of being human, solidarity of being . . . A person is . . . all of humanity in one, and whenever one man is hurt we are all injured. The human is a disclosure of the divine, and all men are one in God's care for

---

literature and art may be, they do mirror 'significant aspects of the human condition in our time'" (*To Deny Our Nothingness: Contemporary Images of Man* [New York: Delta, 1968], 21).

11. See Harold Kasimow, *Divine-Human Encounter: A Study of Abraham Joshua Heschel* (Washington, D. C.: University Press of America, 1979), 82. The foreword to this published version of my dissertation was written by Maurice Friedman.

12. Parenthetical page references are to "No Religion Is an Island" as reprinted in *Disputation and Dialogue: Readings in the Jewish-Christian Encounter*, edited by Frank E. Talmage (New York: Ktav Publishing House, 1975).

man. Many things on earth are precious, some are holy, humanity is holy of holies.

To meet a human being is an opportunity to sense the image of God, *the presence* of God. (347)

[O]n the level of faith we experience in one another the presence of a person radiant with reflections of a greater presence. (348)

The purpose of religious communication among human beings of different commitments is mutual enrichment and enhancement of respect and appreciation rather than the hope that the person spoken to will prove to be wrong in what he regards as sacred.

Dialogue must not degenerate into a dispute, into an effort on the part of each to get the upper hand . . .

Does not the all-inclusiveness of God contradict the exclusiveness of any particular religion? . . . Is it not blasphemous to say: I alone have all the truth and the grace, and all those who differ live in darkness, and are abandoned by the grace of God?

Is it really our desire to build a monolithic society: one party, one view, one leader, and no opposition? Is religious uniformity desirable or even possible? Has it really proved to be a blessing for a country when all its citizens belonged to one denomination? Or has any denomination attained a spiritual climax when it had the adherence of the entire population? Does not the task of preparing the kingdom of God require a diversity of talents, a variety of rituals, soul-searching as well as opposition?

Perhaps it is the will of God that in this aeon there should be diversity in our forms of devotion and commitment to Him. In this aeon diversity of religions is the will of God . . . The ultimate truth is not capable of being fully and adequately expressed in concepts and words. The ultimate truth is about the situation that pertains between God and man. "The Torah speaks in the language of man." Revelation is always an accommodation to the capacity of man. No two minds are alike, just as no two faces are alike. The voice of God reaches the spirit of man in a variety of ways, in a multiplicity of languages. One's truth comes to expression in many ways of understanding.

Holiness is not the monopoly of any particular religion or tradition. Wherever a deed is done in accord with the will of God, wherever a thought of man is directed toward Him, there is the holy. (357)

What then is the purpose of interreligious cooperation? . . . [It is] to cooperate in trying to bring about a resurrection of sensitivity, a revival of conscience; to keep alive the divine sparks in our souls, to nurture openness to the spirit of the Psalms, reverence for the words of the prophets, and faithfulness to the Living God. (359)

In a letter written to me on July 17, 1986, accompanying his manuscript on Heschel, Friedman says: "I think no reader can doubt what I say: that we are in astonishing agreement and that what I write is very much in his spirit." In *Touchstones of Reality*, one of his most personal books, Friedman states: "The reality of pluralism must be the starting-point of any serious modern faith. We should give up looking for the one true religion and consider our religious commitments as unique relationships to a truth which we cannot possess. We should also give up the notion that some men possess the spirit and others do not."[13]

These statements by Friedman and Heschel make it clear that for them no one has a monopoly on God. God is found in human hearts everywhere, not just in the Jewish tradition. What is most critical for Friedman and Heschel is not what religion an individual belongs to but how human he or she is. What is most significant is not the tradition an individual follows but how the individual acts in his or her everyday life in order to enhance the power of human love, the power of peace, and the power of justice.

The affinity between Friedman and Heschel in their approaches to members of other faiths may seem surprising to many who know of Friedman primarily as the friend of and the foremost authority on the life and thought of Martin Buber. What is less known is that Friedman was also a friend and near-disciple of Heschel. The relationship between them was one of affection and friendship. In the conclusion to his article, "Abraham Heschel among Contemporary Philosophers," Friedman speaks of his indebtedness to Heschel: "The evaluations that I have made of Heschel's thought from the standpoint of an American raised in a tradition of liberal Judaism give no adequate indication of my great intellectual and spiritual indebtedness to him in the course of more than a quarter of a century of personal friendship. To Heschel I owe my

---

13. Friedman, *Touchstones of Reality*, 214. The last time I saw Rabbi Heschel was on June 13, 1972. He told me how moved he was by Friedman's book *Touchstones of Reality*, a manuscript of which was on top of one of his piles. I later read a statement that Heschel gave to Friedman's editor at Dutton in which he describes this work as a "deeply moving account of a personal pilgrimage of a highly sensitive and rich soul."

understanding of prayer, *kavanah*, *hasidut*, wonder and awe, the Psalms as a part of daily living, the Sabbath as a holiday of joy, and many other things Jewish."[14]

As we study the life and thought of Friedman, we begin to see that Heschel became a very important touchstone for him. But Friedman, who wrestled intensely with Heschel's vision of Judaism, could not accept Heschel's view of Jewish law, which was based on a different understanding of revelation. On this critical issue, Friedman's view is much closer to that of Martin Buber. Friedman agrees with Heschel that revelation is a dialogue between the prophet and God and that the prophet is "not a passive recipient."[15] But Friedman did not accept Heschel's stress that the content of revelation is as important as the event of revelation. In his interpretation of Martin Buber's position on Judaism and law, Friedman states that for Buber "the laws of the Bible are only the human response to revelation, and, therefore, are not binding on future generations."[16] I believe that this is also Friedman's own position, which is quite problematic for Heschel, who for many years encouraged Friedman to accept Jewish law (*halakhah*). Although Friedman could not agree with Heschel on this issue, the friendship between these two Jewish philosophers lasted for nearly thirty years, until Heschel's death on December 23, 1972.[17]

I first met Maurice Friedman in 1968 when I enrolled in his course on Jewish and comparative mysticism. For this course, I wrote my first paper on Heschel, one titled "Mystical Elements in the Thought of Abraham Joshua Heschel." I also wrote a review essay on Martin Buber's "The Place of Hasidism in the History of Religion" in which Buber compares Hasidism with Zen Buddhism.[18] I certainly did not have the faintest idea at that time that thirty-five years later I would still be immersed in such a study.[19] At that time, however, I was very taken by Buber's tales and wrote a paper titled "My Encounter with the Hasidic Tales" for the

14. Friedman, "Heschel," 303.

15. Heschel, *God in Search*, 259.

16. Friedman, "Martin Buber," 1433.

17. For a detailed account of the great affection that developed between Friedman and Heschel, see chapter one ("My Friendship with Abraham Joshua Heschel") in Friedman's book *Abraham Joshua Heschel and Elie Wiesel: You Are My Witnesses* (New York: Farrar, Straus, and Giroux, 1987).

18. Buber, "Place of Hasidism," 219–39.

19. See *Beside Still Waters: Jews, Christians, and the Way of the Buddha*, edited by Harold Kasimow et al. (Wisdom Publications, 2003).

literature and existentialism course which Friedman offered in the fall of 1969.

My favorite Hasidic tale is the story of Eizik, son of Rabbi Yekel, who travels from Cracow to Prague in search of treasure. He ultimately discovers, after meeting with a Christian, that the treasure is in fact buried in his family's home in Cracow. Thus, it is a member of a different religious tradition who helps Rabbi Eizik to find the treasure in Judaism, to perceive more profoundly the depth and the uniqueness of the Jewish tradition. Friedman, in his interpretation of this tale, states:

> Perhaps if we had not gone to "Prague," we should not have discovered that the treasure was hidden beneath our own hearth. There is meaning in our searching, even when it takes us far afield, if it enables us to come back home to the unique task which awaits us . . . This was my own experience in relation to Judaism. Brought up in a liberal Judaism of a very thin variety, I could never have returned to Judaism and established a new and deeper relationship with it had I not gone through Hinduism, Buddhism, Zen, Taoism, and Christian mysticism. Nor have I lost these other touchstones. They are part of the way in which I came to Hasidism and relate to it.[20]

Friedman, who was deeply influenced by the Hebrew Bible, Hasidic spirituality, Buber, and Heschel, and who considers himself to be a neo-Hasid, was also deeply touched by other religious traditions. As I write this essay, I realize that a number of the crucial touchstones of reality for Friedman have also become touchstones of reality for me.

I was born a few years before the Nazi occupation in a small village near Vilna in a traditional Orthodox Jewish family, although my mother's family belonged to the Lakhovich-Koidanov Hasidic dynasties of Lithuania. My education was also very traditional. When I arrived with my family in the United States after the war, I studied at Yeshiva Salanter, and then at Talmudical Academy of Yeshiva University. My Jewish education continued at the Jewish Theological Seminary and at the University of Jerusalem. Today, after nearly thirty-five years of study of other religious traditions and having participated in a number of meditation retreats under the direction of Zen Buddhist masters in the U.S., Canada, and Japan, I believe that I have developed a deeper understanding of and attachment to my own tradition. Although I consider

---

20. Friedman, *Touchstones*, 169–70.

myself to be a committed Jew, I am also a pluralist deeply influenced by both Friedman and Heschel. The Jewish tradition is my tradition, the one which is most precious to me, but I do not believe that it is the only valid religious tradition. I am firmly convinced that the Jewish tradition is not incompatible with religious pluralism. As I come to the conclusion of this tribute to my teacher and friend Maurice Friedman, I am aware that I am even more indebted to him than I have ever realized.

BIBLIOGRAPHY

Bokser, Ben Zion. "The Bible, Rabbinic Tradition and Modern Judaism." *The Bulletin* 48:2 (1968) 16.

Buber, Martin. "The Place of Hasidism in the History of Religion." In *The Origin and Meaning of Hasidism,* edited and translated by Maurice Friedman, 219–39. New York: Harper & Row, 1960.

Friedman, Maurice. "Abraham Heschel among Contemporary Philosophers: From Divine Pathos to Prophetic Action." *Philosophy Today* (Winter 1974) 303.

———. *Abraham Joshua Heschel and Elie Wiesel: You Are My Witnesses.* New York: Farrar, Straus, and Giroux, 1987.

———. "Martin Buber." *Encyclopedia Judaica* 4. Jerusalem: Keter, 1971.

———. *Touchstones of Reality: Existential Trust and the Community of Peace.* New York: Dutton, 1972.

Heschel, Abraham Joshua. *God in Search of Man: A Philosophy of Judaism.* New York: Farrar, Straus, and Cudahy, 1955.

———. "No Religion Is an Island." In *Disputation and Dialogue: Readings in the Jewish-Christian Encounter,* edited by Frank E. Talmage. New York: Ktav, 1975.

Jakobovits, Immanuel. In *The Condition of Jewish Belief: A Symposium Compiled by the Editors of Commentary Magazine.* New York: Macmillan, 1966.

Knitter, Paul F. *Introducing Theologies of Religions.* Maryknoll, NY: Orbis, 2002.

Küng, Hans "Christianity and World Religions: Dialogue with Islam." In *Toward a Universal Theology of Religion,* edited by Leonard Swidler. Maryknoll, NY: Orbis, 1987.

Maimonides, Moses. *The Epistle to Yemen,* Abraham Halkin, trans., in *Crisis and Leadership: Epistles of Maimonides* (Philadelphia: Jewish Publication Society of America, 1985), 99.

Polner, Murray, and Naomi Goodman, editors. *The Challenge of Shalom: The Jewish Tradition of Peace and Justice.* Philadelphia: New Society Publishers, 1994.

Spicehandler, Ezra. In *The Condition of Jewish Belief: A Symposium Compiled by the Editors of Commentary Magazine.* New York: Macmillan, 1966.

Van Buren, Paul. "Reply" to Michael S. Kogan, "Toward Total Dialogue: The Next Step in Interfaith Dialogue: A Conversation in Print." Reprint of "National Dialogue Newsletter" 6:2 (1990–91) 31.

11

Touchstones of Reality

Understanding Genocide and the Absence of Dialogue

ROYAL E. ALSUP

T HE METAPHOR OF TOUCHSTONES of reality, so perceptively and sensitively discovered, developed, and presented by Dr. Maurice Friedman, is an excellent tool to synthesize the work of Dr. Friedman with the Native American experience. This paper shows the amazing relevance that Dr. Friedman's ideas have to an understanding of the Native American experience of genocide and racism. His writings and ideas have much to offer to the development of the ability to work within a world racked by genocide and racism without losing touch with love, compassion, and community.

> In my book *Touchstones of Reality* I speak of "touchstones of reality" as momentous events that imprint our attitudes and life stances in such a way that we bring them with us into all our future encounters. A touchstone cannot be passively received. It must be won by contending, by wrestling until dawn and not letting the nameless messenger go until he has blessed us by giving us a new name. Walking on our path, we encounter something that lights up for us—an event, a teaching, a breathless view of nature, an hour of unusual calm. Touchstones of reality are like insights, except that they are closer to events. To touch is to go through and beyond subjective experiencing. The very act of touching is already a transcending.[1]

---

1. Friedman, *Heschel & Wiesel*, 91.

This paper presents the negative touchstone of the genocide of Native American children in the schools and at the hands of mental health professionals, court systems, and welfare departments. In over twenty years of working with and for Native American children and their families, I have witnessed the horror and trauma that genocide and racism inflict upon Native peoples. The work of Maurice Friedman on the touchstones of reality presents a way of viewing this trauma without getting subjectively stuck in passionate judgments or becoming objectively insensitive to human suffering. The touchstones of reality give us an existential view of the concrete misery that neocolonist systems force American Indian children to endure.

This paper presents three perspectives in dialogue—a dialogue of touchstones consisting of the different touchstones of reality presented in Maurice Friedman's work, the unique touchstones of reality of Native American people, and the touchstones of reality that developed out of the author's encounters with both. In this ongoing dialogue of touchstones, I do not give an interpretation of Maurice Friedman's philosophy, nor of Native American thought per se. The aim is to contribute to a new understanding of both Friedman's work and Native American experiences as they are held in the tension of creative dialogue. This paper endeavors to clarify the dynamics of genocide not by bringing an accusation of collective guilt but by synthesizing and illuminating a correction that will increase love and compassion in our world. No implication is made that individuals are evil, but that dysfunctional systems cause individuals to be ignorant and to inflict harm on others.

MEETING THE MAN, MAURICE FRIEDMAN

My dialogue with Dr. Maurice Friedman started in the late 60s, when, as a teacher's assistant at a California university, I used *Martin Buber: The Life of Dialogue* by Maurice S. Friedman as a text for a course on existential psychology. I was fascinated at that time, and have been ever since, with trying to establish a child developmental psychology based on a dialogical approach. At various times in my career I have just missed meeting Dr. Friedman. Several years ago, while presenting at an Indian Health conference in San Diego, I noticed announcements that Dr. Friedman was to speak at a different event in the same hotel. After my presentation, I ran downstairs to catch him, but he had just left. It was frustrating because I had always wanted a face-to-face dialogue with the man whose work had become a touchstone of reality for me.

In 1991, Dr. Ilene Serlin asked me to speak on American Indian psychology in Humanistic Psychology Division 32 at an American Psychological Association Conference in San Francisco. I noticed that Dr. Serlin had also scheduled Maurice Friedman to speak. I told Ilene that I had been trying to meet Dr. Friedman for many years and that I wanted her to introduce us. The introduction was made and Maurice, my wife, Dr. Patricia Alsup, and I had a lengthy conversation. I was interested in Maurice as a person and as a philosopher. More than twenty years of working with American Indians had trained me to be more concerned about a person's personality and relationships with others than to be impressed by status, position, or reputation. Maurice's humanness and knowledge, his humor, and his ability to relate in a caring, concerned conversation made me aware that I was in the presence of a great teacher. Dr. Friedman demonstrated the integrity of his writings by standing his ground while maintaining his openness, his spontaneity, and his ability to listen and to carry on a dialogue of depth. Maurice's accessible humanity has never disappointed me.

My relationship with Dr. Friedman continued at the Saybrook Institute residential conference in 1995, at Rohnert Park, California, when Stanley Krippner and I presented him with the Saybrook yearly award for Outstanding Humanistic Scholar. During that conference Maurice and his wife, Dr. Aleene Friedman, along with my wife and I, had intensive conversations about philosophy and religion. My dialogue with Maurice from that point on has given me a more profound depth of understanding of his existential, dialogical philosophy.

TOUCHSTONES OF REALITY: A SYNTHESIS

Dr. Friedman's touchstones of reality emerged out of his dialogues with different great world religions. He writes that "My metaphor of 'touchstones of reality' originally evolved, as we have seen, as an approach to religion. From there, however, it moved into an approach to education and communication, and finally, over the course of time, to psychotherapy. As such, 'touchstones of reality' represents in itself a unique meeting between psychology and religion."[2] Touchstones in Dr. Friedman's

2. Friedman, *Heart of Wisdom*, 215.

experiences also included socialism and mysticism. His experiments in his life have made his relationship to touchstones of reality an ongoing appreciation of old touchstones and openness to the spontaneous discovery of new touchstones.

For twenty-two years, I worked to develop a mental health program with relevant cultural touchstones for American Indian children and their families. An effective and culturally relevant mental health program must address the horrible psychological genocide being perpetrated against American Indian children by welfare agencies, mental health professionals, probation officers, and law enforcement organizations throughout the United States. Dr. Friedman's metaphor of touchstones of reality enabled me to work with American Indians in a manner that employed a profound appreciation of their resiliencies and strengths. It allowed me to have an open dialogue among the agencies, the tribal members, and myself without defining or interpreting specific American Indian philosophy and religion. Standing on my own ground in my own culture and listening to American Indians define for themselves their touchstones of reality helped me to create an American Indian mental health program that was not static, demanding a receptivity and spontaneity that allowed new touchstones to be discovered to help explain the Native American way. This is the vital ground of Dr. Friedman's dialogical existentialism pragmatically used cross-culturally.

In his book, *Abraham Joshua Heschel & Elie Wiesel: You Are My Witnesses,* I discovered Friedman's metaphor of a *negative touchstone of reality.* The plight of American Indian children is a negative touchstone of reality for me. The metaphor has been useful in describing my contact with the racism and emotional and mental genocide that are experienced by American Indian children. This is where Maurice Friedman's work touches the heart of my work and brings our touchstones into what Dr. Friedman calls a *dialogue of touchstones.*[3]

The concept of negative touchstones existentially describes the way that American Indian children lose their self-esteem, their self-efficacy, and, ultimately, their motivation. Ongoing and negative concrete events in the lives of American Indian children that take place in schools, psychotherapy rooms, court rooms, and juvenile halls are negative touchstones that destabilize American Indian families and are probably involved in an increasing suicide rate among American Indian children.

3. Friedman, *Heschel & Wiesel,* 91–92.

GENOCIDE, PAST AND PRESENT

The General Assembly of the United Nations adopted the Convention on Genocide, which came into force in 1951 after being ratified by twenty nations. The Convention states that:

> Genocide means any of the following acts committed with intent to destroy, in whole, or in part, a national, ethical, social, or religious group as such:
>
> a) Killing members of the group.
>
> b) Causing serious bodily or mental harm to members of the group.
>
> c) Deliberately inflicting on the group conditions of life calculated to bring about its physical destruction in whole or in part.
>
> d) Imposing measures intended to prevent births within the group.
>
> e) Forcibly transferring children of the group.[4]

The early Christian colonialists, who had no idea of a dialogue of touchstones, neglected and could not acknowledge the aboriginal cultural touchstones of reality of the native peoples they encountered. They wanted to suppress and destroy indigenous people who refused to accept their alien Christian touchstones of reality. As a result, millions of native people were killed. The history of this colonization with its accompanying genocide has been well documented. For the last five hundred years, we have seen the *manifest destiny* of a race that feels called to rule the world through its own civil religion. This same destruction of American Indian children continues in present time through sophisticated and devious means. There has been a serious psychological, emotional, and physical genocide of American Indian children within Indian Country perpetrated by the United States and her army of soldiers, police, doctors, psychologists, anthropologists, and psychiatrists. I have been a witness to this horrible evil that has been inflicted, and is still being inflicted, on tribal peoples and their beautiful, sacred children.

Tribal psychologies are grounded in a cosmology that includes a center of the world for each local tribe. Each tribe's psychology and sociology evolve out of their dialogue with their own tribal lands. Sacred

4. Simpson and Yinger, *Minorities*, 20.

place and sacred land are touchstones of reality for Indian people that have far-reaching effects on their whole being and on their unique cultures. Mental health, welfare, probation, and education systems are often ignorant of the fact that each tribe may have a vastly different psychology, sociology, and system of religious practices and beliefs.

Over the years, and even during the twentieth century, the Bureau of Indian Affairs forced American Indian children to attend church-based boarding schools and schools that the BIA funded. During a conference at which I was presenting on a large Indian reservation, a 70-year-old Indian woman told us that when she was a little girl she was kidnapped out of her front yard and was taken to a boarding school far from her home. She did not have a chance to say good-bye to her family. She never saw her parents again because they died before she was released from the school and could return to the reservation. Hearing about the institutionalized kidnapping of American Indian children that was as close to us as this living woman's past was profoundly upsetting. Many American Indian families have intimate stories from their living elders that keep alive the horror of being discounted and treated in ways that deny one's legitimate yet differing touchstones of reality.

Religious, government-backed schools forced Indian children to cut their hair and to stop speaking their Indian languages. The most genocidal aspect of their treatment in the boarding schools was that they were forced to forget their so-called pagan religion, to read the Bible, and to become Christian. Needless to say, most traditional religious and communal tribal customs were suppressed. This has caused American Indians to mistrust the United States educational system. Indian resistance to the forced kidnapping and non-traditional education of their children has led to the mistaken belief, however, on the part of many educators and school boards that Indian parents do not want their children educated. This is simply not true.

The psychological genocide of American Indians has continued into present time. Welfare agencies, educational departments, and court systems use their teams of professionals who are willing to use culturally inappropriate evaluation tools to assess American Indian children and their families. Such instruments are used to substantiate the supposed mental health problems of Native Americans. Negative psychological evaluations and assessments of Native American children and families, even when they are arrived at by culturally inappropriate means, enable officials to remove American Indian children from their homes and to place them in non-Indian homes.

The American Indian Religious Act of 1978 and American Indian Child Welfare Act of 1978 slowed down, but did not stop, the spiritual and psychological genocide of American Indians. The American Indian Child Welfare Act states that if it is found to be necessary to remove American Indian children from their homes, they must be placed in another Indian home, with first priority going to a family member's home or to another Indian home in the same tribe. If such a home were not available, then another Indian family home not of their own tribe would be appropriate. The welfare agencies and their doctors or therapists most all of the time find ways to nullify the Indian Child Welfare Act and attempt to place Indian children in non-Indian homes. Of course, welfare departments often find Indian families to be dysfunctional because of the use of value-laden neocolonist tools of evaluation that are prejudiced and biased against the touchstones of reality of American Indian families. If American Indian children and their families and tribal members are evaluated according to their own touchstones of reality, they are more apt to be perceived as being functional. Mental health professionals who are not aware of Native children's traditions and their cultural viewpoints of the world force a perspective on these children through assessment and treatment that is mentally harmful to them. In many cases, the family is diagnosed as unfit for a child to stay in the home, and the Indian Child Welfare Act is nullified. In this way the welfare system and their mental health professionals inflict genocide on American Indian children by committing the following parts of the Convention on Genocide: Causing serious bodily or mental harm to members of the group, deliberately inflicting on the group conditions of life calculated to bring about its physical destruction in whole or in part, and forcibly transferring children of the group.

The negation of another person's touchstones of reality aborts the possibility for what Maurice Friedman calls *imagining the real* to take place. In a true dialogue, each person stands his or her own ground and thereby calls the other person into being present. Friedman calls this process *making the other present*, and he stresses that it is not empathy. Each person has a perspective that represents his or her own unique view of the world while the other person, through an I and Thou dialogue, confirms that view. Ruptured or broken community, confusion,

depression, and mistrust on all sides are the sad harvest of a lack of dialogue of touchstones that involves the disconfirmation of the uniqueness
of American Indian touchstones of reality. When one people are being
grossly disconfirmed and abused by another, the process is the opposite
of the partnership that Maurice Friedman describes in *Touchstones of
Reality*. "Those people who relate to the world only as a function of their
own becoming will not change no matter how concerned they are about
changing. But those people whose trust is grounded in the partnership of
existence are changed every time they go out to meet another."[5] The real
value of the dominant culture's confirming the touchstones of reality of
American Indian families and children is that it makes possible a social
process that creates an I and Thou relationship and establishes a true
partnership of existence between races and ethnic groups. Dr. Friedman
affirms that by authentic communication based on true dialogue and
love, one can overcome the obstacles and barriers that cause what he
calls *mismeetings*. Such communication brings about reconciliation between ethnic groups and races.[6]

The existential philosophy of touchstones of reality and the I and
Thou relationship create a positive approach to repairing and bringing about a genuine community through a healing dialogue. Indian
children who have had positive Indian parenting based on an I and
Thou relationship with their parents, siblings, and tribal members have
a resiliency that protects them from complete disconfirmation by the
negative evaluations of educators, mental health professionals, lawyers,
and judges in courts and welfare agencies. Such American Indian children are encouraged to develop their individual touchstones within the
family and tribal settings. The confirmation of individual touchstones
for children and adults within a democratic family setting is what Dr.
Friedman means by being *truly confirmed*. Dr. Friedman emphasizes
genuine confirmation throughout his works, and it is the same as that
which Indian people refer to as respect for life and love for their people.
The love that is generated in American Indian families through *genuine
meeting* increases the Indian child's self-esteem, self-efficacy, and motivation. Maurice writes that, "To be confirmed in personal uniqueness
is to be confirmed directly. That is dialogue. To be confirmed only as a
certain social role is to be confirmed indirectly. That is dialectic. Both

5. Friedman, *Touchstones of Reality*, 310.

6. Friedman, *Healing Dialogue*, 207.

are necessary. We cannot altogether dispense with the idea of social role, though we can guard ourselves against taking it as a reality in itself."[7] American Indian children experience the confirmation of their true otherness, rather than of a social role, in families and tribal communities that confirm them based on their unique expression of their touchstones of reality. It is true that social roles are important and necessary in the tribal community to get tribal business accomplished. Although a strong conformity factor is maintained, it is based on true dialogue. Maurice Friedman would call the tribal community a *community of otherness* because tribal tradition allows a plurality of touchstones that creates a true dialogue of touchstones.

INDIAN CHILDREN, EDUCATION, AND THE NEED FOR A DIALOGUE OF TOUCHSTONES

I am in agreement with Dr. Friedman concerning the importance of the confirmation of touchstones in education. He maintains, "True education is an education in the communication of touchstones. Touchstones of reality always include the component of our unique response to them."[8] The Bowlus study, "An Examination of Factors Responsible for Low Achievement in Indian Elementary School Students" (1973), examines the reasons why American Indian children fail or drop out of the school system. Bowlus, Miles, and Tarbet (1973) confirm that American Indian children do as well on achievement tests as do Caucasian children. This finding eliminates the possibility of lower IQ scores as the determining factor in Indian child school failure. The report demonstrates the importance of unconscious behavioral cues in an ethnic contextual school environment. It indicates that American Indian children fail, fall behind, or drop out of school because they have difficulty reading the teachers' behavioral cues. Such cues arise out of a Euroamerican value system and are therefore difficult for the American Indian child to interpret. For example, imagine that a teacher is preoccupied with her own preparation of lesson materials before class and an Indian child comes into the room. If the teacher ignores the Indian child, the child might read that cue as meaning that the teacher does not like her. She might read the cue in this manner because of the relationship orientation of American Indian culture.

---

7. Friedman, *Dialogue with Dialogue*, 29.

8. Friedman, *Healing Dialogue*, 208.

The lack of confirmation for the Native American child's touch-stones of reality causes profound difficulties for the child to succeed in school. The Bowlus research indicates that there is a conflict of touch-stones between home and school that results in an I and It relation-ship in school, but the child's touchstones are confirmed at home in an I and Thou environment. The child-school conflict makes the child feel disconfirmed because of the mismeetings among the school staff, the child, and the child's family. Evidence of the effect of the lack of confirmation is manifested when the child begins to fall behind in his or her schoolwork in the earlier grades. I have observed that by the eighth grade many American Indian children drop out or, in my opin-ion, are pushed out of school. In some Native American communities, "school dropouts are rated as high as 70 percent."[9] The disconfirmation of touchstones is not a simple matter of ignoring or downplaying the essence of another person. It is the terrible destruction of the unique gloriousness of a human being.

The goal of individual achievement is a powerful touchstone of the non-Indian worldview. American Indian students try to accept the competition-based institutional values by working for achievement and individual success. In the process of trying to succeed in school, how-ever, the Indian child's touchstone of cooperation is shattered. The result of such a conflict of touchstones is that Native American children's self-esteem and self-efficacy begin to erode by the fourth grade. By the end of grammar school, many Indian children drop out of school because the stress caused by this cognitive dissonance is simply too painful.

The following description of a therapy session I had with a fifth grade Native American girl illustrates some possible psychological ef-fects of genocide and racism caused by conflict in the dialogue of touchstones.

> The child and I were involved in an art therapy project of making collages of pictures cut out from magazines. The topic of the art therapy process was about her feelings concerning school. During the session she saw a picture of Ronald Reagan, and threw the magazine across the room, saying, "I hate this man. He doesn't like Indian people." I did not respond and the child continued, "He's white. You can see by how he talks on TV that he doesn't like us." I thought that comments such as hers were probably made in

9. Duran and Duran, *Native American Psychology*, 24.

her family when President Reagan appeared on television. Her childlike understanding of the influence of dominant cultural attitudes was obvious when she spoke of her pain. She went on to say, "The teachers are white just like him, and if he liked Indian people he wouldn't let them talk bad about our dances. When we don't have to go to school on a holiday for a white president or on Columbus Day, but we don't get out of school to go to our own dances, it makes me angry. Besides, I don't see the teachers at my dances. The white Christian teachers think our dances are silly."[10]

The anger, fear, resentment, and subtle self-hatred that she poignantly expressed and strove to explain can be shaped and formed in a child who experiences psychological genocide and racism. The conflict of touchstones between the girl's tribal religious ceremonies and the teachers' lack of appreciation for the spiritual importance of the dances made it difficult for her parents to force her to go to school. The Indian parents wanted their child to go to school and to succeed, yet they saw how the school was disconfirming her and that she was suffering because she was being taught values that conflicted with her family values and tribal values.

Psychotherapy that uses true dialogue can bring about healing in situations that seem insurmountable. The girl was able to express her conflict of touchstones in a therapy session that confirmed her own values and raised her self-esteem and self-efficacy. As Friedman affirms, "to be confirmed in personal uniqueness is to be confirmed directly. That is dialogue."[11] She felt safe and secure in the therapeutic setting because she felt genuine caring coming from the therapist. She felt her personal uniqueness as an Indian person being confirmed in an open dialogue where the caring relationship became the touchstone of reality.

A recent development in the United States education system is the increased use of home schooling to deal with Indian students who find it difficult to attend school. Home schooling as a remedy for the systemic problem of Indian student school failure is on the increase because schools are able to receive funding for home-schooled students. The use of home schooling has become an effective and devious means of increasing the Indian student dropout rate.

10. Alsup, "American Indian Child," 16.

11. Friedman, *Dialogue with Dialogue*, 29.

Some American Indian children develop school phobia, a mental health disorder that causes behaviors that are often misunderstood by teachers, administrators, and parents. Parents have difficulty believing that their child's desire to avoid school is indicative of a legitimate emotional disorder, and they may assume that their child is faking. School officials are no more understanding of this commonly experienced emotional reaction to the disconfirmation of touchstones that occurs in the schools for Indian children. Schools punish children for their attempts to avoid being in school, which triggers the anxiety and panic attacks that characterize school phobia.

The following case study of an Indian adolescent describes a shattering of touchstones that was perpetrated by an insensitive high school principal. The Indian girl's touchstones of reality involved the interaction of her immediate family, extended family, tribe, and ancestors in what Dr. Friedman would call a *partnership of existence*.[12] The young woman was 15 years old and attended high school in the tenth grade. She spoke with me in psychotherapy about her fears of attending school. She said,

> I go to school and when I arrive my heart starts beating fast and I feel like I'm going to die. On Sunday nights, I start getting stomachaches and I vomit when I think about going to school the next morning. I start praying to Grandfather or Grandmother so I can try to feel safe. If I can go to school and cooperate with the teachers, my parents and the principal will be happy. But the closer I get to the school and when I enter the school grounds, I feel like I am going to vomit and pass out. When I feel this way the principal says I'm faking and that I have my parents fooled and that nobody prays to Grandfather and Grandmother in the modern world. My father and mother will not believe me and they send me to school anyway. So, I go to school and I can't stand the fear. Sometimes my prayers don't help me, so I want to run. A couple of times when I felt this way the principal took me into his office and threatened me. One time he told me if I kept behaving this way, he would take me away from my parents and put me in juvenile hall. Then I was really frightened. My heart started beating, I felt like I was going to pass out and I started screaming. The principal said I was a spoiled brat and threatened to punish me if I did not stop screaming. So, I became more frightened. Dr. Alsup, please don't make me go back to that school.[13]

12. Friedman, *Touchstones of Reality*, 304–5.
13. Alsup, "American Indian Child," 18.

When I looked into this case, the principal threatened me. He called the agency I was working for at that time and tried to get me removed from the case. He convinced the adolescent's parents to not have me work with their child. The intimidation of the young woman by the school principal persisted, and he began to threaten the parents. The situation escalated and was on the brink of violence. The parents were angry at the institutional abuse by the principal against their daughter, and they subsequently asked me to resume treatment of their child.

The principal and parents found it difficult to believe that the shattering of a child's touchstones of reality could cause such a strong phobic reaction. The touchstones of reality for the principal were secular and materialistic whereas the touchstones for the American Indian child and her parents were ancestral and supernatural. The conflict of touchstones for the principal came from his lack of belief in the supernatural. He refused to understand or accept the legitimacy of the Indian girl's touchstones of praying to Grandfather or Grandmother and that help from her ancestral spirits could help her cope with her fear of going to school. The principal accused the child of lying and of making excuses for not wanting to attend school, and he incorrectly assumed that the parents did not want to let go of their child. In reality the Indian parents were hopeful that she somehow would gain the courage and desire to go to school. They were angry at her for trying to stay home. In fact, they were the ones who encouraged her to pray so that she could cope with her fears of being in school.

The principal's bureaucratic *I and It* relationship with the girl was the focus of his handling her problem, and this disrupted the child's trust in the school. He was having a monologue with his own touchstones and, therefore, could not have a dialogue with this Indian teenager. The impersonal school bureaucracy of the dominant culture comes up against the Native American personal orientation to life. American Indian traditional education is nonintrusive and has sensitivity toward others. It has more of a sense of a *we* orientation in contrast to the dominant culture's individualistic attitude and perceived need to be tough-minded in one's personal development—a *me* orientation to life. Such an approach stresses touchstones of hardiness, self-elevation, and independence rather than the Indian child's touchstones of cooperation, concern for family, and interdependence.

TOUCHSTONES OF REALITY AND PSYCHOTHERAPY

American Indian children and adolescents who are experiencing school problems are often referred for psychotherapy. The need for culturally sensitive psychotherapy based on a true dialogue of touchstones is readily apparent. Native American children feel disconfirmed in psychotherapy when the therapist unconsciously has a monologue with his or her own touchstones and the treatment is not centered on the client's touchstones. The monologue disrupts mutuality and interferes with the therapeutic alliance between client and therapist that is necessary for healing to take place in psychotherapy. Dr. Friedman's concept of dialogue of touchstones brings the therapeutic relationship into a true existential partnership between client and therapist. Such a dialogue of touchstones is neither encouraged nor experienced in major psychotherapy approaches.[14]

Most psychotherapy approaches that American Indian children encounter do not allow the therapist to get beyond the Euroamerican monologue. Such treatment is based on a worldview and paradigm that is antitherapeutic, because it discounts the American Indian child's touchstones of reality and causes the iatrogenic disease of maintaining mental health problems and school-related problems rather than implementing a cure. Monological and insensitive treatment subtly shifts the child's attitude toward a worldview that is not his or her own, causing confusion, feelings of inferiority, alienation, and withdrawal.

The concept of the shadow that interferes with healing became a reality for Maurice when he experienced Jungian psychology as a touchstone of reality. The archetypal world and the Jungian shadow remain touchstones in Dr. Friedman's worldview.[15] When therapists or teachers are not aware of their own shadow, they project it on another person who seems different from them and who may give witness to different touchstones. When therapists and teachers do not address the shadow problem, Indian children are not perceived as individuals giving unique expression to their cultural touchstones, and the therapists and teachers become psychic police for the society by making the children conform to the dominant cultural touchstones. The therapist or teacher who is unable to confirm an American Indian child in his or her touchstones is practicing what the United Nations Charter defines as genocide.

---

14. Friedman, *Healing Dialogue*, 211.

15. Friedman, *Touchstones of Reality*, 62.

GENUINE RELATIONSHIP

Professionals who treat and advocate for American Indian children, and who possess an appreciation of the unique personal and cultural touchstones that give the children's lives meaning and direction, need to be prepared to receive the same racism and mistreatment from mental health, welfare, probation, and educational systems that ethnic people receive. The pain of injustice that their fellow professionals inflict upon them is what keeps educational and mental health professionals from working with American Indian children. However, that pain helps professionals who do work with and for Native American to understand Indian people's lives as seen from their eyes and as experienced in their emotional and psychological reactions to racism. Dr. Friedman calls this phenomenon *imagining the real*.[16]

True inclusion of genuinely accepting the touchstones of reality of a group that is other than one's own and allowing that group to speak from its own original voice confirms the presence of the otherness of the other in true dialogue. My experience of being in dialogue with American Indian people has not only made them present, but it also has called me forth and made me present, bringing out strong values and potentials of which I was not aware until I responded.

The genuine relationship about which Dr. Friedman writes throughout his work is an integral part of American Indian values and thinking. It is the ever-present love of Indian people between individuals, with their community and with all of creation, seen and unseen. Friedman wrote that "hallowing the everyday and going out to meet the world with one's whole being meant, to the Hasidim, loving one's fellows. All Hasidic life takes place within community, and community is both matrix and product of love."[17] Hasidism became a touchstone of reality for Maurice, and he used it as a metaphor to explain his genuine community—the community of otherness. American Indian life and Hasidic life takes place in a community that shapes the Hasid and the Native American to experience a *we* psychology built on respect and love for the other person.

Native American philosophy does not separate the sacred and the profane, with unseen forces as well as the manifest world being inter-

---

16. Friedman, *Religion and Psychology*, 177.

17. Ibid., 29.

dependent and in relationship. American Indians experience and describe a concrete mysticism. The Indian child addresses the Eternal Thou in the particular and everyday concrete events of the I and Thou experience. The American Indian life position of making everything sacred is the same as Friedman's concept of hallowing the everyday—a mysticism of the concrete. Friedman writes:

> I should define mysticism, rather, as immediacy and presentness plus presence—a strong sense of the immanence of God not as doctrine but as immersion in a directly experienced reality of divine presence. Mysticism includes not only personal contact with God but also the presence of the spirit of God . . . Put in terms of modern Jewish philosophy of religion, mysticism includes both Martin Buber's dialogue with the "eternal Thou" and Abraham Heschel's "awareness of the ineffable." Our existence is not only God's address and our answering response; it is also discovering ourselves in the presence of God, knowing ourselves as known by God. Mysticism is not only "the lived concrete" it is also joy and praise, wonder and awe.[18]

For Indian people, the spiritual experience of the human and his or her encounter with the other is the I and Thou relationship of respect for the divinity in the between that is love in action. All relationships are sacred.

Friedman again describes a reality similar to that of the Native American orientation to life when he writes that "God is immanent—not in the sense of being some universal essence inside of particulars but in the sense that each thing that we meet can be a *Malach*, and angel or messenger that speaks to us of God, a burning bush that tells us that the ground on which we stand—the ground of the everyday—is the ground of hallowing."[19] Friedman's meeting of the divine within the physical world echoes that Great Spirit being experienced in an existential, concrete everyday world.

On a vision quest, the Native American receives a message from one of a vast cast of characters, such as an animal, a rock, a tree, or a bird—a part of nature that goes beyond nature. To the Native American the importance of the sacredness does not lie in the messenger, nor in the one seeking the vision, but in the relationship of the between.

18. Friedman, *Touchstones of Reality*, 152–53.
19. Friedman, *Human Way*, 80–81.

The Great Spirit and the holy ground are experienced through the dialogue of the one in search of a vision with the messenger. The feeling of divinity and of being given a gift of knowledge in the relationship is the sacredness of the between.

The materialistic, successful human image of the dominant culture is different from the American Indian image of the real or complete person. In northern California the Yurok Indians' image of the *pegerk*, or spiritually wealthy person, is similar to the human image that Maurice Friedman unconceals when he describes Lao-tzu's *sound man*, another touchstone that left an imprint on Maurice's experience.[20]

The American Indian human image includes a respect for life and for all of creation. Religion is a way of living, not a fragmented segment of life. The Native American way of being-in-becoming resonates with Dr. Friedman's presentation of the sound man and the Tao. The Tao is another way of describing how the American Indian experiences the Great Spirit that flows through everything and envelops all creation but cannot be pinned down within creation. Indian people are both panentheistic and pantheistic. The Indian person stands his or her own ground and has a dialogue with creation in a relationship where the transpersonal is experienced within the concrete reality of everyday life. The Indian human image of being-in-becoming is opposed to the dominant society's obsession with doing. The conflict of touchstones between American Indian people and the dominant culture happens when the non-materialistic, mystical pragmatist encounters the theoretical skeptic who is trapped in a materialistic existence.

Maurice Friedman discovered a trust in God or in existence itself through his experiments in life with different touchstones of reality and out of his dialogues with various religions. Dr. Friedman's touchstone of reality of the biblical covenant is an important aspect of his work. The biblical covenant includes the assurance of basic trust, existential trust, trust in existence, and a profound trust in God.[21] The transpersonal reality that is expressed through such trust is a concrete mysticism brought into community that works to increase love and compassion in the world.

---

20. Friedman, *Hidden Human Image*, 122.
21. Friedman, *Touchstones of Reality*, 131.

CONCLUSION

Friedman's position reveals a basic trust in existential reality and in God that enables him to continue to hope and to love in the same world that has been a home for oppression, genocide, and the Holocaust. This love and compassion appear throughout the works of Maurice Friedman when he talks about everything and everybody being redeemable. He writes, "In the end redemption is neither the action of man alone nor of God alone but the completion of the dialogue between them."[22] The purpose we are fulfilling by hallowing our everyday concrete reality is the trust required to stand in the world in spite of the experience of the Holocaust and to bring everything of our existence that is in exile into dialogue with God. As long as we bring every part of our reality into a dialogue with God, every part of our reality can be redeemed. "The love between man and God, like the love between man and man, is not a matter of merit or unearned grace but of the "between": If one loves less, then the other should love more for the sake of the relationship itself."[23]

Maurice Friedman's works and Native American ideologies both embrace an existential spiritual life that gives witness to the touchstone of a revelatory world and earth. Revelation comes in the encounter in the between of God and man, of man and man, and of man and nature. In both Hasidism and Native American views of the world, happiness is not assured and the world is not evolving to some great paradise. Maurice Friedman and Native American spirituality state that reality has to be dealt with, to be confronted in the present and in the moment. Both the Hasidic person and the Native American are aware that the presentness of concrete reality addressing them in the moment demands a response. An approach to reality based on revelation in spite of genocide brings about basic trust and hope. A revelatory world reassures man that God, the Great Spirit, intervenes in history and time, in place and event, to give a person the courage to contend with world and community and to wrestle with what seems to be unchangeable.

The world is a dangerous place for Native American children. Racism and genocide are manifested in far too many Indian children's lives by their being forcibly transferred out of their homes to non-Indian foster homes and by being pushed out of schools because they cannot

22. Ibid., 171.
23. Ibid., 172.

bear the stress and psychological and emotional trauma of trying to succeed in a system that does not honor their touchstones of reality. When
they are made to see mental health professionals who do not cherish
their worldview or their culture, their self-esteem is further lowered,
which may be part of the reason for the escalating suicide rate among
American Indian young people. Conditions of life are inflicted upon
American Indian children that are calculated to bring about the destruction of the tribe completely or in part. This violates all of the aspects of
the United Nations Convention on Genocide.

Maurice Friedman's negative touchstones of reality offer a way out
of this dilemma of the destruction of the American Indian child. The
practice of confirming the American Indian child's touchstones of reality will restore the child's self-esteem, self-efficacy, and motivation. A
confirmation of touchstones will bring the American Indian child and
the American neocolonist back from exile, and it will redeem them both
by bringing them into a dialogue with God. In this way, all people involved will be hallowed and redeemed, establishing a true dialogue of
touchstones and a true partnership of existence.

BIBLIOGRAPHY

Alsup, R. "California School System: The Destruction of the American Indian child." Paper presented at the American Indian Mental Health Conference, Logan, Utah, July 1989.

Bowlus, K. R. et al. *An examination of factors responsible for low achievement in Indian elementary school students: part I.* Eureka, CA: Northern Indian California Education Project, 1973.

Buber, Martin. *I and Thou.* Translated by R. G. Smith. 1958. Reprint, New York: Macmillan, 1987.

Duran, E., and B. Duran. *Native American Postcolonial Psychology.* Albany: SUNY Press, 1995.

Friedman, Maurice. *Abraham Joshua Heschel & Elie Wiesel: You Are My Witnesses.* New York: Farrar, Straus, Giroux, 1987.

————. *Dialogue and the Human Image: Beyond Humanistic Psychology.* Newbury Park, CA: Sage, 1992.

————. *Encounter on the Narrow Ridge: A Life of Martin Buber.* New York: Paragon, 1991.

————. *The Healing Dialogue in Psychotherapy.* Northvale, NJ: Jason Aronson, 1985.

————. *A Heart of Wisdom: Religion and Human Wholeness.* Albany: State University of New York Press, 1992.

————. *The Hidden Human Image.* New York: Dell, 1974.

————. *The Human Way: A Dialogic Approach to Religion and Human Experience.* Chambersburg, PA: Anima, 1982.

————. *Martin Buber: The Life of Dialogue.* New York: Harper & Row, 1955.

————. *Martin Buber and the Eternal.* New York: Human Sciences, 1986.

————. *Martin Buber's Life and Work.* 3 vols. Detroit: Wayne State University Press, 1981–83.

————. "My dialogue with dialogue." Manuscript. 1995.

————. *Problematic Rebel: Melville, Dostoievsky, Kafka, Camus.* Rev. ed. Chicago: University of Chicago Press, 1970.

————. *Religion and Psychology: A Dialogical Approach.* New York: Paragon, 1992.

————. *To Deny Our Nothingness: Contemporary Images of Man.* Chicago: The University of Chicago Press, 1967.

————. *Touchstones of Reality: Existential Trust and the Community of Peace.* New York: Dutton, 1974.

————. *The Worlds of Existentialism: A Critical Reader.* New Jersey: Humanities Press International, 1964.

Simpson, G. E., and M. J. Yinger. *Racial and Cultural Minorities: An Analysis of Prejudice and Discrimination.* 5th ed. New York: Plenum, 1985.

12

Strelisk

ELIE WIESEL

WAS HE REALLY AN angel of fire whose voice was heard in heaven and on earth? Did he really make people's souls tremble in fear and ecstasy? It is said that he was a holy man for whom terrestrial matters meant less than the movement of a tree caught in a storm? Surely, he was different from his peers. That is what many people were thinking, and some people were saying.

Have you heard of the strange incident that occurred at his funeral, one week before Rosh-Hashana? Listen:

Under a dark sky, in the presence of a large number of disciples and followers, his son, reb Shlomo, began reciting the kaddish . . . and stopped after the first words. It's the pain, someone whispered. Pain can make one lose one's voice. After what seemed to be an endless silence, the old rabbi of the community ordered the son to continue. In a halting voice, reb Shlomo completed the solemn prayer which, as we face death, makes us proclaim God's majestic right to be glorified.

Later, a commentator explained the interruption in the following manner: what is the purpose, the aim of the kaddish? To help the soul of the departed climb higher and higher toward purity. But was such help necessary for Rabbi Uri, the Seraph of Strelisk? His soul had already attained the highest degree of holiness; it needed no assistance from anyone here below—be it his son. That is why reb Shlomo had paused in the middle. He was convinced that even when his saintly father was alive, he had succeeded unaided in transcending his earthly condition, that even in this world, under God's watchful yet clement eye, he had evolved in

191

celestial spheres, tempted by nothing but the absolute, getting closer and closer to God. So extraordinary a human being was reb Uri during his lifetime that, even after his death, he continued to fascinate those who had been devoted to him.

Listen further: during the week of mourning that followed, reb Shlomo astonished his visitors with his good mood. At times, his face was radiating as if illuminated by a secret joy, drawn from an invisible source. Clearly, he did not accept the death of his father. He even said so openly. "Father is not dead," he said. "Don't you see that the holy Seraph is still part of this world, even as his soul roams around the highest, most inaccessible spheres in heaven? A man like him cannot die, a spirit like his cannot vanish. A soul like his is stronger that the Angel of death."

When the "Shiva"-week was over, the old members of the School of Strelisk began talking to him about succession. They wanted him to ascend the throne and thus become their new Master. He refused. Why? Simple: how could he succeed his father, since his father was still alive?

True, other Hasidim—the Bratzlaver, for instance—also maintained that their Rabbi had remained among the living. Still, when he died in Oman, his followers had observed the laws of mourning. They believed that though dead, Rabbi Nachman was alive. Not so Reb Shlomo. He really believed that his father did not die and that therefore he could not succeed him. His Hasidim argued? So what. He knew best.

In the end, he won. He did not succeed his father, not really, as leader of the Strelisker Hasidim. Another pious man inherited both the title and the crown. For Reb Shlomo only briefly survived his father. Four months after Reb Uri's death, the son was gone as well . . .

But tonight, we intend to talk about the father, not the son. Reb Uri: one of the truly great Hasidic Masters of his generation, and perhaps of all generations. We shall try to scrutinize the principle elements of his life and legend: why was he called, why is he still called the Seraph, the man of fire whose soul was aflame? I confess my affection and admiration for him. Firstly—because he incites us to dream fiery dreams. And then—because he is linked to the first rebbe of Kossov, the founding father of the Wizsnitzer school—and whenever Wizsnitz is mentioned I do not hide my bias: I have a special affection for it.

Strelisk taught us that Hasidism is the glorification not of poverty, but of the poor. Not of ignorance, but of simplicity. Hasidism in Strelisk is what it was for the Besht: the despairing sigh of a poor cobbler who cannot afford to send his children to school weighs more than the most brilliant study of the most erudite but heartless scholar. Any human being weighs more than all the books in the world. That was how Rabbi Levi-Yitzhak of Berditchev saw it: one day he instructed his most faithful disciples to gather at a secret place in order to unite their forces and hasten the coming of the Messiah. They were all there on time—not he. An hour passed, two hours passed. When he finally appeared, he apologized: On my way here, he said, I heard a child crying; he was alone; his mother was sick or at work. What could I do? I went in just for a moment, to see whether he needed food or water. But what about the Messiah? One of the disciples cried out. Oh, said the great Rabbi Levi-Yitzhak who was even more different than all the different masters, you must understand: when a Jewish child is crying—I have to take care of him. But still, what about the Messiah? Asked another disciple. Oh, the Messiah? said the Berditchever. When a Jewish child cries, the Messiah can wait.

But . . . those who came late . . . cannot.

Why the nickname? Why the Seraph? There exist two versions. Here is the first: after the passing of his first wife, Freidele, Rabbi Uri seemed disconsolate. He could not stop weeping. He was asked: is this not overreacting? Wasn't the tragedy that had befallen him the will of God? His answer: if my Freidele had stayed with me for seventy years, I would have ascended into heaven alive. Having said that, he turned to one of his Hasidim and asked him to reveal what he had witnessed. Said the hasid: one day I followed our holy Master out of town, deep into the woods; suddenly I saw him growing and growing, until his head penetrated the sky. I got scared. Panic-stricken, I seized a corner of his caftan and held him back. And the Rabbi regained his normal size.

Second version: a certain Reb Eizik decided to spend Rosh-Hashana with the holy Seer of Lublin. On his way, he stopped over in Strelisk where he spent the night at reb Uri's House of Study and Prayer. Around midnight he saw the Master enter the room and—as was his custom—check on those who slept there, making sure they they needed nothing. Unnoticed, Reb Eizik watched as the Rabbi walked back and forth, back and forth his face glowing like burning coal. At one point, when the Rabbi had his back to Eizik, Eizik was startled; he discovered that the Rabbi had *another* face in the back. If only he had dared to question the Rabbi, but he did not. Well, he said to himself, I shall ask the Seer. He knows everything, he will explain this mystery too. But woe unto Eizik, when he reached Lublin, so moved was he by the sight of the Seer, that he forgot the question. He remember it only after the High Holidays when the time came to take leave of the Seer who looked at him severely and said: "on your way home, stop again in Strelisk. Tell Reb Uri that I know he has *two* faces." "But Rabbi," exclaimed Eizik, "that is what I wanted to tell you!" "Knowing and talking are two different things," answer the Seer. "Do what I tell you." Naturally Eizik did. Reb Uri's answer? He quoted the prophet Ezekiel: "And the Seraph's have *four* faces." And that is why he was called the Seraph.

A Master like many others? A man like any other man? Perhaps a bit better than most? Yearning for greater purity and devotion? No Reb Uri is truly special. All right, I know, I say that of all Hasidic Masters, and I think I am right in each case. But more so in the case of reb Uri. He truly *is* different. On many grounds. One: he does not belong to any illustrious line. Two: he was not appointed or chosen by a great Master for his exceptional scholarship. In a way, he is a typical Hasidic Rabbi. Beloved by his followers who bask in his love for God and for them. He helps the needy, in general, through prayer. Miracles? He is suspicious of miracles. His followers are encouraged not to rely on the supernatural. You know the old Yiddish saying: "*Farlozt zich nisht oif kein nissim, sogt thilim*: do not rely on miracles, say the Psalms." And yet—when nothing else seems to work, he too is ready to perturb the laws of nature for the sake of a desperate father or mother: what doesn't one do for a smile on the lips of a sick child? But then—in what way is Rabbi Uri of Strelisk different? Actually, the story of his birth and rise to glory is typically Hasidic. One finds in it hidden innocence, naïve goodness and divine reward. In God's book, everything is related. No gesture is lost, no tear forgotten. Weep and someone will hear you. Cry out, and your voice will reverberate in heaven. Take the hand of someone who drowns in solitude and angels will smile at both of you. Like marriages, all encounters are planned up above. That was surely true of Reb Uri's parents.

Listen: on the surface, Pinhas and Rivkele Klughoipt who lived in Lianov, a small village near Lvov, had not much in common. A poor orphan whose grandmother died of grief when her husband was beaten to death by pogromtchiks, Rivkele worked as a maid in an inn for coachmen. The innkeeper and his wife had noticed this man Pinhas who did not speak or behave like the others; he neither drank nor cursed. They decided that Pinhas and Rivkele ought to get married. By coincidence—

one more—the great Maggid of Mezritch happened to be there for the engagement ceremony. When they got married, Pinhas changed jobs and became a tailor. The couple was poor and had to work hard for a living. Was it a happy marriage? It does not seem so. Rivkele was probably more pious and refined than her husband. Was it mental incompatibility? Or some other kind? One source states that "*Aharei ha-khatuna,* after the wedding, *lo yakhla lisbol et tahaloukhot baala,* she could not tolerate her husband's behavior." What behavior? What could the simple tailor of Lianov have done to provoke such anger or resentment in his duly wedded wife? Rivkele considered divorce which, at the time, was extremely infrequent in Jewish life. She first went to consult the great Maggid of Mezritch. He remembered her engagement party: "Do not even think of divorcing, he reprimanded her. You will have a son who will bring joy and consolation to our people." And he sent her back to her husband. When she became pregnant, she returned once more to see the great Maggid who stood up to welcome her. Hasidim say: he stood up because he knew she was carrying Reb Uri in her belly. It is also possible that he stood up simply because Jewish tradition orders us to stand up before *every* pregnant woman. Why? The child in her womb may be the Messiah.

Anyway, Rivkele went home totally reassured. If she was pious and charitable before, she became more so now. She kept away from whatever was not kosher. As a young mother, she prevented her child from even noticing whatever was impure. Shielded by his mother's extreme precautions and inspired by the Maggid's prediction, there appeared to be no way for Reb Uri to avoid the glorious destiny that was awaiting him inside the Hasidic kingdom.

Still, Rabbi Uri must have had problems with his father. At one point, he is said to have remarked: "Had my father gone to the mikva—the ritual bath—once, at least once, before my birth, I could have accomplished much more." But he, Reb Uri, made up for it: he went to the mikva very often. I do not suggest we follow him there, but let us visit him at his home.

Who is he?

Born in Lianov in 1757—three years before the passing of the Besht—he had a normal childhood—I mean: normal for a lonely melancholy Jewish child with an overprotective mother in a Russian village where few Jews could be found. He himself later told the story of his father shedding bitter tears for not being able to gather a minyan for his son's circumcision.

For an entire week, Pinhas tried to find ten men. He could not even find nine or, for that matter, eight, five or four. He went from village to village, from one marketplace to another, in vain. On the morning of the eighth day, as he was sitting in front of his hut, lost in thought, wondering how his son would be brought into the covenant of Abraham, how, without a minyan for the ceremony, his son would become Jewish, he began to sob uncontrollably. Suddenly, he heard the sounds of a carriage approaching. As it pulled up in front of him, he saw that its passengers seemed in a good mood. Why are you upset? the coachman asked him. Isn't God our father? Yes? Then what troubles you? Reb Pinhas explained his predicament. God had blessed him with a son; but now, eight days after his birth, it was time to circumcise him and there was no minyan. That's all? exclaimed the coachmen. Rejoice, dear man, your worries are over. Aren't we all Jewish? Look here: the ten of us are just returning from a wedding; and we have brought food along, enough for two minyanim. So what are we waiting for? Well—never in Lianov had there been such a circumcision ceremony . . . It seemed that one of the passengers happened to be a mohel, another a teacher, a third a singer . . . And all night long, there was a prying, singing and dancing . . . Can you guess who they were? Asked Reb Uri. No? well let me tell you: the teacher was Moses, the mohel Abraham, the singer was King David and Prophet Elijah was the "Sandek," the godfather . . .

With such guests, and their blessings, the child had to do well. He did. So precocious was he that one day when he was heard sobbing, and his parents ran out to see what happened, they found him in the field, staring at the sky. Why are you crying? They asked him. Did you fall? No. Are you sick? No. Are you afraid? No. Then why the tears? I feel sorry for God, he answered. He has so many children—and they are all so far away from him . . . At three, he was able to read the Bible, at five he was discovering the depths of Talmud. Some considered him an *Ilui*, a child prodigy. Of his first tutor, various tales have been told, such as the following: since the tutor frequently wasn't paid, he would frequently punish his pupil. He would punish him when he knew his lesson "too well:" "You see?" he would shout, you see the quality of my teaching . . . and your father doesn't even see fit to pay me." On the other hand, when the young pupil did not know his lesson, the tutor would punish him, shouting: "You don't pay and you don't even learn! That's too much!" Later the young Uri also studied Kabbala but not practical Kabbala: "whenever he would see an angel," says a text, "he would close his eyes."

Hasidic legend tells us that he was befriended by the lord of the village. How did that happen? Listen: that particular lord was a learned, enlightened man who had once been visited by a Jewish renegade who told him that he planned to become a missionary. Why don't you try your debating skill on young Uri? Asked the village lord. The renegade accepted the challenge. As Uri was known to frequently walk alone in the woods, they decided to wait for him there. When he appeared, the renegade engaged him in conversation. "Why don't you give up the Torah? Don't you see it is obsolete and useless? It only brings trouble for those who believe in it." At first, Uri kept silent, afraid of offending the lord of the village. But when the latter ordered him to answer, he said: "When God gave the Torah, the entire Jewish people stood at Sinai to receive it. Thus it would take the entire people to decide to give it back. No Jew may do it on his own. So—you know what? Gather all the Jews from all over the world—and you and I will debate the question before them." Hasdism say that reb Uri's answer made the lord of the village smile.

As an adolescent, he may have met the great Maggid of Mezrtitch who died in 1772. We know that he was searching for a Master, he met Rabbi Elimelekh of Lizensk and left him for Ostraha where the famous Reb Yevi received him with great affection. But that was not what he needed then. He left Ostraha for Koretz where Rabbi Pinhas simply refused to be his Master. For there he traveled to Neshkhiz: would Reb Mottele be his teacher? On he went to Onipol: where he was asked to stay as Reb Zusya's disciple. He did not. Instead he continued to Karlin which was to be his last stop.

Why didn't accept the other offers? Were the other Masters less pious, less impressive than Reb Shloimele Karliner? No acceptable theory has been advanced. The truth is that a secret bond exists between the soul of a Master and that of his disciple. And no one knows its root or reason. Just as there is love at first sight, there is "*Hitkashrut*" at first sight. The Hasid has only one Master and for the Master every Hasid is the only one. It is as though their bond were older than Creation itself.

Some commentators say that Reb Uri was suspicious of some Masters. That he thought they were not careful enough and could fall prey to vanity which, in Hasidic literature, is considered a sin and a malediction; it pushes on to the precipice without warning. "Better throw yourself into a burning furnace than become famous," said Reb Uri.

He was once asked: How is it that today's rebbes take so much money from their followers, whereas their distant predecessors were satisfied to receive much less? With tongue in cheek, he replied: "How much does a living rooster cost? Pennies. But a sculpture or painting of a rooster, the illusion of a rooster, a fake rooster, costs a lot." Another time he wondered aloud: "How can people be vain? Whatever we possess belongs to God; it is only given to us on loan. Even our piety comes from Him . . ."

Anyway—he eventually became Reb Shloimele Karliner's disciple. How did it happen? During a lesson in mysticism? No. During prayer perhaps? No. Listen: when Reb Uri arrived in Karlin, he saw Reb Shloimele sitting on a rock in the street. "Peace unto you," said Reb Shloimele. And that was sufficient. Reb Uri felt he had reached his destination. Tradition has it that he stayed there seven years. His first wife—Freidele—worked as a maid in wealthy homes. Later she opened a grocery store. After her death, he married Blimele, Reb Mendel Kossover's sister. They were so poor that when Reb Uri came home for Passover, they could not afford to have their own Seder and therefore celebrated at the table of the local rabbi. Later he had his own disciples, most of them just as impoverished as he. He disliked and mistrusted the rich. Of his followers, only one was known for his wealth, a certain Reb Wolfe from Lvov. I like you, Wolfe, he once told him. But I would like you even more if you were poor. No, no, protested the frightened Hasid, don't change things, Rabbi; leave them alone; if I were to lose even a shoelace, I would be unable to pray properly. So—the Seraph allowed him to keep his money. Since he needed it for prayer . . .

But other Hasidim had no problems with prayer though they were all poor, almost destitute. They were not alone. Most Jews, especially those in the villages, lived in misery, fear, and—fortunately for them—hope.

Let us have a closer look: what was their situation? What was happening outside the Hasidic universe while Reb Uri worked on his prayers?

The world had entered a period of violent and bloody convulsions, oddly accompanied by cultural renaissance. Reb Uri was a contemporary of Friedrich the Great and Scarlatti, William Blake and Diderot, Gainsborough and Schiller, but was he merely aware of their existence? Did he perceive the burning impatience of history? Did he ever realize that Europe was going through endless turbulence and that Western civilization was enduring fundamental mutations? Prussia and Great Britain are constantly at war; in America, there is the Revolution and the War of Independence; in Russia, Czars and Czarinas succeed one another on Ivan the Terrible's throne. Poland is divided once, twice, three times. The French Revolution produces great orators who, in the name of freedom, fill the prisons with former and future adversaries; in the name of life, they send hundreds of men and women to die on the guillotine. The *Ethics of our Fathers* seems to have foreseen everything: the killer will be killed; the king's judges will be judged. Danton, Robespierre, Marat: in the end, there is only one victor: Death. Death alone can boast the lasting triumphs. It ridicules covenants and alliances, it imposes its will on sovereigns and dictators. And God in all that? His name—or other names—are invoked by those who die as well as by those who kill. Is it because the century is nearing its end? The pace accelerates. Denmark is ruled by a madman, Christian the seventh. Berlin is burned by Russian soldiers; Bengal suffers from starvation. Napoleon undertakes the conquest of the Orient. Kant and Rousseau, Goethe and Goya and Mozart build spiritual cathedrals while Europe drowns in oceans of blood and sinks into darkness. Oh yes, history in on the move. It moves forward, then jumps backward. What will the nineteenth century be like?

While all these forces are at work, the Hasidic kingdom continues to serve as a haven, both enchanted and blessed, to God-fearing men and women who still believe in non-violence, in the importance of the sacred element in human relations, who still believe in the beauty and depth of each moment that passes.

They are poor? So what. They are oppressed? So what. They have their own "kings," their own ideals. They too are fighting, but their means are different. Their victories are of a spiritual nature; for a hasid, what matters is the spiritual, nothing else. But what about one's daily worries? They must be transformed. But what about bread for hungry children? What about hope for desperate prisoners? Hunger implicates all those who have bread and do not share it; a prisoner, in his or her cell, implicates all those outside who are still free. Every problem must be examined from a moral aspect. This moral aspect must govern the hasid's conduct. One must look at one's fellow human being, one must listen to him, one must help him. Who among us does not need help?

In those times, all Jewish communities needed help and comfort. Especially those scattered in the forsaken corners of the Ukraine, Poland, Hungary, White Russia and Romania. And even in France where the French Revolution of 1789 had given human rights to its citizens, but had forgotten its Jews. True, there were not many Jews in France then: approximately five hundred in Paris and some forty thousand elsewhere. A delegation of Jews said, to argue their case before Parliament, and I quote: "Aren't the Jews human beings like all the others?" Of course, it was worse in Eastern Europe. But there, Jews knew where to go for help; they had their rebbes who offered them hope and consolation, who helped them live and survive.

The various Masters attracted large numbers of disciples from all parts of Eastern Europe: that was the great Maggid's formidable victory; he had foreseen the political changes and taken appropriate measures. He had sent his best disciples to the four corners of Central Europe with the mission to enlarge the movement. More and more schools were created where Masters and disciples sought to develop and enrich Jewish thought and memory. Each and every Master had his distinctive approach. What was Reb Uri known for? His opposition to the popularization of Kabbala? His passion for the poor? We know that *his* son Reb Shloime was born in a cellar and that many guests *were* invited to the circumcision; all attended. But Reb Uri could not afford the customary meal that follows the ceremony. He was heard saying: "And what if I cannot offer food and wine to my guests, is that a reason for a Jewish child not to become a part of the Jewish people? " Among his guests, there was a certain Reb Leib Dimeles, the Seer's brother-in-law, who was known for his wealth and generosity. When he saw the poverty of his host, he sent out for the best food and drinks available. He then offered Reb Uri valuable gifts and clothes and money, and promised him to take care of the entire family. When Reb Uri protested, Reb Leibel said: "I am not giving it to you, but to your son." That very night Reb Uri decided to leave Lianov and move to Strelisk, known for the misery of its Jewish population.

When did he become rebbe? After the death of his beloved teacher, Reb Shloimele, who was killed by a Cossack while reciting the Amida prayer. Hence the extraordinary importance Reb Uri attached to prayer. To his disciples he once said: "You wish to learn my teaching? Start praying."

Masters and teachers came to attend his "lessons": he welcomed them with a test; they were made to drink two or three glasses of vodka; if they couldn't handle it, he told them that they still had much to learn.

Once, when wealthy Hasidism appeared before him, he ordered them to go outside to the well and bring in two pails of water. "Why is he doing this?" wondered Rabbi Bunam. "To teach them humility," answered a disciple who had just returned from Strelisk.

Not surprisingly, soon only poor Hasidim remained in Strelisk. A Tzaddik from out of town could not hide his astonishment: since the Seraph of Strelisk could accomplish miracles, why didn't he help his followers become rich? "Soon you will understand," answered Reb Uri. "Look at my followers; invite any one of them to join us." The tzaddik motioned to a man asking him to come closer. "Listen," said the Seraph. "This moment is special; it is a moment of grace. Tell me your most ardent and secret wish; I promise you: it will be accomplished." It took a while for the hasid to control himself: "My wish? The rebbe wants to hear my real wish? It is to be able to say at least one of the prayers the way the rebbe does." In other words: prayer in Strelisk was not a means to attain a goal; prayer was *the* goal.

One day, the Seraph interrupted the morning service exclaiming: "I know your needs; I know you need money to pay the butcher and the baker, the cobbler and the healer. So—whoever wants money, let him put his hand in my pocket, he will get more than he needs." All remained motionless. Their mind was in another world as was their heart. Their soul was not in their pocket.

It is in Strelisk, that Reb Uri perfected, so to speak, his concept and practice of prayer. Like Rabbi Akiba, he would leave this world during prayer, detaching himself from reality, extracting himself from time itself. His soul would travel in celestial spheres where it met other souls, all attracted by the same light. Only when Reb Uri ascended into heaven, he took others with him, allowing them to see what he saw. When Reb Sholemke of Belz came to visit him on Shavuot, he was invited for an aliyah. Shaking with fear and awe, he literally saw the Torah as it was written in the time of Moses: white fire on black fire. Reb Uri's ecstasy was so powerful, it is said, that every day before services he put his affairs in order, and bid farewell to his family as though he were seeing them for the last time. To his wife and children, he would repeat his last will. To a devoted disciple he would say: "If you do not see me again,

remember: the written notes on my table are not mine, but my teacher's."
Reb Sholemke's comment: What did I learn from him? The art of prayer.

A few words may be in order to remind us who his teacher, Reb Shlomo Karliner, was.

Rabbi Asher of Stolin said of him: "When reb Shlomo prays, he has one of his feet in this world, and the other in the world to come; and it is on the other one that he is leaning."

As for Reb Uri, he testified: "The Heikhal Haneguina, the sanctuary of melody, is the smallest of the sanctuaries, but none is as close to man. Enter it and you will be in the presence of God. However, Rabbi Shlomo Karliner did not need it; he approached God on his own. Through prayer."

And Rabbi Shneur-Zalman of Ladi commented: "Not one could be compared to Reb Shlomo; for not one prays like him. When he prays, he is higher than all of us."

One day the king issued a decree forbidding Jewish communal prayer. Naturally, Jews everywhere moved heaven and earth to revoke the decree. They made such a noise that the heavenly court itself became troubled. After long deliberation, it was decided to ask Rabbi Shlomo Karliner to render his judgment. Said he: "*Vaani tefila*" does not mean 'I pray,' but 'I *am* prayer.' Who and what would the Jewish people be without prayer?" As a result, we are told, the decree was soon abolished.

Toward the end of his life, Reb Shlomo moved to Ludmir which was under Russian occupation. It happened during the month of Iyar. A special squad of Cossacks had arrived in town to disarm a band of Polish insurgents. While searching for them, its commander stumbled upon a gathering in a house. He did not know that Jews had assembled there to celebrate Shavuot which that year fell on Shabbat. The officer entered the shtibl. Reb Shlomo, lost in prayer, did not notice his presence. Not even when the officer stood next to him. Reb Shlomo's grandson wanted to yell, but dared not make a sound. Finally, he shyly pulled his grandfather's caftan. Without success. Reb Shlomo, absorbed in prayer, remained motionless. Thereupon, in an outburst of anger, the officer fired at him pointblank, hitting him in the hip. The rebbe fell to the ground. "Why did you bring me down?" he asked, opening his eyes. His Hasidim carried him to his room. Nobody knows if he realized that he was dying but we do know that he asked for the Zohar and began reading it. And that he died while delving into its mysteries.

As his worthy follower and disciple, Reb Uri of Strelisk also placed a strong emphasis on prayer. But then, wasn't this—isn't this—part of Hasidic teaching? With the exception of Reb Mendele Kotzker, all Hasidic Masters believed in the power of prayer. But with the exception of Reb Shlomo Karliner, none went as far as the Seraph of Sterlisk. Praying, for him, was a constantly renewed statement of being ready to die for God. Why did God accept Abel's offering? Because he gave of himself. To pray means to become offering and sacrifice. Unfortunately, said Reb Uri, we have forgotten how to pray. We must learn again. King David knew how to write Psalms, said Reb Uri; all I know is to say them. But, in truth, no one said them like him. No one had his fervor, his passion, his flame. Thus Strelisk became a new center in Hasidism: a center of ecstasy where his followers forgot their links to the material world and attached their being to the divine Being.

With the strength of his prayer, Reb Uri succeeded in saving not only the living, but the dead as well. Hasidic legend has it that he held the keys to hell in his hands. Every Shabbat, the angels in heaven would wait for him to end the Havdala prayer before they could usher the sinners back into Hell. That is why he made a special effort not to hurry.

Does all this sound supernatural? Like most Masters, Reb Uri was versed in mystical studies: what would Hasidism be without its mystical component? But . . . there is a but. Though inspired by mysticism, Reb Uri was opposed to its popularization fearing its trivialization. He was against publishing mystical books. As a result, he entered into open conflict with other great Masters—such as Reb Tzvi-Hersh of Ziditchoiv—who publicly encouraged the study of the Zohar and the Lurianic commentaries. Reb Uri believed that the study of Kabbala for the uninvited was too dangerous. The debate split the movement. When Reb Tzvi-Hersh declared that he knew the entire Zohar by heart, Reb Uri responded in the third person: "Uri is satisfied to know only one verse; it offers me enough food for thought for a thousand days."

Listen to some of his favorite sayings:

The Torah is composed of six hundred thousand letters, one for each soul of the people of Israel. Omit one letter and the entire Torah is "psula," unfit for use. The same is true of the Jewish people: eliminate one of its children, and the people will not be the same.

Also:

Why are letters and words separated from one another in the Torah? To illustrate our occasional need for solitude. True, we must all belong to the community; but, at times, we must also belong to ourselves.

Another saying:—he loved to speak of himself in the third person— Uri is not afraid he'll be asked why he wasn't Abraham or Moses but why he wasn't Uri . . .

When his son Reb Shlomo—named after Reb Shlomo Karliner— got married, he began building his own "*Daven shtiebel.*" Just at that time, messengers came to his father asking for contributions for a House of Study to be established in the name of the holy Ari in Safed. "I will not give a penny, said Reb Uri of Strelisk. Firstly—when the Messiah will come and the holy Ari will finally come to his synagogue, there will be not room for me. Secondly: my son also needs money. And lastly: I have no money . . .

A saying: examine a person's palm and you will read his or her mind.

Another: every person must go through a thousand worlds every day.

And another: people came to me . . . they know where *they* are going—but where am I going?

And the most beautiful of all: truth remains true even if we do nothing.

He said: I know nothing, nothing at all. All I know is that I must envelop myself in the talit and shout: Shema Israel, hear oh Israel. And once he shouted Shema Israel with such force and exuberance that the ceiling broke over his head.

We are now in 1827. The Hasidic kingdom has grown; it is now an immense movement with many centers, many capitals: Kozhenitz and Riminov, Lublin and Pshiskhe, Lizensk and Rizhin and Kotzk. The great Masters of the earlier generations are gone. As are gone the three participants in the holy conspiracy for redemption, who paid with their lives for their daring experiment: God's hand cannot be forced with impunity. Having lived and worked, studied and taught for seventy years, the Seraph of Strelisk is aware that the end is near. Members of his immediate family, of his intimate circle of faithful disciples, come from near and far to be with him. Physical pain and mental anguish have not left him for weeks and weeks. What will happen, when . . . What happens to a kingdom when it loses its crown? Psalms are being recited from morning to evening, from evening to morning.

A rumor spreads through the community: he has just lost consciousness. Only his lips are moving, but it is difficult to hear what he says. Probably a prayer. Will his prayer be received? His agony seems endless. From time to time Reb Yehuda-Tzvi of Stretin—his favorite disciple and probable successor—opens the door, looks at the Master and closes it again. At one point, he enters the room and fails to reappear. His sobs break the silence. Everyone is now sobbing.

Reb Yehuda-Tzvi was asked later: how did he know that it was indeed the end? He answered: it is written in the Bible: "*lo yireani haadam vehai*"—no one could see God and live. When I opened the door I realized what he saw.

The House of Strelisk was in mourning. Following tradition, older Hasidim sought to crown the son, Reb Shlomo, as their new Master. He refused. Anyway, he survived his father by only four months. Reb Yehuda-Tzvi of Stretin was thus unanimously elected to the throne. That may well have been the wish of Reb Uri. Between Master and disciple there existed a powerful affection that people compared to the one that had once linked Moses to Joshua. Rabbi Itzhak-Eizik of Kalev—the Hungarian Tzaddik who would buy shepherd's songs and sanctify them as mystical tunes—asked Reb Yehuda-Tzvi to tell him of the Seraph of Strelisk. I cannot, answered Reb Yehuda-Tzvi. Since the Kalever Tzaddik insisted, Reb Yehuda-Tzvi opened his shirt, pointed to his heart and exclaimed: "Kalever tzaddik, look! Look well into my heart and you will see whom I was fortunate to have had as my Master and teacher."

In conclusion—for tonight's excursion into Strelisk—a commentary that tradition has preserved in the name of Reb Uri:

The Midrash tells us that, together with Abraham, his nephew Haran also entered a burning furnace. Abraham who went first, emerged unscathed whereas Haran, who followed him, did not. How are we to explain the miracle of the one and the tragedy of the other? It is simple, according to the Seraph of Strelisk. Abraham said to himself: if I want the idols to be smashed and burned, I must prove my conviction by throwing myself into the flames; and because he had thus risked his life, he was saved by God. But Haran was both more practical and skeptical. He thought: I will see what happens to Abraham; if he comes back alive and healthy, I too shall go into the flames, if not . . . Well, he was not ready to risk his life for God, and that is why he lost it.

The moral of the story? One must risk everything for the sake of one's beliefs, one's faith. In the final analysis—who is a hasid? Someone who is faithful—someone who is filled with faith. Faith in God and in His words. Faith in His community and beyond it, in the larger human community composed of the living and the dead, thus offering promise to the first and benedictions to the latter. Faith in memory helps the individual transcend his or her condition, faith in the future must be justified by memory.

The greatness and holiness of the Seraph of Strelisk? He knew how to reconcile his love of God and his love for his fellow human beings. He remained faithful to both—but never at the expense of either God or His creatures.

To an opponent of Hasidism who criticized the Seraph, the great Rabbi Ziskind Landay remarked:

—You criticize him for not being sufficiently erudite? Well, I want you to know that there are various geniuses among rabbis. There are those whose specialty is the domain of the pure or impure, others who know everything about marriage and divorce, still others who are teachers in the field of compensation. The Seraph of Strelisk is a genius in the domain of *Yirat Shamayim* and *Ahavat Hashem*—the fear of God and the love of God.

But then, you may ask: how is one to teach these essential virtues? The son of his successor, Rabbi Abraham ben Reb Yehuda-Tzvi was asked this question, and he said: Fear of God is something I cannot teach you. But I can teach you love of God.—And what is it? he was asked.—Oh, he sighed. It is love for the person next to you . . .

I know. You may say: that is all? It is so easy . . .

Easy? Did you say: easy?

Then . . . why not try it?

12

Strelisk

Introduced by a Dialogue on Hasidism
between Elie Wiesel and Maurice Friedman

EW: How did you discover Hasidism?

MF: Well, you know, I had been in this camp for conscientious objectors, and I had become a mystic. A fellow camper who had gone to Yale and studied philosophy said to me that I ought to read Buber because he combined mysticism and social action. But for a year and a half I immersed myself more and more in Hinduism, Buddhism, and Taoism, and only then did I read *I and Thou* and *The Legend of Baal Shem*. It was *The Legend of Baal Shem* that spoke to me emotionally.

EW: But you, you introduce yourself inside Hasidism. If Buber became known in America, it is thanks to you. How did it change your life? Hasidism is life changing.

MF: Heschel once said to me that everyone has something they consulted. And for me, he said, it was Hasidism. More often than not it's not one tale or another that comes into my mind but . . . I'll tell you a story. I was Visiting Professor at Hebrew Union College in Cincinnati in 1956, and one of my students became a rabbi of a large reform temple in Dallas. He invited me to come to give a lecture and after the lecture—it was Shabbat, so there was an Oneg Shabbat. After the lecture, a woman came up to me, and she said, "Well you talked a lot about Hasidism, but you're not a Hasid." So I said to her, "You mean because I have no *peot*, no *yarmulke*, no *streimele*? I have no caftan?" Then I said to her, "There was one Hasidic rebbe who said, 'The way of life is like a knife's edge.

There is doom on either side of the way of life lies between.' I do that, can you?" Then I went on, "Another Hasidic rebbe said, 'There are three basic attitudes of the Jew: silent screaming, upright kneeling, motionless dance.'" I said, "I can do that; can you?" Of course I didn't mean that I was a great Hasid, but what I meant was to me the basic attitudes are what is essential to Hasidism.

This is the paradox. My grandfather was a Lubovitcher Hasid in the old country, but I had never heard of Hasidism until I was 24. My mother had been so disturbed by his letting my grandmother raise thirteen children and support them while he spent his time on prayer and study that she rebelled against it, and that's why she became a Reform Jew. I wasn't bar mitzvahed because they didn't have such a thing in the Temple in Tulsa, Oklahoma, when I was growing up. I was a prize Sunday school student, yet the whole time they never mentioned Hasidism. Hasidism wasn't rational, it wasn't liberal, it wasn't enlightened. When I was 24 and came home on furlough, my mother broke down and told me about Hasidism. That's when she asked me to see the Conservative rabbi in Tulsa who sent me to see Rabbi Simon Greenberg who later sent me to meet Abraham Joshua Heschel.

When I was at Hebrew Union College in Cincinnati in 1956, we had a Havdalah ceremony. I was enormously struck by the fact that it was only after the candles were extinguished that we said "Eliahu" as if only in the secular week do we wait for the coming of the Messiah because . . .

EW: We are supposed to wait for him *everyday*.

MF: Yes, but, when we have to, during the week, we have to . . .

EW:—**prepare** the Sabbath. Do you feel at home among Hasidim?

MF: Yes. You know Heschel sent me to Williamsburg in 1950. I stayed with a friend of his who was a Hasid there, and I went to the Satmar Rebbe's place. There were about 150 people in a very small room, and they were tearing at each other to get part of the *shrirayim*. All of them had black hats and long *peot*, and I just felt so out of place. When the rebbe was going through his meal, I thought, "Gee, it would be nice if he would send me a drumstick, but dressed like this, I'm the last person he would send something to." Then someone gave me a drumstick and said, "The Rebbe sent this for you." That should have converted me, but I didn't feel at home. I felt that they had a childlike relation to the Rebbe and I as a Westerner could not have. When I came back, Heschel said many times how he envied me. "Well, why don't you go and live there?" I asked him. Heschel said, "I can't; I'm a Western man."

On the cover of my book *A Dialogue with Hasidic Tales* there is a picture of a former student and disciple and friend of mine, David Lichtman, who followed me from Pendle Hill all the way out here to San Diego. He took a course from me in Contemporary Jewish Thought. He was deeply influenced by Franz Rosenzweig, and he came to me and asked, "How was it you decided to become a professor and not a Jew?" I said, "I didn't know the two were incompatible!" Then to my astonishment he decided to apply to Hebrew Union College. HUC sent him to Israel, and then he disappeared. He told me later that he got tired of talking about God and he went to Mea Shearim. He was there with the Bratzlaver Hasidism. Now he's back. He lives in Brooklyn, and he's become a Satmar Hasid—this man who grew up without any Judaism. David Lichtman would be very happy if I followed in his footsteps. But I cannot. I'm caught in tension between form and attitude.

EW: Has your concept of Hasidism changed since age 24 because of meetings that you had, books that you have written?

MF: Yes, it has changed. Of course, at first, as I have said, I was struck—I still am—by the fervor. That is very important to me, but it has a lot more form and richness. Then I was struck by the ecstasy. I think I would say now a way of preserving ecstasy while hallowing the everyday together.

EW: And yet ecstasy is a moment—it lasts but a moment.

MF: That's right, and I feel that very strongly but . . .

EW: Maybe two minutes . . .

MF: As you know, I wrote a book called *Touchstones of Reality*. Sometimes people ask me if a touchstone of reality is like Abraham's Maslow's "peak experience," and I say no, because with a peak experience you have it and then you come down from it. I want something that you can come back to again and again in the worst times as well as in the best times.

Of course meeting you has changed me. As I have written, even a negative touchstone of reality such as the Shoah is important. I cannot see Hasidism without thinking of what you said: in 1839 the Kotzker rebbe went into retirement just 100 years before the Second World War. In the Kotzker story the Sacred Goat lost his black horns by bending down and giving everyone a piece of them to make snuff boxes. Yitzhak of Vorki comes to see him. He calls him Rebbe.

EW: But the Kotzker responds, "I'm the Sacred Goat."

MF: He calls himself the Sacred Goat. "I'm the Sacred Goat." It's almost as if he's saying, "I passionately long to connect earth and heaven, and all these people with their little concerns like snuff boxes . . . "

EW: The Kotzker was an elitist. "You give me ten men, and I will go on a trip on the roofs over the houses," he said. "And I would shout that God is God!" He wanted only the best, and he drew to him the best—the elite. He believed that people, normal people, common people were not for him—he really meant what he said.

MF: He has an obscure saying that there were seven—Baal Shem Tov and so on, and he was seventh . . .

EW: "I was the seventh—I'm Shabbat."

MF: He was Shabbat.

EW: They all were great, but the Kotzker Rebbe surely was the most original. The other was Rebbe Nachman.

MF: Could it be that the Kotzker Rebbe did not really believe in hallowing the everyday?

EW: Well, he believed that we must separate the sacred from the profane. He believed that in order to attain sacredness we must give up everything. I even think that he gave up what we would call sanity—what *we* would call sanity. In the end, of course, he was sane, more sane and lucid than many others. He entered solitude and remained there for twenty years.

MF: He runs out and curses his followers.

EW: Even there, but then—he is different. He believed that man must make a choice between God and his creation, and the only choice is not to live with the creatures in order to live closer to God.

MF: Maybe that's why Heschel thought of him in connection with Kierkegaard. In his book *A Passion for Truth*, Heschel put together the Baal Shem Tov, Kierkegaard, and the Kotzker Rebbe. In the preface he wrote: "I was taught about inexhaustible mines of meaning by the Baal Shem; from the Kotzker I learned to detect immense mountains of absurdity standing in the way." That gave me a clue to Heschel that I never had before. That he wasn't just lyrical . . .

EW: No, he was a philosopher. He suffered really in the seminary because people didn't think he was philosophical enough.

MF: I think so too.

EW: His anguish obviously was profound. You, you were close to Heschel. Heschel respected you. He liked you very much. He spoke about you often, and you are now older than he was when he died. Has the Hasid in you aged?

MF: That's a good question. Yes, in the sense of experience, of life-experience and suffering. Perhaps you're asking am I still holding on to what I was when I was 24. No. *The Legend of the Baal Shem* was more exalted—that's Buber's early writing, and the later tales are much more stammering. Now I find that I appreciate every nuance. For example, we were discussing Rabbi Barukh of Mezbizh last Sunday at our Hasidic Tales group . . .

EW: The rebbe's melancholy . . .

MF: That's right. I picked the last tale. It's called "The Twofold World." Rabbi Barukh said, "What a good and bright world this is if we do not lose our hearts to it, but what a dark world it is, if we do!" I choose that take because it was always intrigued me.

EW: Personally.

MF: Personally—that's right. I do not get a finished teaching out of it. I don't think it just means you distance yourself and are not involved, and yet somewhere in it he says something very profound.

EW: The Kotzker was a desperate person. Rabbi Barukh was a melancholy person.

MF: Do you remember the man that you met who was also from Sighet, who accused you of lack of faith. You asked: "Hasn't this changed anything for you?"

EW: Yes.

MF: And you said you weren't talking about faith, so in a way you were saying real faith has to also accept the reality of what has to be . . .

EW: It needs to be tested.

MF: It has to be tested.

EW: Sure. It's tested for me; it's tested for everyone—without a doubt. Except I believe that my religious test is conditioned by my other test with regard to human beings. I think God is testing me just as I am testing Him.

MF: It's like your fate then?

EW: Oh, yes, and that is one aspect of Hasidism. The first question according to the Talmud—the first question asked in heaven is: "Did you handle your business relations honestly?" The celestial tribunal doesn't ask, "Do you believe in God? Did you wear *tefillin*? Did you observe the Sabbath?" They want to know: "Were you honest in your business dealings?" Then the second question is, "Were you waiting for salvation?"

PART THREE: AFTERWORD

Dialogical Knowing

To stimulate dialogues with and about ideas presented in Part Three you may wish to consider the following questions (whether general or chapter-specific) about the central concepts of each chapter. How would you respond to these questions if, for example, you were speaking to the author of that chapter? How, for instance, do the concerns raised by these questions implicate your life-situation? How would you, assuming you were writing an essay about a similar concern, construct it differently? What materials, which authors, what stories would you select to clarify and deepen your stand? Moreover, if you were personally addressing the authors of these chapters, what question would you ask of them?

Friedman (chapter 7): Is your dialogue with religion part of your everyday sphere—how does religion influence your life, if it indeed does? Can existential trust accept and overcome the social and existential mistrust that robs us of the courage to respond? Do you see religious interdictions as guidelines or rules, and why or why not?

Moore (chapter 8): Do you agree with Moore's assertion that for Friedman trusting in God is "a trust in the very meaning of existence?" If so, where do the consequences of this trust manifest most significantly in your life? If not, why not?

Katz (chapter 9): Katz posits that Friedman believes that "meaning was neither in the mind of the perceiver nor in the object perceived." Does this hold for you? If meaning only happens in the space of the between—i.e., the text-reader interaction—what does this mean for religion?

Kasimow (chapter 10): The major religions of the world have historically been at odds with each other, but Kasimow points out that each religion is grounded in the belief or selling point that *this* particular religion is the best. What does this point of focus bring into clarity about the "differences" of organized religion?

Alsup (chapter 11): One of the central conflicts between the Native Americans and white settlers has been the differences between the two cultures—of which religion has played a large part. What about religion, historically, has disabled the ability to create a dialogue with indigenous cultures or religions?

Wiesel (chapter 12): Is it possible to hear the voice of and have a dialogue with someone who is no longer living on earth? Is this possible only if you have known the person, and if so, what kind of dialogue would it be? How does Wiesel come to know Reb Uri of Strelisk's great power of ecstatic praying?

Another way to engage in dialogue with the ideas and concerns presented here would be to imagine yourself as a student in one of Professor Friedman's classes. The purpose of education, for Friedman, is to establish a "learning community," one in which there is genuine concern for the otherness of the others. The true teacher has always been aware that, above all, he or she is confronting students with images of the human and that it is precisely through this confrontation that the student is educated. The unique response of every student to the image of the human is that which draws forth the potentialities of becoming and transforms students into "educated" persons who are able to embody and express tradition and thereby become more uniquely human.

In order to understand the values, reasoning, and points of view of his students, Friedman assigned personal academic journals with four steps.

- **Step one** is for the student to select from the reading something that strikes him or her and to write it down in the journal.

- **Step two** is to try then to put it in one's own words, not by translating the quotation into familiar categories or constructs, but by swinging imaginatively over to where the other person is speaking from.

- **Step three** is coming back to one's own side and entering into dialogue with the author's words—both intellectually and emotionally—from where one is.

- **Step four** is to relate what one is commenting on to ongoing issues of the course and of one's life.

How would you apply this journal strategy, either by thinking through or writing about a specific passage that really engages you? To arrive at a more integrated understanding of Friedman's interdisciplinary humanism, you may wish to compare your response with his essay in this part to your response to his other chapters.

PART FOUR

Psychotherapy as Dialogue

"DIALOGICAL PSYCHOTHERAPY IS NOT a school of therapy but a movement that has had its representatives and pioneers in many major schools of psychotherapy. By dialogical psychotherapy I mean a therapy that is centered on the vital relationship between the therapist and his or her client or family as the central healing mode, whatever analysis, role-playing, or other therapeutic techniques or activities may also enter in."

—Maurice Friedman

13

Healing through Meeting

Dialogical Psychotherapy

MAURICE FRIEDMAN

"HEALING THROUGH MEETING" IS the heart of what a number of psychotherapists, including myself, call "Dialogical Psychotherapy."[1] By "dialogical psychotherapy" we mean a therapy that is centered on the *meeting* between the therapist and his or her client or among family members as the central healing mode, whatever analysis, role-playing, or other therapeutic techniques or activities may also enter in. It is more of an approach than a school of psychotherapy because it belongs to no one school and has had its representatives and pioneers in many major schools of psychotherapy. If the psychoanalyst is seen as an indispensable midwife in bringing up material from the unconscious to the conscious, this is not yet "healing through meeting." Only when it is recognized that everything that takes place within therapy—free association, dreams, silence, pain, anguish—takes place within the context of the vital relationship between therapist and patient do we have what may properly be called dialogical psychotherapy.

Dialogical psychotherapy is not a school of therapy but a movement that has had its representatives and pioneers in many major schools of psychotherapy, most of whom have been directly influenced by the great

1. The Institute for Dialogical Psychotherapy was founded in 1984 in San Diego, California, and co-directed by Maurice Friedman, Richard Hycner, and James DeLeo. The Institute rests upon the conviction that at the core of human existence is our interconnectedness with others—the interhuman dimension.

Jewish thinker Martin Buber's philosophy of dialogue—the study of the wholeness and uniqueness of the human person. What is essential in his thought is not what goes on within the minds of the partners in a relationship but what happens *between* them. For this reason, healing through meeting is opposed to that psychologism that wishes to remove the reality of relationship into the separate psyches of the participants. The inmost growth of the self, writes Buber, does not occur, as many assume, through inner awareness, but through entering into genuine relationships with others who are willing to enter into genuine relationship with you.

The uniqueness that one partner experiences in genuine dialogue with another is hidden from the individual who comes merely as objective observer, scientifically curious analyst, or prying manipulator. We cannot and will not allow another to "see into our soul" if we sense a prying, unsafe or indifferent presence. If we sense that someone is trying to "psych" us out or find out what makes us tick, we shut off precisely those parts of us that make us unique persons.

Healing through meeting, therefore, is a two-sided event that is not susceptible to techniques in the sense of willing and manipulating in order to bring about a certain result. What is crucial is not the skill of the therapist but, rather, what takes place between the therapist and the client and between the client and other people. To become aware of a person, Martin Buber points out, means to perceive the dynamic center that stamps on all utterances, actions, and attitudes the recognizable sign of uniqueness. Such an awareness is impossible if, and as long as, the other is for me the detached object of my observation, for that person will not thus yield his or her wholeness and its center. It is possible only when he or she becomes present for me as a partner in dialogue.

THE BETWEEN

In my therapeutic practice, I have drawn upon ten elements of healing through meeting. The first is the *between* or the *interhuman*—the recognition of an ontological dimension in the meeting between persons that is usually overlooked because of our tendency to divide our existences into inner and outer, subjective and objective. The sphere in which person meets person has been ignored because it possesses no smooth continuity. For Buber, the between is that which we cannot get hold of, cannot reify. It is neither subjective nor objective; it is not me or you; it is neither inner nor outer. What I call the "touchstone of reality," Buber finds again and again in the between.

The between is difficult to understand precisely because one cannot make an object of it, cannot make a thing of it and hold it up. For this reason, its experience has been annexed to the soul and to the world, so that what happens to an individual can be distributed between outer and inner impressions. But when two individuals "happen" to each other, there is an essential remainder which is common to them but which reaches out beyond the special sphere of each. That remainder is the basic reality, the "sphere of the between."

In an essential relation the barriers of individual being are breeched. The two persons participate in one another's lives not merely psychologically, as images or feelings in one another's psyches, but ontologically as a manifest, even if not continuous reality of the between. For such relationship to be possible, each must be a real person in his or her own right. A *great* relation not only breeches the barriers of solitude of each of those persons, claims Buber, but is stronger than death.

Something takes place between persons which takes place nowhere else in nature. One person turns to another as this particular being in order to communicate with the other in that sphere of the between that reaches out beyond the special sphere of each. In that sphere what happens cannot be exactly distributed between an "outer" event and an "inner" impression. This realm of the between exists on the far side of the subjective and on this side of the objective on the "narrow ridge" where I and Thou meet. This sphere of the interhuman is where the human comes into being.

THE DIALOGICAL

The second is the recognition of *the dialogical* as the essential element of human existence in which we relate to others in their uniqueness and otherness and not just as a content of our experience. The unfolding of that sphere, which is both ontological and existential, manifests through the dialogical. From this standpoint the psychological is only the accompaniment of the dialogical and not, as so many psychologists tend to see it, the touchstone of reality in itself. The meaning of this dialogue is found in neither one nor the other of the partners, nor in both added together, but in their interchange.

The distinction between the "dialogical" and the "psychological" constitutes a radical attack on the psychologism of our age. It makes manifest the fundamental ambiguity of those modern psychologists who affirm the dialogue between person and person, but who are unclear as to whether this dialogue is of value in itself or is merely a function of the individual's self-acceptance and self-realization. By pointing to dialogue as the intrinsic value, and self-realization as only a corollary, by-product rather than the goal, Buber separates himself from those existential psychotherapists like Binswanger and May who tend to make the I-Thou relationship just another dimension of the self, along with one's relation to one's self and to one's environment.

The distinction between dialogue and monologue that Buber makes is not, as in the theater, between two people speaking and one person delivering a soliloquy on stage, such as Hamlet's "To be or not to be." In dialogue I allow the other person to be in his or her uniqueness, whereas in monologue the other person is only part of my experience and I shut out their uniqueness, their otherness. Dialogue, therefore, is not a question of how many people one encounters but with *really* encountering the unique other.

The unique is known only through dialogue. Only in genuine dialogue do I relate and respond to the other for the sake of our relationship and not as a function of knowledge. But the converse is also true. Every genuine dialogue is unique. An ever-renewed presentness and presence can be fully concrete and meaningful only in so far as it is unique. There is no essence of dialogue that can thread its way through the world of particulars as some ideal universal. The proper understanding of dialogue includes uniqueness; for it is only in uniqueness that there is real mutuality, presentness, and presence. Dialogue means a mutual sharing in reciprocal presentness of the unique.

Buber believes that there is a personal direction to which we are called—our created uniqueness. "I don't know any other way to put it," Buber says. I only find my direction time and again by concretion—in my relationship to what meets me in the world. My personal direction is not a destiny I perform on the world. The world exists before my destiny. On the contrary, my direction of movement is dialogical in the full sense of the term. I can find it only when I come again and again as far as I can with my whole being to the meeting with the world.

DISTANCE AND RELATIONSHIP

The third element is the recognition that underlying the I-Thou, as also the I-It relations, is that twofold movement of *setting at a distance* and *entering into relation* that Buber makes the foundation of his philosophical anthropology. Only through our setting at a distance do we have a world that can be whole and one, a world that we can have a synthetic appreciation of over against us, and that gives us the universal structure. Thinking of this as a dynamic swinging rather than a fixed thing, one moves away into distancing and then one moves back into relationship. An animal, Buber suggested, has only what it needs for its organic life—it has an environment, it does not have a world; it does not set anything as independently opposite from itself. It is through setting at a distance that we become selves with other selves; the self only exists in this distance, where the distance from me to you and the distance from you to me is completed. Distancing, therefore, is the presupposition for entering into relationship, although entering into relationship does not necessarily follow distancing.

These two primary movements—distance and relationship—are the ground of the bifurcation of I-Thou and I-It. The first one Buber called the primal setting at a distance—by which he did not mean physical distance—and the second that he called entering into relationship. Only through our setting at a distance do we have a world that can be whole and one, a world that we can appreciate over against us, and that gives us its universal structure. If one thinks of this as a dynamic swinging rather than a fixed image, one moves away into distancing and then one moves back into relationship. It is through this double movement that we become selves with other selves.

Using this approach, it is important that we view each other as independent persons. This enables us to enter into relationship as *individual* selves with those like ourselves. The very essence and meaning of the self is this interrelatedness. I am called into being by you and you by me. When you embrace me as the unique person that I am and when you confront me in your own uniqueness, we confirm each other as the unique persons we are called to become. This direct contact between whole human beings gives rise to the sphere of the *between*. A true event in our lives is neither inner nor outer but takes up and claims the whole of us. In the sphere of the between. I meet you from my ground and you meet me from yours, and our lives interpenetrate. Our very sense of ourselves comes only in our meeting with others.

HEALING THROUGH MEETING

These elements lead in turn to the fourth element—the recognition that the basic element of healing, when it is a question not of some repair work but restoring the atrophied personal center, is *healing through meeting*. Buber says in *I and Thou* two things which have always struck me as being very central to life: "all real living is meeting," and "by the graciousness of its comings and the solemn sadness of its goings [the I-Thou relationship] teaches you to meet others and to hold your ground when you meet them."[2]

One of the most important issues the approach of healing through meeting addresses is the extent to which healing proceeds from a specific healer and the extent to which healing takes place in the "between"—in the relationship between therapist and client or among the members of a therapy group or a family. When it is the latter, is there a special role, nonetheless, for the therapist as facilitator, midwife, enabler, or partner in a "dialogue of touchstones?" To what extent does healing through meeting imply that meeting must also be the *goal* as well as the means to that goal? And to what extent are we talking about a two-sided event that is not susceptible to techniques in the sense of willing and manipulating in order to bring about a certain therapeutic result.

Real presentness means presence—being open to what the present brings by bringing oneself to the present, allowing the future to come as it comes, rather than attempting to turn it into a predictable replica of the past. The life of dialogue realizes the unity of contraries in meeting others *and* in holding one's ground when one meets them. This is the existential trust that "all real living is meeting," that meaning is open and accessible in the lived concrete, that our true concern is not the unraveling of mysteries but the way of the human person in partnership with creation.

Another important problem that healing through meeting encounters is that of the limits of the responsibility of the helper. To what extent should therapists feel themselves a success if the patient is healed and a failure if he or she is not? Finally, in healing through meeting therapy

---

2. Buber, *I and Thou*, 11.

should not proceed from the investigation of individual psychological complications but rather from the whole person and the relation between persons. The patient must be summoned to bring his or her inner being to unity so that one may respond to the address of the being or beings that face one.

THE UNCONSCIOUS

The fifth element of dialogical psychotherapy is *the unconscious* seen, as Buber saw it, as the wholeness of the person before the differentiation and elaboration into psychic and physical, inner and outer. Freud, and after him Jung, made the simple logical error of assuming that the unconscious is psychic since they denied that it was physical. They did not, Buber holds, see this third alternative and with it the possibility of bursting the bounds of psychologism by recognizing that the division of inner and outer that applies to the psyche and the physical need not apply to the unconscious. Here, in contrast, there might be direct meeting and communication between one unconscious and another.

The unconscious is a state out of which the physical and the psychical have not yet evolved and in which the two cannot be distinguished from each other. The unconscious is our being itself in its wholeness. Out of it the physical and the psychic evolve again and again and at every moment. The unconscious is not a phenomenon. It is what modern psychology holds it to be—a dynamic fact that makes itself felt by its effects, effects the psychologist can explore. But this exploration, as it takes place in psychiatry, is not of the unconscious itself but rather of the phenomena that have been dissociated from it. We cannot say anything about the unconscious in itself. It is never given to us. The radical mistake that Freud made was to think that he could posit a region of the mind as unconscious and at the same time deal with it as if its "contents" were simply repressed conscious material that could be brought back, without any essential change into the conscious.

Dissociation is the process in which the unconscious "lump" manifests itself in inner and outer perceptions. This dissociation, in fact, may be the origin of our whole sense of inner and outer. Our conscious life is a dualistic one, as we know it; our objective life is not dualistic, but we do not know this life. We can, to some extent, be conscious of the coming together of our forces, our acting unity, but we cannot perceive our unity as an object. The unconscious has its own existence: we do not have a deep freeze that keeps fragments. The patient with the supervision, help, and even initiative of the therapist can accomplish the radical change that comes with dissociation. The patient, in any case, brings up something that she senses is wanted of her, something that is the product of her relationship with the therapist.

Since the material that the patient brings forth in therapy is made and produced rather than simply brought up from the unconscious, the responsibility of the therapist is greater than has been supposed. The deciding reality, Buber declares, is the therapist, not the methods. At times when the unique person of the patient stands before the unique person of the doctor, the doctor might properly throw away as much of her typology as she can and accept the unforeseeable happening that goes on between therapist and patient. The usual therapist imposes herself on her patient without being aware of it. What is necessary is the conscious liberation of the patient from this unconscious imposition of the therapist—leaving the patient really to herself and seeing what comes out of it. "It is much easier to impose oneself on the patient than it is to use the whole force of one's soul to leave the patient to himself and not to touch him. *The real master responds to uniqueness*"[3]

It is Hans Trüb who has best spelled out the implications of this approach to the unconscious for healing through meeting. Repression, instead of being a basic aspect of human nature or an inescapable manifestation of civilization and its discontents, becomes the early denial of meeting, and its overcoming means the reestablishment of meeting, the breakthrough to dialogue. As Trüb states: "The unconscious touched by us has and takes its origin from that absolute "no" of the rejected meeting behind whose mighty barrier a person's psychic necessity for true meeting with the world secretly dams itself up, falls back upon itself, and thus, as it were, coagulates into the "unconscious." . . . . What is meant by the unconscious is precisely the personal element that is lost in the course of development . . . that escapes consciousness."[4]

In the relatively whole person, I believe, the unconscious would have a direct impact, not only on the conscious life, but also on others, precisely because it represents the wholeness of the person. In the relatively divided person, on the contrary, the unconscious itself has suffered a cleavage so that not only are there repressed materials that cannot

3. Buber, *Humanism*, 168.
4. Friedman, *Worlds of Existentialism*, 504.

come up into consciousness, but what does come up does not represent the wholeness of the person but only one of the fragments. As the unconscious of the relatively whole person is the very ground of meeting and an integral part of the interhuman, the unconscious of the relatively divided person is the product of the absence or denial of meeting. From this we can infer that the overcoming of the split between the repressed unconscious and the conscious of the divided person depends on healing through meeting. This includes such confirmation as the therapist can summon from the relationship with the client to counterbalance the "absolute no" of the meeting rejected or withheld in childhood.

This approach to the unconscious applies to dreams too, I hold, which from this standpoint are never just the raw material of the unconscious but, upon being remembered, have already entered into the dialogue between therapist and client and between the client and others. The result of this approach is the possibility of having dialogues with our dreams themselves, as with any other person or thing that comes to meet us. Dreams have a certain continuity and connection of their own, but we cannot understand this connection or compare it to that of the waking world. The dreamer, so long as he or she is dreaming, has no share in the common world and nothing, therefore, to which we can have access. Dreams are the residue of our waking dialogues. Not only is there no real meeting with otherness in our dreams, but even the traces of otherness are greatly diminished. We cannot speak of dream relations as if they were identical with relations to persons in waking life. What we can say is that having set the dream over against us, thus isolated, shaped, elaborated, and given form as an independent reality, we enter into dialogue with it. From now on it becomes one of the realities that address us in the world, just as surely and as concretely as any so-called external happening.

One cannot interpret the dreams of one patient by the same methods as one interprets the dreams of another. The therapist must be ready to be surprised. From this type of "obedient listening," a new type of therapist may evolve—a person of greater responsibility and even greater gifts, since it is not so easy to master new attitudes without ready-made categories.

EXISTENTIAL GUILT

The sixth element of dialogical psychotherapy—*existential guilt*—is not basically inner or neurotic but an event of the "between." Existential guilt is guilt that you have taken on yourself as a person in a personal situation. Freud's guilt is repressed into the unconscious; you do not know it. But existential guilt you do know. Only it is possible that you no longer identify yourself with the person who committed the injury. It is just here, in the real guilt of the person who has not responded to the legitimate claim and address of the world, that the possibility of transformation and healing lies. Guilt does not reside in the person, says Buber. Rather, one stands, in the most realistic sense, in the guilt that envelops one. Similarly, the repression of guilt and the neuroses that result from this repression are not merely psychological phenomena, but real events between persons.

Existential guilt also arises, writes Buber from injuring the common order of existence, the foundation of which we know—at some level—to be the foundation of our own and of all human existence. Each of us understands, I maintain, in terms of our family, our friendships, the people we work with, our social groups of whatever kind—what it means to injure the social realities in which we share.

Buber puts forward three steps that can be taken toward overcoming existential guilt. The first is illuminating this guilt: "I who am so different am nonetheless the person who did this." Secondly, we have to persevere in that illumination—not as an anguished self-torment but as a strong, broad light. If we were only guilty in relation to ourselves, the process might stop there. But we are always also guilty in relation to others. Therefore, we must take the third step of repairing the injured order of existence—restoring the broken dialogue through an active devotion to the world. If *we* have injured it, only we can restore it. We may not be able to do so with the person we injured; yet there are a thousand places where we can restore the injured order of existence.

What can the therapist do? In *The Healing Dialogue in Psychotherapy*, I suggest a few paradoxes. The first is that most therapists do not even recognize existential guilt. Second, even if the therapist does recognize it, it is intrinsicably mixed in with neurotic guilt. The third is that most people shy away from coming to know their own guilt. Here Hans Trüb helps us with his suggestion that the therapist distinguish two stages. In the first stage, the person before one has been disconfirmed by the community, and the therapist needs to be the confidant who understands and helps this person who has been disconfirmed. In the second stage, which does not exclude the first, at some point one has to help bring this person back into a dialogue with the community, place the demand of the community upon them, as it were, not through moralizing at them but simply through the fact that one is another person oneself.

INCLUSION

The seventh element *inclusion*, or *"imagining the real,"* must be distinguished from that empathy that goes to the other side of the relationship and leaves out one's own side and that identification that remains on one's own side and cannot go over to the other. Therapy too rests upon the I-Thou relationship of openness, mutuality, presence, and directness. Imagining what you are perceiving, thinking, feeling, and willing is how I include you in genuine dialogue. I can be empathetic or intuitive in our relationship, but unless I swing boldly and wholeheartedly in your direction I will not make you fully present to myself. Any lesser action on my part will result in my including you in part—keeping you at a distance by way of distraction or disinterest. If you have ever been the object of someone's undivided attention, as I have, then you have experienced inclusion in genuine dialogue.

The therapist with years of experience and the knowledge of the many case histories that are recorded in the literature will naturally think of resemblances when a client tells her something. But if she is a good therapist, she must discover the right movement back and forth between her patient as the unique person he is and the categories and cases that come to her mind. She cannot know through scientific method when a particular example from case histories, her earlier clients, or even her own experience applies. This is where true intuition, where imagining the real, or "inclusion," comes in.

It would be misleading to think that inclusion means that I should be so taken with you that I lose my own sense of being grounded in the relationship. Buber's term inclusion is not synonymous with being symbiotically joined. Inclusion is "imagining the real" which means to experience the other side of the relationship while not losing your own ground in the process. It is in the process of being fully present in relationship to you that I initiate genuine dialogue. When I see you in your unique and separate way of responding to a situation that is common to us both, I am practicing inclusion.

Inclusion, or "imagining the real," does not mean at any point that one gives up the ground of one's own concreteness, ceases to see through one's own eyes, or loses one's own "touchstones of reality." In this respect it is the complete opposite of empathy in the strict and narrower sense of the term. Empathy attempts to get over to the other while leaving oneself; identification tries to tune in to the other through focusing on oneself. Neither can grasp the uniqueness of the other person, the uniqueness of oneself, and the uniqueness of the relationship. Neither empathy nor identification can really confirm another person, since true confirmation means precisely that I confirm you in your uniqueness as a really other person. Only inclusion, or imagining the real, can confirm another; for only it really grasps the other in his or her otherness and brings that other into relationship to oneself.

We find ourselves as persons through going out to meet the other, through responding to the address of the other. But we do not lose our center, our personal core, in an amorphous meeting with the other. If we see through the eyes of the other and experience the other side, we do not cease to experience the relationship from our own side. We do not understand the other's anger because of our anger; for the other may be angry in an entirely different way from us. But we *can* glimpse something of the other's side of the relationship. This is because a real person does not remain shut in herself or use her relations with others merely as a means to her own self-realization.

The I-Thou relationship in dialogical psychotherapy can never be fully mutual. There is mutual contact, mutual trust, and mutual concern with a common problem but *not* mutual inclusion. The therapist can and must be on the patient's side too and, in a bipolar relationship, imagine quite concretely what the patient is thinking, feeling, and willing. But the therapist cannot expect or demand that the patient practice such inclusion with him or her. Yet there *is* mutuality, including the therapist sharing personally with the client when that seems helpful. For this reason, I call the eighth element of dialogical psychotherapy *the problematic of mutuality.*

MUTUALITY

The amount of mutuality possible and desirable in therapy depends not only upon the stage of the relationship, but also upon the unique relationship between this particular therapist and client and upon the style and strength of the therapist. Many therapists testify to bringing their feelings into the therapeutic encounter to a greater or less degree, and many testify to themselves being healed through that encounter or at the very least growing in creativity and wisdom. None of this changes the basic fact that the dialogical therapist's expression of emotion ought always be made in the service of the therapy and never in the service of the healing of the therapist or of mere self-indulgence on the part of the therapist.

There is undoubtedly a meeting of the unconscious of the therapist and that of the patient. What the patient picks up in this way may become the subject of the therapy, as the Jungian analyst Marvin Spiegelman and the relational therapists stress. The healing relationship must always be understood in terms of the quite concrete situation and life-reality of those participating in it. It is not always necessary or even helpful, I feel, to label the client by such terms as "schizophrenic," "neurotic," "obsessive-compulsive," "borderline" or any of the other categories of the DSM Manual. But it is necessary to recognize that in the healing partnership one person feels a need or lack that leads him or her to come to the other for help and that the other is a therapist or counselor who is ready to enter a relationship in order to help. This excludes neither Erich Fromm's nor Harold Searle's conviction that the therapist him- or herself is healed in some measure through the relationship between the therapist and the patient nor Carl Rogers' feeling of the equal worth and value of the client. But it does exclude accepting the therapist's *feeling* of mutuality as equivalent to the actual existence of full mutuality in the situation between therapist and patient.

Having stressed this limitation, we must also stress the fact that healing through meeting *does* imply mutuality between therapist and patient, that the therapist is called on to be present as a person as well as a smoothly functioning professional, that the therapist is vulnerable and must take risks, that he or she is not only professionally *accountable*, but also personally *responsible*. The professionally oriented therapist tends to regard those of his or her patients who commit suicide as his personal failures and those who get better as his personal successes, as if the patient's actions were simply the effect of which the therapist is the cause. Healing through meeting, in contrast, accepts the reality of the *between* and recognizes that it is not entirely to the therapist's credit if the therapy goes well, or to his or her discredit if it does not.

CONFIRMATION

Only the bipolar relationship in which the therapist is simultaneously at his or her own side and at the same time at the patient's side can produce the ninth element—*confirmation*. Being made present as a person is the heart of confirmation. Confirmation is basic to dialogical psychotherapy. It begins with the affirmation that development of the self, of the person, emerges in confirmation. According to Buber, the inmost becoming of the self does not take place through our relationship to ourselves, as people like to suppose today, but by being make present by another and knowing that we are made present by them.

Together with the mutuality of acceptance and affirmation, confirmation is interhuman, but it is not simply social or interpersonal. Unless one is confirmed in one's uniqueness as the person one can become, one is only seemingly confirmed. The confirmation of the other must include an actual experiencing of the other side of the relationship so that one can imagine quite concretely what another is feeling, willing, and knowing. This "inclusion," or imagining the real does not abolish the basic distance between oneself and the other. It is rather a bold swinging over into the life of the person one confronts, through which alone I can make that person present in his or her wholeness, unity, and uniqueness.

Confirmation—receiving a Yes from another human person which allows us to be—is so central to psychotherapy that I once taught a graduate seminar at Temple University whose main theme was the issue of "confirmation" and its relationship to the philosophy of genuine dialogue. As a part of the course syllabus, each student was given the following questions to ponder and discuss.

1. Can I make you present through experiencing your side of our relationship without empathy or identification?

2. Can I accept you as you are yet refuse to confirm you when you are unfaithful to the person you are called to become?

3. Can I expect my child or my student to confirm me as well as I them?

4. When is interhuman conflict an obstacle and when a gateway to mutual confirmation in depth?

5. Is there an existential confirmation that we experience *through* and *beyond* the personal and social?

6. Does the courage to address and respond make possible the "courage to be" or the other way around?

True confirmation means that I confirm my partner as this existing being even though I may oppose him or her as the person that I am. To meet others and to hold our ground when we meet them is one of the most difficult tasks in the world. We tend, as a result, to alternate between two opposite forms of not meeting: "meeting" others through leaving our ground—taking on other peoples' thoughts and feelings while losing our own—and "protecting" our own ground through closing ourselves off and holding others at arm's length.

If confirmation is central to human and interhuman existence, then it follows that disconfirmation, especially in the early stages of life, must be a major factor in psychopathology. Instead of finding the genesis of neurosis and psychosis in frustrated gratification of drives, à la Freud, we shall find it more basically and more frequently in disconfirming situations in the family that impair the child's basic trust.

Accepting and confirming a person *as he* or *she is* is only the first step. The therapist is also concerned with the potentialities of this person and can directly influence their development. Healing does not mean bringing up the old, but rather shaping the new. It is not confirming the negative but rather counterbalancing with the positive. For this reason a part of the confirmation the therapist brings to the patient may be wrestling *with* the patient, *for* the patient, and *against* the patient.

Confirming means that as a therapist I may have to struggle with you, for you, to help you find your personal direction in life. It is not that I am imposing it on you, of course, but in relationship with you I can sense it, nonetheless, and help you in your struggle between the part of the being that wants to take personal direction and the other part that does not. The client who confronts the therapist is not a whole being but is someone who, as it were, is moving in one direction or another, not moving in opposite directions but simply failing to take direction. To Buber these are corollaries—our wholeness as a person and whole decision-making and responsibility go together.

Caring often means a contending with the patient within the dialogue with him. Hans Trüb helps us understand the meaning of confirmation in therapy through his conception of the two stages. In the first stage the person who comes before the therapist is the person who has been unconfirmed, disconfirmed by the world, a person who needs a confidant, a big brother or sister, someone who really hears and who "imagines the real" while listening. The second stage is made necessary because a part of the patient's sickness is that through the fact of this non-confirmation, the person has withdrawn from active dialogue with family, friends, and community. At some point, therefore, without putting aside the first stage, the therapist must enter a second stage in which she helps the client resume the interrupted dialogue with the community. The therapist represents and bears the community values that he or she embodies. Without this second stage—not replacing, but combined with the first stage—there can be no real healing.

DIALOGUE OF TOUCHSTONES

The tenth and last element of dialogical psychotherapy is *the dialogue of touchstones*. This element takes up into itself both inclusion and confirmation. Through his or her greater experience in inclusion and imagining the real, the therapist enables the patient to go beyond the terrible either/or of remaining true to one's unique "touchstones of reality" at the cost of being cut off from the community or of entering into relation with the community at the cost of denying one's touchstones of reality. The therapist must help the patient bring his or her touchstones of reality into dialogue with really other persons, beginning with the therapist himself. Touchstones of reality and the dialogue of touchstones offer an alternative to the either/or's of objective versus subjective, absolute versus relative, mind versus body, and the rejection of the "schizophrenic" versus the romantic glorification of her.

The terrible dilemma of the "sick" person is having to choose between giving up his or her touchstones in order to communicate or giving up communication in order to retain one's unique touchstones. Such a person needs the help of someone who can glimpse and share the unique reality that has come from this person's life experience and help this person find a way of bringing it into the common order of existence so that he or she too may raise what has been experienced as "I" into the communal reality of "We." Such persons need the help of a therapist who can "imagine the real" and practice inclusion in order to help them enter into a dialogue of touchstones."

While working as a dialogical psychotherapist and as Co-Director of the Institute for Dialogical Psychotherapy and co-teacher of its training program, I discovered an important role for what I call the "dialogue of touchstones." In communication, education, and interreligious dialogue this role modifies the full mutuality of the dialogue of touchstones in the direction of what Buber calls a "normative limitation of mutuality." There are people who are faced with the impossible choice between either not giving expression to their unique touchstones of reality in order to be accepted by the community or affirming their touchstones in the face of rejection by the community. For this reason, I suggest that a therapist who has experience in what Buber calls "inclusion," or "imagining the real" can help such persons bring their touchstones of reality into a dialogue with the community.

From the standpoint of the dialogue of touchstones much of what we call "mental illness" can be seen as something that has happened to distort, objectify, or make merely cultural our touchstones of reality. Touchstones and the dialogue of touchstones begin in, and are renewed by, immediacy. Sickness is what prevents the return to immediacy. From this standpoint mental and emotional "health" is not "adjustment," becoming rational or emotional, but rather coming to a firmer grasp of one's own touchstones of reality in dialogue with the touchstones of others. In this sense the dialogue of touchstones may be the goal of therapy as well as the means. This goal helps the therapist avoid three equally bad alternatives—adjusting the client to the culture, imposing his or her own values on the client, or accepting whatever the patient says and does as healthy and romantically celebrating it.

Speaking of Hans Trüb, of his spiritual destiny, and of his approach to healing, Buber writes: "this way of frightened pause, of unfrightened reflection, of personal involvement, of rejection of security, of unreserved stepping into relationship, of the bursting of psychologism . . . of vision and of risk . . . which Hans Trüb trod." [5] Surely, Buber concludes, there will not be wanting persons like him who will take this path and extend it further.

---

5. Buber, *Humanism*, 142.

BIBLIOGRAPHY

Buber, Martin. *A Believing Humanism: My Testament*. Translated by Maurice Friedman. New York: Simon & Schuster, 1967.

————. *I and Thou*I. Translated by R. G. Smith. 2d ed. New York: Scribner, 1958.

Friedman, Maurice. *The Worlds of Existentialism: A Critical Reader*. 3d ed. Atlantic Highlands, NJ: Humanities Press International, 1991.

14

Dialogical Psychotherapy

The Seminal Influence of Maury Friedman

Richard Hycner

WITHOUT MAURY FRIEDMAN IT is unlikely there would be a dialogical psychotherapy. He has been the linchpin between Martin Buber's philosophy of dialogue and the formalized application of that philosophy to psychotherapy. His seminal influence has been through a lifetime of original multidisciplinary thought, coupled with translation, interpretation, and explication. Virtually single-handedly he has laid the foundation for understanding the thoroughgoing implications of Buber's philosophy for psychotherapy. Furthermore, he has striven mightily to incorporate the principles of dialogue into his personal and professional life.

Despite all of this, or because of this, I cannot talk about Maury Friedman's influence on psychotherapy without also discussing the profound effect he has had on my life and work. The way he dealt with me early in my professional life demonstrated in a concrete human manner many of the principles of dialogical psychotherapy. In many ways, I am able to separate my experience of Maury from my understanding of dialogical psychotherapy only in recent years—the two early on were so intertwined.

PERSONAL REFLECTIONS

In 1965, I was a college freshman desperately seeking answers to my existential questions—questions that bore the weight of life and death

237

for me. A Jesuit priest, whom I greatly respected, suggested that I read Martin Buber's *I and Thou* as a way of addressing these concerns. I tried to do so. Failing to grasp the deep meaning that I sensed must be there, yet respecting the opinion of this priest, I sought out some secondary sources to explain this work to me. The main secondary sources I kept coming across, and the ones that spoke most clearly to me, were written by a Maurice Friedman. In reading Friedman's explications of Buber's philosophy of dialogue, I began to grasp the profound meaning presented in *I and Thou* as well as the richness of the poetic form in which it was written. Reading Buber gave me hope: Reading Friedman gave me the understanding of how this philosophy could be applied to daily living. The two together presented me with a new way of understanding the interhuman. In a sense, I had been in a "dialogue" with Friedman from that early date. Later, in my Master's program in phenomenological psychology at Duquesne University, I clearly saw the need for a radically different philosophical foundation for psychotherapy, especially utilizing insights from the philosophy of dialogue as articulated in Friedman's writings. I continued to immerse myself in his and Buber's writings. Both inspired me to explore further within this perspective. Implicitly, they both pointed to far more that needed to be done in this field.

In 1973, at another desperate stage of my life, I entered a newly created doctoral program at the California School of Professional Psychology in San Diego. In registering for my first courses, I noticed a course entitled "Confirmation of Otherness" being taught by a Maurice Friedman. The course certainly sounded like something that *the* Maurice Friedman would teach, but I knew that he was at Temple University in Philadelphia, so this couldn't be the same person—though the coincidence was titillating. With little expectation I signed up for the course. To this day I will never forget the first class meeting. At the appointed time, the teaching assistant (Dick Stanton) came in to announce that the instructor would be a little late. Shortly thereafter a man walked in looking all askew in a rumpled jacket and tie and carrying an open and overflowing briefcase in the palms of his hands. As he entered the room, he tripped forward and most of the books and papers flew out of the briefcase in every direction. My immediate response was, "This can't be the great scholar Maurice Friedman." But it was. Thus inauspiciously began a relationship that would have a profound impact on my life and would continue to the present day, and would forever tie me to exploring the implications of a dialogical psychotherapy approach.

Even in that first class meeting what came across immediately was Maury's Friedman's profound humanity and unselfconsciousness. This was by no means an act, but rather was at the core of his character. I quickly learned that this unassuming quality was readily channeled into great interest and concern about the experiences and lives of his students. This world-renowned scholar unhesitatingly made himself available to his students in a way I had never experienced a professor doing so before. He had such an incredible and genuine openness to so many different perspectives, as well as a wonderful generosity of spirit. He valued the uniqueness of each student. It was a genuine "turning toward the other." Students felt listened to at an enormously deep level. He was interested in "having a dialogue" with his students. He treated us with respect.

In that first year of doctoral studies, I was faced with a serious dilemma. For the previous two years, despite, or perhaps because of my love of books, I had suffered from anxiety attacks whenever opening a book. It was only because I so valued Maury, and that at that time he was a model for me, that I was willing to slowly force myself to read the material he assigned. However, we were supposed to do a paper for the final grade for the course. Though by the end of the course I was able to read somewhat, I knew I was incapable of writing a paper without becoming totally overwhelmed. I risked explaining this to Maury, and asked him if he would be willing to give me an oral exam. He was more than willing to do that. In fact, the exam turned into something that was in fact quite therapeutic for me. I felt deeply respected and "confirmed" by this man whose opinion I so respected. That experience gave me an entirely different sense of what academic achievement can be—a dialogic pedagogy—one in which there can be academic learning as well as personal healing. Maury was a man who tried to do both with many of the students he came in contact with.

An even more significant event for me occurred in that first year of doctoral work: One that clearly demonstrated the incredible humanity of Maury and his deep caring for his students, as well as his willingness to go far beyond the normal limits in furthering the personal and academic development of these students—for the person and the teacher were one. A requirement of that first year was that we were to have a dissertation chair, or we wouldn't get credit for the research course. My dilemma was that I didn't even have a general idea as to what I was going to do, much less how I was going to go about it. With a bravado coming out of a naiveté as well as sheer desperation, I asked Maury to be my chairperson, confessing that I didn't have any formed topic at that time. He magnanimously agreed to be my chair. It was an incredible act of faith in someone who had yet to demonstrate any sustained abilities in this area. This faith in me (which I sorely lacked in myself) was so confirming, that deep inside I knew that I would have to do a dissertation that fulfilled that faith. I had to live up to the potentiality that he clearly discerned in me, but which I could barely sense. His act of faith called up something in me that stirred my spirit to new heights of intellectual and emotional exploration.

Displaying incredible generosity with his invaluable time, Maury agreed to meet with me every Monday morning at his home in the hills of Del Mar. I was awed that this world-renowned scholar would take the time to meet with someone like me who didn't have the slightest idea what he was going to do for a dissertation, much less had ever published a paper. I felt I had so little to offer to him in return. There was no way I could ever return the favor. I would always be indebted to him; and the only way I could repay such human kindness was to have that kind of faith in someone whom I could later teach and mentor. To this day, I well remember my trips up to Del Mar on those often fog-enshrouded mornings near the Ocean. We would meet in his home office. From there we could see the vast Pacific Ocean spread out far below us. I remember thinking that this was all unreal. There was something almost mythopoetic about those meetings, looking out at the ocean, shrouded in the fog, and meeting with a mentor of great personal and scholarly depth and wisdom. There was for me the ongoing project of trying to overcome despair and rebuild a life from a new base. This reminds me of Buber's quote; "What do we expect when we are in despair and yet go to a man? Surely a presence by means of which we are told that nonetheless there is meaning."[1]

What stands out about those meetings was the marvelously "inclusive" sense that Maury had about me, and my struggles. In a way I had never experienced with anyone else, he was genuinely interested in my touchstones of reality—those events of my life that defined me and by

1. Buber, *Meetings*, 46.

which I defined myself. For someone experiencing profound existential anxiety, someone who even questioned whether these events should be so influential, that was a marvelously validating experience. Rather than asking questions about my research, the purported reason for our getting together, Maury would ask me about my life. He was interested in me in a manner I had previously never experienced with anyone else. It was also very clear that he was able to "meet" me in a manner to which I was unable to reciprocate. There was truly a sense of what Buber referred to as a one-sided "inclusion," that ability to go over to the other's experience without losing your own, and without requiring that it be reciprocated. Yet, there was never the sense that Maury felt shortchanged. He was generous in his spirit without regard for reciprocity.

Most of all he seemed to understand my "dynamic center," that core part of me that defined the character of my personal existential reality. What Hans Trüb once said of how Buber had listened to him in person would best describe what my experience with Maury was like; his listening to me was as if he were "letting a soft tone sound and swell in himself and listening for the echo from the other side."[2]

What was perhaps most extraordinary about this entire experience was that out of Maury's deep listening to me, sensing with experience and wisdom what I had not yet become conscious of, that at the end of our meeting he would often suggest readings for me; that in itself would not be unusual for such meetings with our avowed purpose. However, what was extraordinary about the readings was that they were addressing the deepest personal and existential issues that were actually blocking my "personal direction"—issues that I was not able to fully articulate, nor even be conscious of. Yet, Maury had this deep sense of me, in a way knowing me better than myself, that he suggested readings which provided guidelines for dealing with my most heartfelt dilemmas. After a while, I realized that in a sense I was in an existential-dialogic "analysis."

Eventually, I felt supported enough by Maury, and that he had been able to sufficiently elicit my touchstones, to be able to begin the daunting task of writing a dissertation proposal. Throughout that process Maury was there for me. I felt that I could stand on the bedrock of his support. His faith in me helped restore my faith in myself. That's the kind of man he was and continues to strive to be.

---

2. Friedman, *Healing Dialogue*, 32.

INTERFACE WITH PSYCHOTHERAPY

When asked how he started applying Buber's thinking to psychotherapy, Maury responded that it started with therapists who were interested in Buber, seeking him out. For example, Leslie Farber (then Chair of the Washington School of Psychiatry) took a trip to New York after Maury published an article in 1954 on Buber's theory of knowledge, and invited him to come down to be a discussant when he was giving a public presentation on Martin Buber and psychiatry. That was the beginning of a very long and fruitful relationship. A year later Farber invited Maury to come to Washington and be part of a seminar with him. For two years Maury was a member of the Washington School of Psychiatry faculty and would visit there every other week. His friendship with Leslie Farber deepened and they became quite close. Maury taught public courses in "Religion and Psychotherapy" and a private seminar on "Evil" with Edith Weigert and Ben Weininger. Similarly, the faculty of the Horney Institute would invite him to take part in the discussion of their papers. It seemed like a number of psychotherapy groups were reaching out to him. As always, Maury was more than responsive in giving of his expertise in applying Buber's philosophy of dialogue to related fields.

Early in the 1950s, Maury got interested in Carl Rogers's thinking. In fact he had a correspondence with Rogers before Maury published his first book, *Martin Buber: The Life of Dialogue* (1955). Rogers sent Maury a number of unpublished papers that later became *On Becoming A Person*, and to which Maury responded in writing. Rogers seemed very pleased with Maury's understanding of his thinking. In fact, in his first book, Maury had a section on Rogers's and Buber's thinking on psychotherapy. He noted a number of remarkable similarities in their thinking (the critical questions about Rogers' theory didn't come till later when Maury moderated the Buber-Rogers dialogue in 1957 at the University of Michigan.)

Maury became friends with Rollo May around 1958. Maury taught for two years at the William Allison White Institute of Psychoanalysis and Psychiatry and Psychology in New York. When the Sullivan Society, which was connected with the Institute, asked him to give a paper, Maury asked Rollo May to be a discussant. Almost without any particular effort on his part (as he reported it) he found himself interfacing with a number of different schools of psychology and psychiatry. This continued as a lifelong endeavor.

Maury had been interested in Erich Fromm for many years, even before he came to Buber's philosophy. Fromm was the topic of an early paper he wrote called "Healing Through Meeting." When he met Fromm in person, Fromm said that he very much liked that title; in fact Fromm said to Maury that his patients heal him. Maury later described this issue as the "problematic of mutuality" in therapy, and it has intrigued him ever since.

Maury feels he was quite fortunate to have an incredible array of contacts and friendships with some of the leading individuals in various schools of psychotherapy. This is obvious from the list of people he had contact with. When Buber came to the Washington School of Psychiatry in 1957, Maury went with him to Chestnut Lodge and Frieda Fromm-Reichmann was there and that for him was a remarkable event. At that time, he also got to know Otto Will and was exposed to his thinking.

Maury taught at a number of schools of psychology and psychiatry. In the first year he taught at the William Allison White Institute, the faculty asked Maury to conduct an extra session in which they discussed existential guilt, and how it applied to their clinical work.

The Association for Existential Psychology and Psychiatry began in 1959, around the time Rollo May asked Maury to review his groundbreaking book *Existence*. Maury was on the Executive Committee of the Association, and he suggested that Leslie Farber be brought in and Farber eventually became Chair. There were some incredible conferences with such luminaries as Medard Boss, Paul Tillich, and Gabriel Marcel coming together for a conference, while at other conferences there were Erwin Straus, Helen Merril Lynd, Paul Ricoeur, Saul Bellow, as well as R. D. Laing.

In 1957, Maury facilitated Martin Buber coming to the Washington School of Psychiatry. Maury was also the moderator at the University of Michigan for the Buber-Rogers dialogue. At that public dialogue, Maury began to see three issues and differences between the two that have remained important to him to this day. Of great importance to him was the issue of full mutuality. He used to think that Rogers was claiming full mutuality, that is, that the relationship between therapist and client was fully equal—whereas Buber believed that by the very fact that the client comes to the therapist, that therefore it is fundamentally an unequal relationship. There was also the issue of self-actualization, that is, that everything in the dialogue was in the service of the becoming of the person, and the dialogue was not valued in itself. Finally, there was the critical issue of the inherent goodness or evil of the human being. For Maury, this dichotomy did not substantially address the wholeness of the person, which is determined more by "personal direction." There is not good or evil per se; rather what is determinative is what one does, for example, with the "evil urge." Personal direction means that there is neither good nor evil, but rather that they are in polar relation to each other.

In 1961 Maury started having more contact with therapists in California through the Association for Humanistic Psychology and the Esalen Institute. He later took part in groups with Frederick (Fritz) Perls. He eventually became disaffected with the encounter group, and so-called sensitivity group, movement because, in its purported pursuit of full humanness, some of the methods paradoxically seemed to contribute to a psychological and spiritual degradation of the person.

In 1969 Maury founded the Religion and Psychology program at Temple University. Interestingly, Barbara Krasner, one of the main proponents of Contextual Therapy, was a participant in the program. Around this time, Maury began teaching more courses reflecting the interface with psychotherapy.

Three of the books he published in the 60s had important psychological content. In 1963 he published *Problematic Rebel*, which was an intensive study of Melville, Dostoevsky, and Kafka. In every section, he had something on the interface between personal freedom and psychological compulsion, motives, and existential guilt. He explicated some of the keen psychological insights that these thinkers provided for modern living.

In 1964, he published *The Worlds of Existentialism*, which had about 130 pages on the relation of existentialism to psychotherapy. This was undoubtedly one of the most extensive overviews of the interface of these disciplines either at that time, or to this day. This work has been pivotal in making known such little known or translated, yet profoundly important, dialogical thinkers such as Hans Trüb and Viktor von Weizsäcker. Trüb was undoubtedly the first therapist to make healing through meeting the central focus for psychotherapy. I suspect that without Maury's translation of Trüb's writings there might not have been any movement that could be described as a dialogical psychotherapy. In 1967 he published *To Deny Our Nothingness*. Around 1967, Maury came into contact with Ivan Boszormenyi-Nagy. Maury started doing multiple family therapy with him and Barbara Krasner. Barbara Krasner was initially a student of Maury's. That remains an active connection to this day.

In 1972, he was at the Center for the Studies of the Person in La Jolla, California. Later that year in a presentation at what was to later become the Saybrook Institute, he began to explore applying his understanding of "touchstones of reality" to psychotherapy. He continued this exploration at the Center for the Studies of the Person with some of its members. Maury has always seen himself in a third position between the extremes of "realism" and "social constructivism." That is, he sees himself as coming from the dialogical perspective, in which nothing is given ahead of time, rather everything needs to be discovered in the encounter between person and person. Over and over again he tries to live up to this philosophy.

DIALOGICAL PSYCHOTHERAPY

It is obvious that from early on, Maury, influenced by Buber's philosophy and informed by his own vast understanding of psychological theories, conceptualized psychotherapy in radically different terms from mainstream psychology. He viewed it within the central dimension of "healing through meeting." Whereas in many therapies, the encounter between therapist and client is ancillary, Maury recognized that this neglected the truly interhuman possibilities for healing. Only in the meeting are we made whole. This makes eminent sense if one understands our ontological ground as an interhuman one, that is, the human reality is neither merely subjective nor merely objective, but is found in the rich ambiguity of the interhuman between. The between is the mysterious ground that permeates all our activities, yet one which for the most part we take for granted. It appears to be an oblique reality to our often unduly individualistic eye. If Maury had done nothing else, the articulation and explication of the between would be a sterling achievement: Yet he has done so much more within the field of psychotherapy.

The psychological, as ordinarily understood as an intrapsychic reality, merely describes one aspect of the interhuman: A dialogical approach to living recognizes that we are human and psychological only by the fact that we are in relation to others. This is the core reality from which Maury's thinking arises and to which it always returns. It is also the central insight that, through Maury, has influenced so many psychotherapists and has helped foster approaches such as contextual family therapy and dialogical psychotherapy.

I-thou and I-it are polarities within the interhuman realm. Much like Buber's recognition of the dangers of objectivism in modern society, Maury is a champion of returning the soulfulness between us, by way of the I-thou experience. In fact, the I-thou relation opens us up to an inherent spiritual reality that takes us well beyond the psychological. It puts the sense of mystery and spirit back into our daily living.

Healing through meeting arises from this ontology of the interhuman, as well as the understanding of pathology as interrupted and aborted dialogues. In a sense we can conceptualize pathology as a monologue in search of a dialogue (though the experience is far from benign). In the extreme, this is an experience of profound disconfirmation. There is a vast chasm of misery that comes from disconfirmation. As Maury constantly reminds us, we're creatures of the between, and our souls require confirmation from those around us in order to become the person we are meant to, and called to, become. Human development does not occur in a straight line, but is a dialectical and dialogical process, that at the core requires the critical milk of human kindness to foster our development. Maury has furthermore made the distinction (arising from moderating the dialogue between Buber and Rogers) between acceptance and confirmation. Confirmation goes beyond acceptance. As Maury is fond of saying, we need to turn toward the other and confirm this person as how he/she is, even when we don't accept this person. We need to confirm that person's personal direction, even when specific actions may not be acceptable.

Maury has helped articulate a "psychology of the other." So much of psychology has focused on the intrapsychic dimension of the individual, with others in that person's life important only to the extent they illuminate projections onto that other. Maury has brought home over and over again the essential need to see the other as *other*, not as some form of our own projection, or psychological type, but rather as the unique being he/she is.

This focus on uniqueness is not to be equated with individualism, as Maury is fond of reminding us. Too often individualism is not uniqueness, but rather the splitting of the individual off from his/her most intimate relations with others (e.g., Kierkegaard). We discover our true uniqueness in relation to these others.

Distance and relation are two essential polarities within the interhuman ontological experience. Each is in dialectical relation to the other dimension. "Setting at a distance" allows the individual to truly enter into relation, and "being in relation" requires the ability to set at a distance and stand as a distinct person.

Maury, furthermore, has articulated and expanded upon Buber's description of inclusion. Inclusion goes beyond empathy. It is "a bold swinging—demanding the most intensive stirring of one's being—into the life of the other." This bold swinging is necessary in order to be able to experience what the other person is experiencing—without losing one's own grounding. Both poles, self and other, are necessary for the possibility of a true dialogue.

THE INSTITUTE FOR DIALOGICAL PSYCHOTHERAPY

In the early 1980's, Maury, Jim DeLeo (also a former student of Maury's, and colleague of mine, who shared a deep interest in Buber's work) and myself began to formally articulate a distinct approach which we called "dialogical psychotherapy." With Maury's support, I started writing articles from within this perspective, and at each step of the way consulted him as to whether my interpretation was faithful to Buber's thinking and Maury's articulation of it. It was he who eventually suggested that these articles could be combined into a book.

By late 1983, I began meeting with Maury and Jim DeLeo in order to discuss how the principles of dialogue might be concretely applied to the psychotherapeutic process. Out of those discussions came the suggestion that perhaps other therapists in the San Diego area would be interested in attending some meetings to discuss the applications of the philosophy of dialogue to psychotherapy. As a result, we began in 1984 the then-named, Institute for Existential-Dialogical Psychotherapy. Later that year we invited Jim Bugental to be the keynote speaker at the first annual conference of the Institute. The conferences continued for eleven years with many illustrious speakers, including Irvin Yalom, Rollo May, and Erving Polster and Miriam Polster. As the approach became even more dialogically focused, we dropped the term "existential" from the Institute's name in order to highlight its distinctive emphasis.

In 1989, we began a training program in dialogical psychotherapy. Maury led the seminars on the theory of the philosophy of dialogue. More than fifty therapists and counselors have participated in the training and more than a thousand people have attended the annual conferences.

The development of the Institute, and particularly Maury's intellectual support, has helped foster presentations and writings on dialogical psychotherapy. For example, after two years as a trainee, Bill Heard continued individual consultations with Maury for at least a year, and as a result has since written the second clinically oriented book explicitly focused on dialogical psychotherapy. Also, over the last few years, a number of pastoral counselors have been drawn to the training program in part because of knowing of Maury's work bridging psychotherapy and spirituality and religion. As a consequence, members of the Institute decided that it would be helpful to have a book specifically focused on how to apply this approach to pastoral counseling. Currently, they are working on a cooperatively produced book—in fact one that truly arises out of a dialogue between and among the group members. The support of the Institute was important for the development of another book, co-authored by Lynne Jacobs and myself applying this approach in an extensive manner to gestalt therapy. Also Jim DeLeo, in his writing, and teaching courses to students at the California School of Professional Psychology-San Diego, has continued to bring Maury's Friedman's thinking to contemporary academic and professional psychology. Barbara Krasner in her Contextual Therapy approach has also undoubtedly been strongly influenced by Maury's thinking.

REFLECTIONS ON MAURY FRIEDMAN—THE MAN

Maury's true genius is that not only does he have incredible mental abilities and an unbelievable memory, but perhaps even more astounding is his ability to make contact with so many of those he meets. He is uninhibited by barriers, sometimes to his own detriment, and those of others. His true genius is his ability to bring together large numbers of seemingly disparate people, to relate to each in a unique manner, and to get each of them intrigued in the views and the person of the other people there. In the finest sense of the term, Maury is always pursuing what is "not there." It is not the objective world that propels him—though that is of infinite fascination to him—but rather what goes on between and within people that truly holds the focus of his inner existential eye. He wants to know people from the inside out—not necessarily in an intrusive manner but rather in a way that allows the "soft tone of the other" to deeply resonate in his innermost being, and for him to respond in kind to that place. That is Maury's Friedman at his best. That is what he has taught those of us who have come in contact with him—who have loved him, wrestled with him and his obstinacy, recognized the breadth of this genius, and the limits of the man. To be around Maury is to not be neutral. He has definitive views, and such an attention-catching personality, that it is impossible to ignore his impact. No one will ever accuse Maury of not having an impact.

He is uninhibited in his search for knowledge. He does not allow barriers of particular disciplinary fields prevent him from pursuing the core issues that have propelled him through life, and that course through his veins, giving life to him, and often to those around him. In fact, it is almost as if those barriers are unconscious challenges for him to break through and transform into the wholeness that preceded their academic division.

For those of us who have been with him these many years, he has taught us much. He has taught us the sparkle of genius and the depth of the human, as well as the steep price that one must pay for having visited these forbidden zones of awareness. Those of us who have followed him, know that there is only one Maury Friedman—he is uniqueness personified.

Those of us who have had ongoing contact with Maury over many years—and the numbers seem legion—have undoubtedly been profoundly influenced by him. Sometimes, I am aware that without him, I certainly would never have been able to explore the dialogical approach to psychotherapy to anywhere near the extent that I have. His support was instrumental in this early fledgling effort. He was always there with another perspective, or a particularly apt quote from Buber, or with an especially relevant philosophical or theoretical issue. But that is never to imply that his thinking is merely academic or abstract. Over and over again, Maury has taught me the necessity of marrying the theoretical with the concrete. It was he who taught me the true meaning of existential in the term "existential-phenomenological." It was he who helped me see over and over again, that it is the concrete experiences of life, the touchstones, which become the true basis for all theorizing and philosophizing. Philosophy and theory must never subsume the lifeblood of the experiential event.

For Maury, the "between" is not a theoretical concept, but rather a way of living. It is not some philosophical learning imposed on concrete lived events; quite the contrary, it is the way he sees, hears and thinks, daily lived encounters. Even currently, like Martin Buber before him, Maury is a perpetual beginner. He is always willing to start afresh—to see the world with fresh eyes—and to behold its majesty. At his best, Maury gives that majesty back to the world. For many of us, he has been a gift and a challenge. It is deserving that Maury, who has often not felt the recognition he warranted, should be given that recognition in this volume.

Maury has taught us to not be limited by the artificial barriers erected by academic disciplines: that the true discipline is pursuing the phenomenon through to its core, irrespective of supposed boundaries. This was explicitly reflected in his last academic appointment at San Diego State University, teaching in the separate departments of Religious Studies, Philosophy, and Contemporary Literature. He is the rare teacher who has great breadth of knowledge with corresponding depth. What is also unusual is that he has continued to be a teacher for so many of us, even though it may have been decades since we might have had him in class; in other cases, he is a teacher for us, even when we never took a class with him. He is a teacher without imposing his will on others—that is not to say that he can't be forceful in his opinions and interpretations, but that he is open to reexamining his views, especially when he feels the entire force of the personality of a colleague behind those views. He respects the fact that others put themselves into their theoretical understandings, and that these understandings are not mere abstractions from lived life.

This is but a beginning sketch of Maury's relationship to psychotherapy. To try to capture the fullness of a life like Maury's is a foolhardy venture. I hope only that I have given some flavor of what he has meant for psychotherapy in general, existential psychotherapy more specifically, and even more explicitly, for dialogical psychotherapy. Like the man, the impact of his writings on all three fields, is immeasurable.

BIBLIOGRAPHY

Buber, Martin. *Meetings*. La Salle, IL: Open Court, 1973.

Friedman, Maurice. *The Healing Dialogue in Psychotherapy*. Northvale, NJ: Aronson, 1985.

15

Engagement

The Strict Sacrament of Dialogue

Barbara R. Krasner

> No voice is without value, no witness without reality. Every voice
> needs to be heard precisely because it represents a relationship to
> a unique reality.[1]

PIGS AND PEOPLE

Toward the end of my PhD program in religion and psychology, the department chair criticized me for taking too many of Maurice Friedman's courses. It never occurred to me to question whether or not his view had merit. It didn't matter. For at the time how and what Maury taught were a matter of life and death to me. They still are. My indebtedness to Maurice Friedman runs so deep that over the past two years I have felt that nothing I might write about him nears the reality of our encounters and their consequences. My life and work have been so impacted by him and his life and work that a part of me is undifferentiated from him—clinging still to the length, the breadth, and the depth of his knowledge; and dependent on a wisdom that inerrantly points to the life of dialogue with all its risks, complexities, and unsolicited demands.

There have been many eventful turns on the paths that Maury and I have trod together. A friend of Maury's, Zalman Schachter, pointed me toward Pendle Hill, a Quaker study center, where I first met Maury. I had

---

1. Friedman, *Religion and Psychology*, 231.

read many of his books but sitting in a circle with him was another kind of learning. I spent a year in that circle saying almost nothing—but there I was to learn the syntax of dialogue. I was to learn something about its limitless facets—difficult to grasp, never to be owned, and necessitating courage as its constant companion. I learned about the tension between a community of affinity and a community of otherness, and between the compulsion to please and merited trust. I learned to plumb the white water between *indebtedness*—what I owe and to whom, and *entitlement*—what I deserve and from whom. I learned that speaking can be monologue and silence can be dialogue, that words can injure and silence can kill. I learned to embrace the realities underlying Buber's philosophy of the word, and to let those realities embrace me. I learned to pick my way on the path from the easy word to the difficult one. I learned of speech as event and event as speech, of the world as word, and human existence as address and response.[2]

I trailed Maury to Temple University during the volatile days of social justice movements. His classes typically held an element of surprise: from song to encounter groups, from hand-to-hand combat to Maury's falling asleep in class—with an intuitive, timely awakening and an instant, attuned response. He began one class by passing a newspaper clipping around the circle. People smiled and looked away from me. When the article finally reached me Maury posed a question. "Who are the pigs and who are the people?" he asked. There in front of me was a picture of several policemen and me, standing in front of a police barricade during a protest against the war in Vietnam. I learned a dialogic way from a teacher who rebuffed certainties, ideologies, dogmas, and absolutes; a teacher who was so invested in an "opening way" that his ground made room for radically different positions—including no position at all.[3]

It was a time of high emotions and recriminations, spirituals and assassinations. I was caught up in a hurricane of hope. I was in a hurry. I was sure that religion had conviction without methodology; that psychology had methodology without conviction. I was searching for Truth fast. I looked elsewhere, everywhere. Nothing was enough. So I dropped out of school two times. I came back—drawn by Maury's confirmation of me, by a response that implied that my voice too might have value.

---

2. Friedman, *Narrow Ridge*, 126.

3. Friedman, *Religion and Psychology*, 216.

Maury began to shape a program in religion and psychology at Temple University. Obstacles and misunderstandings got in the way. Faculty members seemed to miss the point. But Maury succeeded in opening up a world of therapists and therapy of which I knew so little. He established internships at Temple through David Reynolds, Department of Educational Psychology, and John Fryer, Department of Psychiatry, among others. When I began my first internship I could not imagine where I was going, and I had a lot of fear about getting there. Maury urged the psychiatrist who would supervise me to make sure that my experience was good. Onlookers warned that I'd have no leverage in either psychology or religion. But Maury reached for my hand and I took it. He tapped a rich network of friends and colleagues. Leslie Farber, Rollo May, Lyman Wynne, and Ivan Boszormenyi-Nagy, among others, were ready resources to students in the program.

Maury introduced Ivan Nagy and me at dinner one night Ivan was taken by the fact that Sal Minuchin had just asked my friend, Lillian Miller and me, to stop teaching in a faculty seminar on black-white relationships at the Child Guidance Clinic. We had allegedly broken group rules by talking to people outside of the seminar. In fact we were challenging the impact of Child Guidance's professional stance in that West Philadelphia community. In any case, Maury and Ivan took delight in the story that may have provided the impetus for future collaboration.

I first saw a tape of Ivan Nagy practicing three-generational family therapy at Eastern Pennsylvania Psychiatric Institute, arranged by Maury for our class. I will always remember the searing impact on me of family members, holocaust survivors, trying so desperately to address each other in the face of invisible loyalties that bade them to silence. That session was to change my life, my family, my thinking, my questions, my direction, the nature of my erratic quest. It marked the end of my search for fast Truth, the beginning of my own professional journey toward the narrow ridge, of a deepening search for many truths, of a way rooted in speech-with-meaning.

Eventually Maury was to train in contextual therapy with Ivan and me at Eastern Pennsylvania Psychiatric Institute; to instruct and enliven conferences on contextual therapy in the United States and Europe; and to make the approach his own. He has written about contextual theory and therapy with a devotion and acuity that has exceeded the attempts of almost everybody. In his books, *The Healing Dialogue in Psychotherapy*

(1985), "Martin Buber and Ivan Nagy: The Role of Dialogue in Contextual Therapy" (1989), and *Religion and Psychology* (1992), as well as in his foreword to *Truth, Trust, and Relationship* (Joyce and Krasner, 1995), he describes, deepens, integrates, and advances contextual theory and therapy.

Maury challenged the use of "self-validation," a term used in conjunction with "self-delineation" to describe the rudimentary stages of dialogue in contextual theory that lead to merited trust. Self-delineation is the stage of dialogue that has to do with making one's self known. Self-validation, on the other hand, is meant to underscore the fact that human motivation gains momentum from the act of giving itself. Doing for others is a way of receiving, in part, because a person can find release and sometimes freedom from investing in another's satisfaction and well-being. It is true that I may receive from the very act of giving to another. It is also true that I receive from another giving to me. How, Maury challenged me, can relational justice devolve entirely on the self to the exclusion of the other? Where is there room for mutuality and genuine consideration between people? Where is there room for real give-and-take? Self-validation leaves room for what happens in and to a person. Due consideration leaves room for what takes place between person and person. Due consideration requires more dialogue, more risk, and less one-sided self-justification than self-validation. The merit of Maury's stance was evident. The use of the term due consideration, in tension with self-delineation, became a truer reflection of a dialogic way, a fuller incorporation of each dialogic partners' initiative, motivation, and longing, and a less unilateral and more multilateral view of what happens between give-and-take.

What characterizes contextual therapy is its powerful distinction between the dialogical and the psychological, a distinction that Maury argues constitutes a radical attack on the psychologism of our age; an attack that makes manifest the fundamental ambiguity of psychologists who embrace dialogue as an ideal but tend to identify this dialogue as a function of a person's self-acceptance rather than as a value in itself.[4] What characterizes contextual therapy is its distinction between *meriting* trust, the ethical dimension of relationship, and *feeling* trust, a transitory experience that may or may not have to do with fairness or relational ethics. Contextual therapy is grounded in the recognition that every

4. Ibid., 11.

human being is part of a multipersonal context whose members are ethically joined and dynamically mandated to help each other discover fairer balances of give-and-take.[5] Whatever the other influences at play in contextual therapy, it most fully bears the philosophical imprint of Martin Buber, and the connective linkages, interpretations, and unique contributions woven by Maurice Friedman.

RELATING WITH THE REAL

> The meaning of the imagelessness of God is that you have no conception, no definition of God, no assurance that he will be merciful but not terrible. Trust in God, like existential trust, is not trust in what God will do for you but simply that unconditional trust that enables one, as long as one has strength to do so, to go forth to meet what comes. It is only trust that gives the real resources to keep going.[6]

Maury points to the intersection between contextual therapy's trust-based stance and Martin Buber's philosophical anthropology. In their emphasis upon restoring *relational* trust and trustworthiness, he writes, Nagy and Krasner converge with that *existential* trust that is central to Buber's (and Maury's) own thought. In turn Buber's life of dialogue is based on a profound religious understanding, one that has to do with an unmediated meeting with the primary Thou. The basic paradox of the Hebrew Bible, Maury writes, is the dialogue between the eternal God and mortal man, between the imageless Absolute and man who is created in God's "image." If that dialogue is to take place, it must take place not in eternity but in the present—in the unique situation of a limited man who was born yesterday and will die tomorrow. Jacob wrestles with the angel, and Job wrestles with God to receive the blessing of this dialogue on which the very meaning of their existence depends.[7]

The meaning of the biblical dialogue is our walking with God on this earth. The trust at the heart of this walking with God is tried, and man is exiled by the facts of the passage of time, sickness and death, and by the very social order that man builds. There is the possibility of renewing this trust, but only if we can bring the exile into the dialogue

5. Joyce and Krasner, *Truth*, xiii.

6. Friedman, *Religion and Psychology*, 11.

7. Ibid., 7.

with God, not if we turn away from the exile or overlook it.[8] Trust accepts the facts that a genuine relationship is two-sided and therefore beyond the control of our will.[9]

The renewal of trust in the service of justice is contextual therapy's goal and mission. Its words can be abstract but its real language invariably points to direct engagement between person and person. However dense its concepts, contextual therapy's grasp of the language of relationship is lucid in its capacity to draw from direct, human experience between person and person. In itself contextual therapy is a freestanding therapeutic modality that is indebted to its roots in revelation and to human encounters with the primary Thou. Contextual theory draws directly on the biological and historic aspects of revelation: 1) on the healing and illumination that come to a single person as he is met and his soul untangles itself from the darkness of illusion, and 2) on the healing and comprehension brought through his agency to his or her organic community. Contextual therapy draws on the language of creation, revelation and redemption, born of human encounter with God. These words point to a direct human experience, not to a theological concept. "All references to the voice of God is highly anthropomorphic—a fact from which theologians have always carefully tried to escape."[10]

The passion with which Buber embraces dialogue clearly reflects his own experienced commission from God: "A man can ward off with all his strength the belief that 'God' is there, and he tastes him in the strict sacrament of dialogue."[11] This taste of God, this mark of engagement, this trust, this *emunah* does not necessarily have a faith content. This trust does not mean security. It does not mean belief in the ordinary sense of the term. It means trust—a trust that no exile from the presence of God is permanent, that each man and each generation is able to come into contact with reality.[12] Only he who himself turns to the other human Being and opens himself to him (who) receives the world in him. Only the being whose otherness, accepted by my Being, lives and faces me in the whole compression of existence, brings the radiance of eternity to me. Only when two say to one another with all that they are,

8. Ibid., 6.

9. Ibid., 9.

10. Scholem, *Messianic Idea*, 293.

11. Buber, *Between Man*, 17.

12. Friedman, *Religion and Psychology*, 3.

'It is Thou,'" is the indwelling of the Present Being between them.[13] The happening is not psychological but objective . . . with a reality of its own which can be accessible to the individuals who truly meet. What Buber termed the objective reality of the between, contextual theorists call the ethical dimension of reality or merited trust.

The passion that Buber invests in covenantal relationship, in speech-with-meaning, trust, reciprocity, confirmation, fair give and take, and address and response is seeded in unmediated meeting with the divine. In the encounter itself, Buber writes, we are confronted with something compellingly anthropomorphic, something demanding reciprocity, "a primary Thou." What Martin Buber has termed "sublime anthropomorphism" is a "bodily nearness which overwhelms man in his encounters with the divine, whether they fill him with awe, transport him with rapture, or merely give him guidance." The religious actuality that emerges in this process is the immediate and direct apprehension of God's presence, an actuality that "is necessarily based on the experience that by its very nature draws man out of the domain of abstract thinking and puts him in actual relation with the real, namely, love." Revelation is an event in which the actual relation with the real is disclosed.

Psychology has long borrowed insights from religious understanding. Bakan describes the linkages between Freud's work and Jewish mystical tradition.[14] Freud's paradigm of the ego, the id, and the superego has its parallel in Kabbalah, in the Zohar's construct of *nefesh*, *ruach*, and *neshamah*: *nefesh*, the animal soul or life force that symbolizes enslavement, *ruach*, the rational soul that symbolizes man's wandering, and *neshamah*, the "super-soul" that symbolizes the "mountain" where trust is disclosed and received. Buber charged Freud with being a simplificator, one who places a general concept of reality in place of the ever-renewed investigation of reality.[15] He charged psychology, particularly Jungian psychology, with promulgating a new religion at the same time that it protests that psychology is a science and nothing more. He claimed that

---

13. Buber, *Knowledge of Man*, 30.

14. David Bakan, *Sigmund Freud and the Jewish Mystical Tradition*. New York: Schocken, 1965.

15. See R.L. Katz, "Martin Buber and Psychotherapy," *Hebrew Union College Annual* XLVI (1975) 413–31.

the new psychology makes the error of mystically deifying the instincts instead of hallowing them in faith.[16]

Maury's program on religion and psychology at Temple University was to crystallize contextual therapy's indebtedness to religious understanding, an understanding that points to a spiritual order in which justice is the course but not the source.[17] At one and the same time contextual theory is the repository of effective therapeutic interventions, and of a vital faith that is manifest in this walking with God, this *emunah* of the Hebrew Bible, this existential trust, this speech-with-meaning on which dialogue takes wing, this healing through meeting that is the unbidden grace of being addressed and knowing it, and the unanticipated courage to respond and be known.

"The courage to respond is not the courage of blind faith but the courage of really entering again into relationship."[18] Actual relation with the real brings with it a reparative way: *tshuvah*, a change of heart and stance, a turning, again and again, toward a world that humanity builds in concert over a thousand generations[19]; to speak with meaning to the injured order of existence. The dynamic leverage for healing through meeting is *tshuvah*—in Hebrew "an act of turning" sometimes described as conversion or repentance. The constituents of turning include an inward movement—an ongoing accounting of the soul (*heshbon Ha-nefesh*), and an outward movement towards repairing and rebalancing the original order of existence—a choice to re-engage, to repair what can be repaired, and rebalance what can be rebalanced (*tikkun*) in the midst of estrangement, polarization, and disengagement, and sometimes despair. Facing, testing, reworking, repairing, restoring, exonerating, and forgiving are each steps in the process of re-engagement, steps that require inordinate courage and conviction in a time when information supplants knowledge, when suspicion erodes trust, and when pretense precludes the word spoken with meaning.[20]

Before I finished my dissertation in 1975, Maury offered a caveat: "I hope you're prepared to be lonely," he said. At the time I was surrounded by friends, colleagues, and family members. I was invested in

16. Buber, *Eclipse*, 137.

17. Heschel, "Mystical Element," 260.

18. Friedman, *Religion and Psychology*, 10.

19. Ibid., 200.

20. Ibid., 4.

my studies. I was propelled by a mission for social justice. My life was crowded if disorderly, vital if overburdened. I remember being touched if confused by Maury's concern. The notion of loneliness seemed off base. At the conclusion of the oral defense of my dissertation, he offered another word: "Welcome to the company of uneducated men," his voice boomed over the telephone from San Diego to Philadelphia within full hearing of the other members of my committee. He was funny but intent. I had heard those words before. In retrospect, his two comments seemed to connect. Loneliness and a life of dialogue go hand-in-hand in a time wired for research and scholarship, for techniques and technology, for instant information that transports people everywhere and nowhere, for penetrating analyses and games of every kind—an era of people poised to engage with anything but the real.

BIBLIOGRAPHY

Buber, Martin. *Between Man and Man*. New York: Macmillan, 1965.

———. *Eclipse of God*. New York: Harper and Row, 1952.

———. *The Knowledge of Man*. Translated by Maurice Friedman and R.G. Smith. New York: Harper and Row, 1965.

Friedman, Maurice. *Encounter on the Narrow Ridge: A Life of Martin Buber*. New York: Paragon, 1991.

———. *Religion and Psychology: A Dialogic Approach*. New York: Paragon, 1991.

Heschel, Abraham. "The Mystical Element in Judaism."In *The Jews*, edited by Louis Finkelstein. Philadelphia: The Jewish Publication Society of America, 1949.

Joyce, Austin J. and Barbara R. Krasner. *Truth, Trust, and Relationships: Healing Interventions in Contextual Therapy*. New York: Brunner/Mazel, 1995.

Katz, R. L. "Martin Buber and Psychotherapy." *Hebrew Union College Annual* 46 (1975) 413–31.

Scholem, Gershom. *The Messianic Idea in Judaism*. New York: Schocken, 1971.

16

Studying Communication, Confirmation, and Dialogue

In Dialogue with Maurice Friedman

KENNETH N. CISSNA

CONFIRMATION

"DEAR PROFESSOR FRIEDMAN: . . . ." That's how our relationship be-gan—with a letter. I had just finished his book, *Confirmation of Otherness*, the first of his books I had read cover to cover. "Your fascina-tion with the implications of Buber's confirmation construct is shared by a growing body of researchers in human communication." It was probably an odd letter to receive, and, in retrospect, seems an odd letter to have sent. He was a well-known philosopher and author of twenty published books. Yet I wrote to him that, in the words of the contem-porary movie *E.T.*, "You are not alone." Confirmation, he had written, was one of Buber's "seminal ideas" that he had "left mostly in seed."[1] As Friedman put it, confirmation involves "the confirming of one person by another through the first person's making the other present, *meaning* him or her in his or her uniqueness, and inducing the other's inmost self-becoming."[2] I had said it a little differently, attempting to translate Buber's philosophical concept into the realm of human communication: "Confirming behaviors are those which permit people to experience

1. Friedman, *Otherness*, xii.
2. Ibid.

their own being and significance as well as their interconnectedness with others."[3] We both thought of confirmation as "central" to "human existence" and to the "emergence of the self."[4]

Prior to writing to Friedman, the highlight of my work on confirmation had been a paper I prepared with Evelyn Sieburg for the 1979 Asilomar Conference honoring Gregory Bateson. The conference was largely organized around invited papers from communication scholars and presentations from present and past members of what has been called the "Palo Alto group," a loose configuration of psychotherapists and others connected either with Gregory Bateson when he was working at the VA hospital in San Francisco or with the Mental Research Institute. Two slots were available for "competitive papers." Not only was our paper selected for presentation, but the conference also included a more informal "Lunch Panel" where interested conferees could discuss issues related to confirmation theory and research. Our paper was selected to appear in the volume that Carol Wilder, conference organizer, edited from the conference papers and presentations.[5]

Yet it felt like lonely work. It seemed as though few people were much interested in it. The literature consisted primarily of doctoral dissertations, most written at the University of Denver. No one of high status in the field had done any work in the area, nor had articles on confirmation appeared in any of the field's most prestigious journals.

I don't know whether it was entirely projection that I thought that *he* might like to know that he wasn't alone in his interest in confirmation. I was certainly pleased that someone had published a book on the topic—and a philosopher, no less, and with close ties to Buber. Although I had been critical of some of the empirical confirmation research,[6] I probably hadn't been critical enough. I knew confirmation was a thoroughly *dialogic* phenomenon, and looking back this paragraph still makes great sense to me:

> Confirming response is dialogic in structure; it is a reciprocal activity involving shared talk and sometimes shared silence. It is interactional in the broadest sense of the word. It is not a one-way flow of talk; it is not a trade-off in which each speaker pauses

3. Cissna and Sieburg, "Patterns," 269.

4. Friedman, *Otherness*, 37.

5. Cissna and Sieburg, "Patterns."

6. Ibid., 272–76.

and appears to listen only in order to get a chance to speak again. It is a complex affair in which each participates as both subject and object, cause and effect, of the other's talk. In short, confirming response, like all communication, is not something one does, it is a process in which one shares.[7]

If confirmation, as we said, was "not something one does" but a "process in which one shares," confirmation couldn't be located in individual utterances and responses to them nor in the self-reported feelings of the human psyche, but was to be found only in the larger give and take of the *between* of human *relationships*. I was ready to think of confirmation in a broader way. I wrote to Maury in that first letter that although "I suspect you will find the work too dominated by essentially positivist assumptions and quantitative empirical methods, I can assure you that our heart is in the right place." I knew these were too limiting, and Maury's book helped me to understand that more fully.

Maury was gracious enough to write back to me—not right away— but a long and detailed letter, much longer than what I had sent him. His remarkable openness and responsiveness—to a young scholar he had never heard of—continues to impress me still. He discussed directly the research that I had summarized, characterizing it in a way I thought very appropriate—as missing "what Buber calls the between." He even suggested that perhaps this called for a dialogue between the philosophical and social science approaches to confirmation. Talk about confirming!

I don't know what he might have meant by such a dialogue, but it sounded good to me. The national organization in communication had recently instituted a category of convention sessions called "Research Seminars" that were designed to allow a small and select group of people to spend an extended amount of time together discussing a significant issue or line of inquiry. I thought a research seminar would be an attractive opportunity for communication researchers who had an interest in confirmation to meet not only with one another but with philosopher Maurice Friedman, who had just written the only book in the world dealing exclusively with this topic.

So, I asked Maury—Professor Friedman, then—if he would be interested in co-directing such a seminar, which we came to call "Directions in Confirmation Research and Theory," at next year's meeting to be held in Denver in November 1985. I was confident, I said, that I could write

7. Ibid., 270.

a proposal that would be accepted and thought we would have a good number of people interested in applying to participate. Looking back, such an invitation seems almost brazen, but he was responsive and graciously agreed. Again, confirmation. Unfortunately, Maury's back problems flared up right before the convention, and he was flat on his back in San Diego while the rest of us enjoyed the talk about confirmation in Denver. When he couldn't make this seminar, Maury suggested that we arrange another. The participants in the seminar agreed, and the 1986 convention saw a seminar focused more narrowly on "Observing Confirmation and Disconfirmation."

I also wrote a review of *Confirmation of Otherness* for one of the communication journals, and I told Maury I had done so. He asked to see it, and I was more than a little nervous about sending it to him. Later, I reported that the journal for which I had written it had turned it down, and that now it would "only occupy a bit of my file space." Maury responded that it was "good and could be tightened" and suggested that I send it to another journal. I know now—having written books myself—that book authors like to have reviews of their books published, especially positive reviews. But his motivation was more than seeking to get a positive review into print. Although his suggestion seems so obvious (now), I had not been able to think of anything else that I could do with what I had written, and Maury broadened my horizon. His suggestion, that my review could find a home in another journal, was confirming, and the review was published.[8]

Tom Porter and I undertook to study an issue Maury raised in *Confirmation of Otherness*. He discussed two closely related problems that complicate the role of confirmation in the development of self. First, in our desire to be confirmed, almost all of us accept a confirmation that comes with "strings attached."[9] We accept an unspoken contract that provides adequate confirmation as long as we are a good boy or girl, student or colleague, church member or soldier. In so doing, confirmation is made conditional. As a person shapes self to conform to the demands of the confirmation of other(s), the genuine meeting of self and other in dialogue becomes less likely. Second, Maury explored difference between confirmation received as a result of one's performance of a behavior or role and the confirmation that recognizes and responds

8. See Cissna, *Southern Speech.*
9. Friedman, *Otherness*, 42.

to deeper levels of one's person. If, initially in our families, we find contingent confirmation, and often receive confirmation for engaging in an approved role, this expectation intensifies as we move into the world of work and pursue broader social relationships. In dialogue, we become most fully ourselves, we realize ourselves most deeply, as we respond to the call of the other—and in dialogue we have not planned what we will say or who we will be. Yet in most relationships we do have expectations for others and they for us. We "know" who we are, and who the other is; we have already accepted one of the "contracts" Maury referred to. The partial confirmation we receive for playing our roles well does not necessarily fully satisfy our human need for confirmation.

Porter and I sought to determine whether people distinguished between the "social confirmation" (and disconfirmation) that comes from performing our roles (which we called acceptance-rejection) and the "personal confirmation" (and disconfirmation) which arises out of one's unique calling (which we called confirmation-disconfirmation) and whether they responded differently to different combinations of these distinct yet related processes. We used a rather novel methodology: We wrote a few lines that we represented as coming from a play, which were identical in all the versions except for the presence of language suggesting confirmation or disconfirmation, and acceptance or rejection. We next asked several hundred people, mostly undergraduates at our institution, to assume the role of playwright and to write the next lines in the play. Two graduate students coded the lines written by the subject-playwrights as confirming or disconfirming and as accepting or rejecting.

We found that respondents distinguished between acceptance-rejection and confirmation-disconfirmation. Not only, for example, did they add different kinds of lines to the play when the previous lines had been confirming rather than disconfirming, and accepting rather than rejecting; but they wrote different lines following confirmation than they did following acceptance (though both were "positive" appearing conditions) and different lines following disconfirmation than rejection (both seemingly "negative" conditions). Further, the respondents seemed to attach greater significance to confirmation and disconfirmation than they did to acceptance or rejection. For example, seldom did our playwrights produce lines that extended disconfirmation, although they often communicated rejection to the other. Disconfirmation was added systematically to the play only in one situation: when the other had "received" confirmation and felt confirmed by it and yet had extended disconfirmation. By contrast, rejection was extended to the other far more often and under far wider circumstances.[10]

All of us are attached to our ideas and roles, and we know that others are as well. This study showed that at some level people also recognize the heightened importance of those deeper aspects of self that reach to the ontological levels of personhood. Although Laing is surely right that *total* confirmation of one person by another is an "ideal possibility seldom realized,"[11] the need for confirmation—as a *person*, and not overly conditional—remains essential to all of us for the emergence of a healthy self and fundamental to any process we can call dialogue.

THE BUBER-ROGERS-FRIEDMAN DIALOGUE

About the same time, Rob Anderson and I wrote a paper in which we attempted to show that the work of Carl Rogers contained a viable and valuable concept of dialogue, which, we argued, was best understood as a philosophical praxis. The editor of the journal we eventually submitted it to told us that the author of an encouraging yet critical three-page single-spaced review had agreed to his revealing the reviewer's identity; of course, it was Maury. He called our paper an "important contribution" and encouraged its publication. Although he disagreed with us in several respects, he did so directly and thoughtfully, withholding neither his disagreement nor his praise. More confirmation. After further revisions, the essay was published, our first on dialogue.[12]

Rob and I wanted to continue to work together, and Maury became instrumental in shaping the direction of our collaboration. We had decided to study dialogue in action based on the published "dialogues of Carl Rogers."[13] We had started work on the project, obtaining tape recordings of several of the dialogues, when Maury invited us "together or separately," he said, to participate in his "International Interdisciplinary Conference on Martin Buber's Impact on the Human Sciences," to be

10. Porter and Cissna, "A Cauffective Model of the Duel Nature of Interpersonal Sequencing"; and Porter and Cissna, "A Cauffective Model of Interpersonal Sequencing."

11. Laing, *Self and Others*, 98.

12. See Cissna and Anderson, "Carl Rogers."

13. See Kirschenbaum and Henderson, *Carl Rogers*.

held at San Diego State University, October 1991. Neither of us had anything ready, and the conference was only four months away, so we decided to focus our attention on the tape recording of the 1957 Buber-Rogers dialogue. Our goal, as I described it in a letter to Maury accepting his invitation, was to examine their interaction "as an effort at dialogue, under rather special and in some ways difficult circumstances. We are trying to see what we can learn about dialogue from examining the efforts of these two gifted communicators to engage in it." Maury said our proposed paper sounded "fascinating." Maury, we were soon to learn, had also written about the dialogue, although we did not see his paper, "Reflections on the Buber-Rogers Dialogue"[14] until after ours was completed.

Initially, Maury asked presenters to prepare papers that would be 50 minutes to an hour in length, but summarizable in 20 minutes. A couple of weeks before the conference he asked us to send along a 20-minute summary so the respondent could read it in advance. We could, he said, send the full paper later. We had not yet quite finished the full paper, and we didn't think we could produce a summary without finishing the full paper. Finally, barely in time, we got the paper—a fifty-page monster—off to Maury in early October[15] and quickly received a brief response. The paper, Maury said, was "marred" by a "tendentious and defensive quality." And it was "much too long for any book we might consider." But he did say he was willing to show us what he meant, and we hoped to arrange an opportunity during the conference not only to discuss the paper with him, but also to interview him, as the only living participant in the dialogue.

We had a couple of pages of questions, and over lunch one day Maury was willing to talk with us about them. He subsequently wrote us five single-spaced pages in which he explained his critique of our paper and his reasons for concluding that we were tendentious. In his concluding paragraph he recognized that he was not being diplomatic, "nor," he said, "have I withheld anything." He said that he was not defending Buber against Rogers, but "defending both of them and their dialogue against what seems to me to be your distortion of it—a distortion based on assumptions about what an ideal dialogue *should* be." Ouch! The conclusion, obviously, hurt; but we were grateful for the attention he had

14. See Friedman, "Reflections."

15. See Anderson and Cissna, "Buber-Rogers Dialogue."

given the paper. We thought he had misunderstood us at some points, and at others that we hadn't expressed ourselves as well as we would have wished. We knew it wasn't a polished final paper—the time crunch to prepare it was enormous.

We wrote back separately—Rob at far greater length than I. Rob explained our points of difference, and some of what we thought was Maury's misreading of our paper. Maury responded again—five more pages. This was, Maury said, a "mismeeting"—Buber's concept to designate "the failure of a real meeting" between people.[16] "I hope this letter can do something to repair the breach, or, again using Buber's terms, the order of the world that I have unwittingly injured." Rob and I didn't agree entirely with all of his specific observations—and still don't—but we respected our points of difference and understood them and each other better. And we valued Maury's willingness to discuss these and his invitation to submit a shorter version of the paper for his contemplated book.

I now think that both Maury's claim of tendentiousness and our objection had some validity. We thought, and still do, that when Maury had written about Buber and Rogers and their dialogue, that Buber had gotten the better and fuller treatment. That is probably as it should be for Maury—he thinks that when they differed that Buber was right, and, since the dialogue, he has emphasized their differences more than their similarities. We think, too, that occasionally his representations of Rogers haven't been as complete or as nuanced as his discussions of Buber. We wanted to tip the scales back a little, and in our effort to argue some of the case that Rogers didn't argue for himself, our hastily written first paper probably didn't express our views as well as we would have wished. As we continued to work on the project, refining one essay and another, and eventually a book and then a second one, we gained a fuller perspective and, I think, provided a more balanced treatment of the dialogue. In defending not only Buber but the dialogue Buber, Rogers, and Friedman created together, we thought Maury seemed to miss what we intended as the most fundamental point of our paper: that dialogue is not an ideal concept but a practical accomplishment enacted within constraints on each occurrence. Because we pointed out limitations of Buber and to a lesser extent of Rogers, Maury read us as adopting an ideal conception of dialogue, when we meant to be saying the opposite.

16. Friedman, *Buber: Early Years.*

After the conference, Rob and I began to divide this lengthy paper into shorter manuscripts that could be submitted to different and appropriate journals. Our first submission was a close analysis of the text of the Buber-Rogers dialogue, which we sent to the *Journal of Humanistic Psychology*. Although the identity of the reviewers was not revealed to us, Maury again wrote a detailed and thoughtful review (we could now recognize his reviews!). He "strongly" recommended publication, while explaining his "questions, corrections, and emendations." Rob and I were especially pleased that the essay appeared in a special issue devoted to dialogue, which also included Maury's essay on their dialogue.[17]

Rob and I wanted to use a chapter, "The Partnership of Existence," from Maury's *Touchstones of Reality* in our edited collection with Ron Arnett, *The Reach of Dialogue*. Maury not only graciously permitted its use (without fee), but Rob reminded me that Maury also expressed satisfaction at seeing this essay, a favorite of his, back in print. In it Maury argues for a very realistic conception of the "partnership of existence," in which "we become our selves *with* one another . . . Paradoxically, we only know ourselves when we know ourselves in responding to others."[18] Through responding to the other, even in disagreement or opposition, we fulfill our responsibility to others. We gain the strength to oppose from being confirmed, and in opposing, directly and honestly, we confirm the other as well. Yet, Maury says, we cannot achieve dialogue by an act of our own will, for dialogue is a two-sided process. In some ways, in this essay, Maury was describing the emergence of our dialogical relationship.

MEETING

My relationship with Maury has been much more "distant" than I suspect is the case with most of the contributors to this volume. I have been neither his student nor his colleague. We have never lived in circumstances that provided regular opportunities for interaction. We met personally and face-to-face for the first time in Chicago at that 1986 convention where we co-chaired the second of the research seminars devoted to confirmation and he served as respondent to a program, "Multiple Conceptions of Dialogue," that I had organized. I recall our having a breakfast or lunch

17. We were pleased that a much revised and abbreviated version of the paper appeared in Maury's book.

18. Anderson et al., *Reach of Dialogue*, 304–5.

together before the seminar, and I imagine we had a dinner as well. We next met five years later at his 1991 Buber conference in San Diego. We didn't spend much time together then—there were fifty or more people at the conference, most of whom, I'm sure, he knew better than he knew me and most of whom were surely far better and more significant Buber scholars as well. He did, however, make time to have lunch one day with Rob and me, and in addition to lunch, he became the first person we interviewed for our project on the Buber-Rogers dialogue.

Another five years later, we met face-to-face again. My national association was going to hold its 1996 annual convention in San Diego, not far from where Maury lives, and I organized a program on "The Future of Scholarship on Dialogue," which was intended to honor Maury for his work on dialogue while enhancing dialogic scholarship in communication. Rather than the usual format of a series of papers in honor of Maury, I asked him to deliver a short address, after which he would join a small panel, seated in a circle, with the audience all around. The panelists would discuss among themselves and with Maury—hopefully, even engage in a measure of dialogue regarding—the implications of Maury's talk for the future of scholarship on dialogue. At Rob's suggestion, I asked Maury to respond to a particularly timely passage from his *Touchstones of Reality*, even though written many years earlier.[19] Rob and I had dinner with Maury and his wife Aleene; and several program participants, including Maury, had lunch immediately before the program.

The next year I was teaching a small doctoral seminar on "Dialogue." A dozen of us were meeting each Tuesday evening. One Thursday I learned that Maury was going to be giving a talk at the University of Florida the following Monday evening. Unfortunately, that day was my younger daughter's seventh birthday, so driving two hours to the lecture was out of the question. But my class met the night following his lecture, and I wondered whether Maury might be available then. I tried to call him in San Diego and learned that he was already in Florida.

---

19. "For the covenant of peace, both the means and the end are the building of true community—the community of otherness. It is not requisite upon a community to forego all action for the sake of a lone dissenter. But much depends upon whether it takes the action as a real community or just as a majority, which is for the moment able to override the minority. The reality of community is polyphonic; it is many-voiced. In real community the voice of the minority is heard because real community creates an atmosphere of trust which enables this minority to make its witness" (Friedman, *Touchstones*, 287).

Fortunately, I was able to reach him, and he readily agreed to come to the class. Rather than asking him to lecture or give a paper, I asked him simply to talk with us. I asked the students to bring questions (about Buber's thought and life as well as Maury's).[20] Everyone was very pleased, and a number of us went out to dinner afterwards.

More recently, Maury came to my campus a second time, in the spring of 2000. Word of how engaging and thoughtful, open and responsive—yes, dialogical—he was with my graduate seminar reached the ears of the dialogically-oriented Associate Vice President for Diversity Initiatives who initiated the effort—and provided most of the funding—to have him return. Maury and I had lunch and, with a group of my students, dinner, as well as a couple of car rides. He gave a lengthy afternoon seminar on "Dialogue and Community," and a University Lecture Series address in the evening.

DIALOGUE

Over twenty years, living on opposite coasts of the U.S., with very different academic backgrounds and departmental affiliations, Maury and I have corresponded much more than we have talked in person. And whether by letter or, more recently, email, our correspondence has been intermittent and mostly related to arranging projects and answering my questions about Buber. We have talked on the telephone only rarely, and we have been together only the five times noted above. For me, each one has been important and memorable.[21]

---

20. We had read, among other books, Buber's *I and Thou*, *The Knowledge of Man*, and *Between Man and Man*, including Maury's introductions to the later two works.

21. Maury has relationships with others in the communication field. In addition to Rob Anderson, whose relationship with Maury is implicated in this essay, his relationship with John Stewart helped us to locate our first copy of the audiotape of the Buber-Rogers dialogue (initially we asked Maury if he could provide us a copy of the tape; he couldn't find it, but referred us to John Stewart to whom he thought he had sent a copy some years earlier). John also attended the 1991 conference on Buber, and served as an associate editor of the *Martin Buber and Human Sciences* volume. Maury wrote the foreword to Ron Arnett's book on *Communication and Community*, and Ron also participated in the 1991 conference. Maury has met with Barnett and Kimberly Pearce to discuss their work with public dialogue (e.g., Pearce and Pearce, "Combining Passions and Abilities," 2001; Pearce and Pearce, "Public Dialogue Consortium's School-wide Dialogue Process"), and he has contributed to Jeanine Czuburoff's work on Buber and dialogue as well (see bibliography, Czubaroff, "Dialogic Rhetoric").

The work that Rob and I have been collaborating on since 1985 is the best and most important scholarly work that I have done.[22] Without Maury, we might not have done it at all, and certainly wouldn't have done it for as long or, I think, as well as we have.

This substantial body of scholarship owes an enormous debt to Maurice Friedman—whether it will have any significant influence is yet to be seen fully, and isn't the point of this chapter. Our work would have been impossible at more than one level without Maury, yet, at times, Rob and I have been critical of Maury. I think we tested him. We argued with some of his interpretations and analyses, and initially expressed our disagreements less artfully than we might have. At first, Maury was, perhaps, a little bit defensive—we were, seemingly, criticizing the host and his intellectual parents and in-laws, and doing so at his own table. But if he was at all defensive, it didn't last long, and Maury soon welcomed our attempts to explore and clarify issues regarding the Buber-Rogers dialogue. He has been a model of graciousness: following one request, providing us relevant excerpts from the Buber-Friedman letters he had at home; following another, giving us written permission to explore their letters in the Martin Buber Archive in Jerusalem; and many times responding to various questions about Buber and Rogers and their dialogue and especially about the thought of Martin Buber. He has read drafts of our work and given us valuable suggestions informally, as well as through the more formal journal review procedures.

Maury has written a lot about confirmation and about dialogue, and he is also a confirming person and a practitioner of dialogue. I don't know how much my work, or Rob's and my work, has influenced Maury. He has now acknowledged what Rob and I called the "enfolded roles" at the center of the Buber-Rogers dialogue, without which, we argue, one can't understand it as a rhetorical and dialogical accomplishment. But I don't think he has changed his mind about much as a result of our work. This is okay. Our work exists in relation to his, but not just as a dialectical counterpoint, for Maury has been willing, more than willing, eager really, to engage in conversation with us about these issues. He hasn't

22. We continued our exploration of the Buber-Rogers dialogue (e.g., Anderson and Cissna, "Criticism and Conversational Texts"; Anderson and Cissna, *Martin Buber Carl Rogers Dialogue*; Cissna and Anderson, *Moments of Meeting*; Cissna and Anderson, "Theorizing about Dialogic Moments") as well as pursuing other dialogue-inflected projects (e.g., Anderson et al., *Dialogue*; Anderson et al., *Reach of Dialogue*; Hammond et al., "Problematics of Dialogue and Power").

relinquished his positions, and he has supported the dissemination of our positions, even when they disagreed with his own. Our relationship hasn't been entirely smooth—we have had episodes of both "mismeeting" and "miscommunication," as Maury described them. But dialogue isn't about smoothness—it is about hanging in there, representing one's own position fully, and being open to others' positions as well. We have confirmed each other, even while disagreeing. Ours has not been a perfect case of dialogue, but there are no perfect or ideal cases of dialogue. Rob and I have shown, I hope, something of how Buber and Rogers developed a dialogic relationship in moments of their brief meeting, despite many obstacles. My relationship with Maury has had elements of dialogue, not as an ideal, but, as Rob and I said of Buber and Rogers, a "practical achievement coauthored anew in each concrete instance."[23]

23. Cissna and Anderson, "Dialogue in Public," 192.

BIBLIOGRAPHY

Anderson, R., and K. N. Cissna. "The Buber-Rogers Dialogue: Studying the Influence of Role, Audience, and Style." Paper presented to the international, interdisciplinary conference, "Martin Buber: His Impact on the Human Sciences," San Diego State University, San Diego, October 1991.

———. "Criticism and Conversational Texts: Rhetorical Bases of Role, Audience, and Style in the Buber-Rogers Dialogue." *Human Studies* 19 (1996) 85–118.

———. *The Martin Buber-Carl Rogers Dialogue: A New Transcript with Commentary.* Albany, NY: SUNY Press, 1997.

Anderson, R., et al. "The Rhetoric of Public Dialogue." *Communication Research Trends* 22:1 (2003) 1–37.

Anderson, R., et al., editors. *Dialogue: Theorizing Difference in Communication Studies.* Thousand Oaks, CA: Sage, in press.

Anderson, R., et al. *The Reach of Dialogue: Confirmation, Voice, and Community.* Cresskill, NJ: Hampton, 1994.

Arnett, R. C. *Communication and Community: Implications of Martin Buber's Dialogue.* Carbondale: Southern Illinois University Press, 1986.

Buber, Martin. *Between Man and Man.* Translated by R. G. Smith and Maurice Friedman. New York: Collier, 1965.

———. *I and Thou.* Translated by R. G. Smith. 2nd rev. ed. New York: Scribner, 1958.

———. *The Knowledge of Man: Selected Essays.* Translated by Maurice and Friedman and R. G. Smith. New York: Harper & Row, 1988.

Cissna, K. N. Review of *Confirmation of Otherness: In Family, Community, and Society.* *Southern Speech Communication Journal* 5 (1985) 89–90.

Cissna, K. N. and R. Anderson. "The Contributions of Carl Rogers to a Philosophical Praxis of Dialogue." *Western Journal of Speech Communication* 54 (1990) 125–47.

———. "Dialogue in Public: Looking Critically at the Buber-Rogers Dialogue." In *Martin Buber and the Human Sciences*, edited by Maurice Friedman, 191–206. Albany: SUNY Press, 1996.

———. *Moments of Meeting: Buber, Rogers, and the Potential for Public Dialogue.* Albany: SUNY Press, 2002.

———. "The 1957 Martin Buber-Carl Rogers Dialogue, as Dialogue." *Journal of Humanistic Psychology* 34 (1994) 11–45.

———. "Theorizing about Dialogic Moments: Postmodern Themes and the Buber-Rogers Position." *Communication Theory* 8 (1998) 63–104.

Cissna, K. N., and E. Sieburg. "Patterns of Interactional Confirmation and Disconfirmation." In *Rigor and imagination: Essays from the Legacy of Gregory Bateson*, edited by J. H. Weakland and C. Wilder-Mott, 253–82. New York: Praeger, 1981.

Czubaroff, J. "Dialogic Rhetoric: An Application of Martin Buber's Philosophy of Dialogue." *Quarterly Journal of Speech* 86 (2000) in press. [ED: check pub]

Czubaroff, J., and Maurice Friedman. "A Conversation with Maurice Friedman." *Southern Communication Journal* 65 (2000) in press. [ED: check pub]

Friedman, Maurice. *Confirmation of Otherness: In Family, Community, and Society.* New York: Pilgrim, 1983.

———. *Martin Buber's Life and Work: The Early Years, 1878–1923.* New York: Dutton, 1981.

———. "Reflections on the Buber-Rogers Dialogue." *Journal of Humanistic Psychology* 34 (1994) 46–65.

————. "Reflections on the Buber-Rogers Dialogue: Thirty-five Years After." In *Martin Buber and the Human Sciences*, edited by Maurice Friedman, 357–69. Albany: SUNY Press, 1996.

————. *Touchstones of Reality: Existential Trust and the Community of Peace*. New York: Dutton, 1974.

————, editor. *Martin Buber and the Human Sciences*. Albany: SUNY Press, 1996.

Hammond, S., et al. "The Problematics of Dialogue and Power." *Communication Yearbook* 27 (2003) 124–57.

Kirschenbaum, H., and V. L. Henderson, editors. *Carl Rogers: Dialogues—Conversations with Martin Buber, Paul Tillich, B. F. Skinner, Gregory Bateson, Michael Polanyi, Rollo May, and Others*. Boston: Houghton-Mifflin, 1989.

Laing, R. D. *Self and others*. 2nd ed. Baltimore: Penguin, 1969.

Pearce, K. A., and W. B. Pearce. "The Public Dialogue Consortium's School-wide Dialogue Process: A Communication Approach to Develop Citizenship Skills and Enhance School Climate." *Communication Theory* 11 (2001) 105–23.

Pearce, W. B., and K. A. Pearce. "Combining Passions and Abilities: Toward Dialogic Virtuosity." *Southern Communication Journal* 65 (2000) 161–75.

Porter, D. T., and K. N. Cissna. "A Cauffective Model of the Duel Nature of Interpersonal Sequencing." Paper presented at the Southern Speech Communication Association convention, Memphis, 1988.

————. "A Cauffective Model of Interpersonal Sequencing: An Ontologically Based Conception of Communication." Paper presented at the International Communication Association convention, Dublin, Ireland, 1990.

PART FOUR: AFTERWORD

Dialogical Knowing

To stimulate dialogues with and about ideas presented in Part Four you may wish to consider the following questions (whether general or chapter-specific) about the central concepts of each chapter. How would you respond to these questions if, for example, you were speaking to the author of that chapter? How, for instance, do the concerns raised by these questions implicate your life-situation? How would you, assuming you were writing an essay about a similar concern, construct it differently? What materials, which authors, what stories would you select to clarify and deepen your stand? Moreover, if you were personally addressing the authors of these chapters, what question would you ask of them?

Friedman (chapter 13): Friedman believes in extending Martin Buber's dialogical theory of being present to healing psychologically. What part does our confirming another in dialogue play in our realizing our personal uniqueness? What can you do, in your everyday dialogical encounters, to be more present for someone else, in a way that you would like them to be present for you?

Hycner (chapter 14): Hycner states that "personal direction means that there is neither good nor evil, but rather that they are in polar relation to each other." Have you found this to be true in your encounters with others, dialogically? If not, why not?

Krasner (chapter 15): In Krasner's essay, the term "sublime anthropomorphism" is defined as a "bodily nearness which overwhelms man in his encounters with the divine, whether they fill him with awe, transport him with rapture, or merely give him guidance." Do you find this to be true in your daily dialogical encounters? Why or why not?

Cissna (chapter 16): How can I live authentically in the tension between personal, social, and existential confirmation? Are the social roles I play and the groups to which I belong the means or the alternative to my being confirmed as a unique person? Cissna's concept of "social confirmation" versus "personal confirmation" underscores the difference between our perception of ourselves and society's perception of us. Do you notice a difference between the self that you are for society, and the self that you find yourself called into becoming? If so, how does that difference affect your life?

Another way to prompt dialogue with the ideas and concerns presented here would be to imagine yourself as a student in one of Professor Friedman's classes. The purpose of education, for Friedman, is to establish a "learning community," one in which there is genuine concern for the otherness of the others. The true teacher has always been aware that, above all, he or she is confronting students with images of the human and that it is precisely through this confrontation that the student is educated. The unique response of every student to the image of the human is that which draws forth the potentialities of becoming and transforms students into "educated" persons who are able to embody and express tradition and thereby become more uniquely human.

In order to understand the values, reasoning, and points of view of his students, Friedman assigned personal academic journals with four steps:

- **Step one** is for the student to select from the reading something that strikes him or her and to write it down in the journal.

- **Step two** is to try then to put it in one's own words, not by translating the quotation into familiar categories or constructs, but by swinging imaginatively over to where the other person is speaking from.

- **Step three** is coming back to one's own side and entering into dialogue with the author's words—both intellectually and emotionally—from where one is.

- **Step four** is to relate what one is commenting on to ongoing issues of the course and of one's life.

How would you apply this journal strategy, either by thinking through or writing about a specific passage that really engages you? To arrive at a more integrated understanding of Friedman's interdisciplinary humanism, you may wish to compare your response with his essay in this part to your response to his other chapters.

Conclusion

Confirmation through Conflict?

Some Questions for the Dialogue of Touchstones[1]

Paul F. Knitter

M y first reading of Maurice Friedman's essay produced much the same effects that are had—today, alas, so seldom—from a good sermon. I was downright inspired and enlivened with new insights and new hopes concerning the contemporary encounter of religions. With his image of touchstones, Friedman avoids academic annotated analysis and provides creative practical theology. Though he does not indicate it through notes or references, he is very well acquainted with the literature and central issues in the contemporary discussion on "the many religions"—how to understand them and how to lead them to a more authentic and effective dialogue.

The particular power of Friedman's proposal is the way it creatively and suggestively searches for a middle path between absolutism and relativism. He realizes that these two "isms" are pitfalls for both conservative exclusivists and liberal pluralists. Though certainly of a more liberal bent himself, Friedman is well aware that typical "liberal" appeals for greater openness, tolerance, and equality among religions are often only steps away from the slippery slopes of indifference and relativism. So with guidance from his "touchstones" of truth, he affirms both radical pluralism and at the same time radical relatedness.

---

1. Used by permission of *Horizons: The Journal of the College Theology Society* ("Editorial Symposium with Maurice Friedman and Paul Knitter") 14.1 (Spring 1987) 97–137.

And he balances both. On the one hand, he chides pluralists (like me!) and urges them actually to recognize and accept what they are advocating—that religious pluralism is real and will not go way, that there will always be many, and especially that one can never find the ultimate system that will finally and neatly interrelate the many. One can never make a "system" out of pluralism (not even a "theocentric" system!) As soon as we have discovered—or imposed—a unifying pattern of interrelatedness, we have, actually, destroyed pluralism. And yet, on the other hand, Friedman does not fall into the incommensurability gap; religions are not so different that they cannot talk to each other. The touchstones touch, and must touch, each other. Within the diversity, therefore, there is a potential (not given) relatedness—the possibility and the necessity of talking to each other. As he puts it, we are "really different and yet really together." And for those of us who are concerned about losing the uniqueness of our own religion or savior, Friedman tells us that we can be both "faithful and diverse"—faithful to out uniqueness, yet embracing and learning from the uniqueness of others. With such images and hopes, he interreligious dialogue can bound forward.

Yet as I bounded with him, I felt myself bounded back by a nagging question. If Friedman can help me clarify this question, I will be able to follow him all the more enthusiastically. Is his vision of dialogue perhaps too irenic or optimistic? This question tugged every time he repeated his reoccurring theme of "a mutually confirming dialogue of touchstones." It seems that for Friedman the encounter of religious believers will be, if not at least basically, confirmed. Now I realize that he does not mean by this a pacific blending of viewpoints. Yet in only one paragraph does he explicitly warn against passive acceptance and tolerance, recognizing that "sometimes the strongest opposition" is necessary. I suggest that Friedman needs to say more about the possibility of a real clash of touchstones, of mutual incompatibilities, of possible ruptures in the dialogue. What happens when "in listening to the other we" do not "hear sometime genuine to which we can respond"? What do I do when the dialogue with another believer does not "point me towards greater openness"? How does Friedman account for such possibilities?

In order to strengthen and clarify his image of touchstones, I think Friedman needs to realize more explicitly that there can be "touchstones of unreality," that religion can provide "detours from reality." The history of religions as well as our contemporary religious scene, seems to indicate how religions can become ideologies—means of self-aggrandizement and manipulation of others. Langdon Gilkey, an ardent advocate of interreligious dialogue, has said that in his experience of dialogue he has encountered some religious views or touchstones that he can describe as nothing else but "intolerable." Friedman, I think, has not sufficiently recognized the intolerable in religion; nor has he said enough about what we are to do when we encounter the intolerable in dialogue.

A related question: would Friedman recognize situations in which I find not that my touchstone of reality is "opened" and "enhanced" through the community of otherness but, rather, placed in question—in radical question? Might I ever be faced with the possibility or even necessity of abandoning my touchstone for another? Indeed, in affirming my touchstone and in trying to relate it to the past and to others, do I not also have to stand ready, at least theoretically or methodologically, to abandon it?

This raises another related and more sticky question: what are the criteria by which we can judge whether the dialogue of touchstones is mutually contradictory rather than mutually confirming—whether another religious touchstone might be intolerable or whether it might be calling me to revise or abandon my own? In judging another touchstone as intolerable and in taking "strong opposition" to it, am I not imposing my touchstone on it? Can Friedman offer us criteria for the truth or validity of touchstones that are more precise and practical than the ones he lists at the end of his essay? Or in making this request, am I falling prey to the enticements of "foundationalism" or "objectivism" and hankering after a criteriological Archimedean point outside the dialogue?

Perhaps Friedman's response to these questions will be as simple as it is engaging: the reason why he finds, or hopes to find, the dialogue of touchstones much more confirming than contradictory, the reason why he believes that even our "strongest opposition" to another touchstone can turn out to be "confirming," is his faith in what he calls "the totally nonobjectifiable myth of the Community of Otherness." Friedman has accepted—or been possessed by—this myth; it is a matter of faith. Panikkar would call it a "cosmic trust" that the incorrigible diversity of religious touchstones is ultimately more unitive than divisive, that despite our differences and even contradictions, it is possible and necessary and beneficial to keep on talking and sharing.

Together with many others, I too share—or want to share—this myth of "the Community of Otherness." Friedman has helped me reaffirm it. I suggest that his help will be all the more valuable if he would follow the suggestions of liberation theologians and show more clearly that and how our Community of Otherness can grow not only through mutual confirmation but also through mutual confrontation, even conflict.

Conflict in the Dialogue of Touchstones

Response to Paul F. Knitter

MAURICE FRIEDMAN

I AM GRATEFUL TO Professor Knitter for his appreciative and thoughtful reply to my article, "The Dialogue of Touchstones: An Approach to Interreligious Dialogue." The questions he raises are central ones.

Professor Knitter asks whether my vision of dialogue is "perhaps too irenic or optimistic." I do not assume that the goal of dialogue is agreement or that dialogue is only of value if it leads to agreement. I believe in dialogue—not as debate or mere intellectual interchange, but as openhearted address and response. But I have no assumptions concerning its outcome. I do not even assume—how could I?—that there will always be genuine dialogue, even though both partners may genuinely desire it. We need to be face to face to talk, but that oppositeness all too often crystallizes into opposition, and we run aground on what Martin Buber calls "the cruel antitheticalness of existence itself." The only perspective from which we can find comfort in the face of such tragic conflict is the Talmudic approach that holds that "every controversy that takes place for the sake of heaven endures." This is completely contrary to Aristotelian logic with its assumption that a statement and its opposite cannot both be truth. To say that *both* sides will endure does not mean that eventually one will be proved right and the other wrong. The knowledge that the other also witnesses for his "touchstone of reality" from where he stands can enable us to confirm the other in his truth even while opposing him. We do not have to liberate the world from those who have different witnesses from us. The converse of this also holds, namely, that each must hold his ground and witness for his truth even while at the same time affirming the ground and the truth of the other.

After I had finished a lecture to two hundred alumni of Union Theological Seminary on Buber's dialogue with Christianity, I was struck by the difference in the spirit in which two people questioned me. One, a minister, said, "I know this is not the right way to put this question, but why is it that Buber and you cannot accept Christ as the Messiah?" Though his question was couched in the terms of his own religion, his hesitation showed that he was trying to reach beyond his own framework to experience the situation from my side. A woman religious educator then asked the same question without the hesitation and added, presumably by the way of persuasion, "I wish Buber and you could understand how much we Protestants all love you." "I am not really lovable enough to be loved by all Protestants!" I exclaimed. What I did not say was that even personal hatred would have been preferable to such an abstract love offered in the name of a total group.

In a "Third Hour" discussion at Emmaeus House between an eminent Catholic theologian and myself, I asserted that Judaism could not be expected to enter fully into dialogue with Catholicism when even after Vatican II the Church still claims to have superseded the people of the covenant as the "true Israel." His complete agreement with what I said was an honest recognition of difference that was already a step toward overcoming it.

If the witness of the other is genuine, it seems to me that it is always possible to respond and to move toward greater openness: I can open myself to what the other says; I can recognize the witness of the other even in opposing it; and I can reaffirm my own witness in dialogue with that of the other.

"Friedman needs to recognize more explicitly that religions can provide 'detours from reality,'" writes Knitter. I title the last chapter of my book *The Human Way*, "Is Religion the Enemy of Mankind?" "The structures of religion—creed, cult and church—more often further a community of affinity, or likemindedness, than they do a community of otherness. What is more, by their very claim to have a corner on the spirit and by their tendency to regard religion as the refuge from the mundane world, religious institutions and groups more often intensify the dualism between spirit and the world than overcome it."[2]

2. Friedman, *Human Way*, 183.

Knitter feels that I have not sufficiently recognized the intolerable in religion. Today I called the head of the Anti-Defamation League in San Diego because I found it intolerable that a Christian minister who preaches five days a week on the national Christian television station should offer his followers in Arkansas the infamous "Protocols of the Elders of Zion"—a poison well of anti-semitism even before the Nazis. On the other hand, I do not find it intolerable that others have witnesses different from my own if they do not try to impose them or use them as a springboard for spreading hatred and violence.

Knitter asks whether I would recognize that my touchstones might be put in question by another's so that I might be forced to change or abandon them. Emphatically yes. Our touchstones help us relate to the new situation, but the situation also modifies our touchstones. However true our touchstone, it will cease to be true if we do not make it real again by testing it in each new situation. This testing is nothing more nor less than bringing our life-stance into the moment of present reality. Any existential truth remains true only insofar as it is again and again tested in the stream of living. My own way from touchstone to touchstone has also included the shattering of all my previous touchstones.

On the other hand, when Knitter asks whether the dialogue of touchstones may not be mutually contradictory rather than mutually confirming, he seems to be changing dialogue into dialectic or debate and submitting lived reality to Aristotle's law of non-contradiction. Similarly, the spirit of the dialogue of touchstones, as I conceive it, has no place for Knitter's question, "In judging another touchstone as intolerable and in taking 'strong opposition' to it, am I not imposing my touchstone on it?" My opposition to the touchstone of the other person has nothing to do with my judging it as "intolerable"; for I confirm the other and the touchstone of the other even in opposing him or her. If I think what the other says is based on error, I may try to enlighten or persuade the other. But if it is a genuine touchstone, I shall not grieve that it is not one that I share. Nor am I in any way imposing my touchstone on the other person by opposing that person's touchstone with my own. As I write in *Touchstones of Reality:*

> We have no right to judge the touchstones of others, whether we mean by judging to evaluate them objectively or morally to condemn them. They are personal revelations and witnesses to existential truth. If we pretend to judge their adequacy by some

objective, universal criteria, it simply means that we have not really listened to the other, that we have used what he said as a pawn in our own mental chess game rather than entering into genuine dialogue with him. If we morally condemn them, then we are excluding the other's reality with his touchstones. We are saying, in effect, "You have no right to make a witness. We have already defined your witness out of existence before it is made." But there is a third sort of "evaluation" which we cannot rightfully escape: we must hear the other and we must respond. He needs to know that he is really coming up against us as persons with touchstones and witnesses of our own. Sometimes the strongest opposition is more confirming by far than someone who defends your right to your opinion but does not take it seriously.[3]

Because our sharing our witnesses with one another is real, it often happens that more than one witness, more than our touchstone is real to us at the same time. When this is so, we cannot exclude either voice, even when they seem to contradict each other. Objectifying, structuring, formulating are essential in the carrying forward of our truths. But if we content ourselves with them alone, we lose our touchstones of reality. We have to take the further step of bringing the old touchstones into the new. Therefore, our ultimate criterion of meaning and truth is not the objectification of a structure but the lived new meeting with reality. To ask for criteria for the validity and truth of touchstones "more precise and practical than this is indeed to hanker after a criteriological Archimedean point *outside* the dialogue! Useful as precision and definition for the exact sciences, the true humanity and the very meaning of the dialogue of touchstones depends upon its being brought back to the fruitful disagreement of lived speech between persons whose meaning necessarily differ because of the difference of their attitudes, their situations, their points of view.

Despite our differences and contradictions, it is indeed necessary to continue talking and sharing; this is the only direction in which we continue talking and sharing; for this is the only direction in which we can hope to reach that "community of otherness" to which I point. In my book *The Confirmation of Otherness*,[4] I do not indeed stress that the community of otherness grows out of conflict—within mutual cooperation, mutual understanding, and ultimately mutual trust. In bedrock

3. Friedman, *Touchstones*, 26–27

4. Friedman, *Confirmation of Otherness*, 1983.

situations even a negative protest may be a positive step toward dialogue if it is done in the spirit of dialogue.

BIBLIOGRAPHY

Friedman, Maurice. *The Confirmation of Otherness: In Family, Community, and Society.* New York: Pilgrim, 1983.

————. *The Human Way: A Dialogical Approach to Religion and Human Experience* Chambersburg, PA: Anima, 1982.

————. *Touchstones of Reality: Existential Trust and the Community of Peace.* New York: Dutton, 1972.

Annotated Bibliography

Books Written by Maurice Friedman

(in order of publication)
Prepared by: Maurice Friedman

Martin Buber: The Life of Dialogue. London: Routledge & Kegan Paul; Chicago: University of Chicago Press, 1959; New York: Harper Torchbooks, 1960; Chicago: University of Chicago Press, Midway Books, 1976.

This was my first book. It grew out of my doctoral dissertation for the Committee on the History of Culture at the University of Chicago (1950), but involved four years of work beyond that in close cooperation with Martin Buber himself. Professor Buber wrote of it: "To synthesize a wild-grown thought such as mine seems to me a remarkable achievement. Friedman has not imposed a unity on my thought but has discovered the hidden one. This is the classic study of my thought." In 2002 it was published in a fourth edition by Routledge in London and New York with two appendices—"Martin Buber and Emmanuel Levinas: An Ethical Query" and "Martin Buber and Mikhail Bakhtin: The Dialogue of Voices and the Word That Is Spoken."

∞

Problematic Rebel: An Image of Modern Man. New York: Random House, 1963.

Problematic Rebel was based on an intensive study of the writings of Herman Melville, Fyodor Dostoevksy, and Franz Kafka. But it was organized according to the main thought categories of the book, e.g., "The Death of God and the Alienation of Modern Man," "The Modern

289

Promethean" (the first either/or type of rebellion against that alienation), "The Modern Job" (the second both/and trust *and* contending type of rebellion), and "The Problematic Modern Man" (the crisis of motives, the problematic of guilt, inner division, etc.). After using *Problematic Rebel* in a graduate seminar at Temple University in the late 1960s, I became convinced that I had subtly violated the spirit of each writer by dividing them up under these thought categories. Fortunately, my old friend Morris Philipson, the director of the University of Chicago Press who had been my editor at Random House, was able to allow me radically to reorganize and enlarge the book so that I could bring all of my commentary on each author together and subsume the thought categories rather than the other way round. I also added a new section on Albert Camus. So the second, radically-reorganized and enlarged edition appeared in 1970 from the University of Chicago Press with the new subtitle *Melville, Dostoevsky, Kafka, Camus*.

∽

The Worlds of Existentialism: A Critical Reader. New York: Random House, 1964; Chicago: University of Chicago Press, 1973; Atlantic Highlands, NJ: Humanities Press International,1991. The last edition includes a long new Preface updating the book.

Although this is a book I edited, I include it here because of its originality and because it entailed an enormous amount of work. Unlike Walter Kaufman's anthology, I did not have chapters representing the main existentialists but subsumed very small excerpts from their writings under the main headings: Phenomenology and Ontology, the Existential Subject, Intersubjectivity, Atheist, Humanist, Religious Existentialism, and Existentialism and Psychotherapy. In the conclusion I brought together my thoughts on such issues as existentialism and sex, intersubjectivity, existentialism and religion. I also included a selection of Martin Heidegger's Nazi writings in order to raise the question of the relation between his existentialist philosophy and his activities as a Nazi. *The Worlds of Existentialism* not only does full justice to the religious existentialists and the existential psychotherapists, as Walter Kaufman's anthology does not. It also brings to the fore an issue that even to this day has not been given adequate recognition: the difference between those existentialists whose touchstone of reality is the centered self

(Kierkegaard, Husserl, Sartre, Tillich, Berdyaev, and [despite his *Dasein ist Mitsein*] Heidegger) and those for whom dialogue or communication is central (Martin Buber, Karl Jaspers, Gabriel Marcel, Franz Rosenzweig, and Albert Camus).

∽

Martin Buber, *The Knowledge of Man: A Philosophy of the Interhuman.* Edited and with an Introductory Essay (Chap. 1) by Maurice Friedman, translated by Maurice Friedman and Ronald Gregor Smith: New York: Harper & Row;s London: George Allen & Urwin, 1965. Harper Torchbooks, 1966. Reprinted, Atlantic Highlands, NJ: Humanities Press International, 1988.

I include *The Knowledge of Man* here because of my major contribution to the book. In addition to what I mention above, I was the middle-man between Buber and Leslie Farber, the Chair of the Faculty of Washington (D.C.) School of Psychiatry, in arranging that Buber come to Washington and deliver the fourth William Alanson White Memorial Lectures. These lectures became Chapter 2, 3, and 6 of *The Knowledge of Man* ("Distance and Relation," "Elements of the Interhuman," and "Guilt and Guilt Feelings"). Except for the first two I translated all of Buber's essays. Buber and I worked sixteen hours together revising R. G. Smith's translation of "Elements of the Interhuman." (At one point when I insisted on breaking up what seemed to me Buber's overlong German sentences, Buber exclaimed, "Grammar is not a subjective matter!" Then he turned to my wife Eugenia, who was present throughout, and said, "Your husband is a very stubborn man." I thought at first he was joking, but when I realized he was not, I exclaimed, "You call *me* stubborn!" Buber was the most stubborn person I had ever met, only I was stubborn about semicolons and periods whereas he was stubborn about major issues such as Jewish-Arab rapprochement!)

∽

To Deny Our Nothingness: Contemporary Images of Man. New York: Delacorte Press, 1967, Delta Books [paperback], 1968. 3rd ed. with new Preface and new Appendices, Chicago: The University of Chicago Press, Phoenix Books, 1978. Reprinted as a Midway Book.

To Deny Our Nothingness continues my concern with the image of man or the image of the human, as I later call it. But in contrast to *Problematic Rebel*, this is an extensive study of many writers rather than an intensive study of four, and the writers included are not only novelists, poets, and playwrights, but also psychologists, social thinkers, philosophers, religious thinkers, and theologians. The starting point of the book is the absence of contemporary images of the human that give us meaningful personal and social direction and the attempt of these writers to respond to that absence. I have created a typology of responses under which my discussions of these writers are subsumed: the Modern Socialist (Malraux, Koestler, Steinbeck, Silone, Carlo Levi), the Modern Vitalist (Bergson, Kazantzakis), the Modern Mystic (Huxley, Eliot, Buber), the Modern "Saint" (Coccioli, Bernanos, Greene), the Modern Gnostic (Weil, Jung, Hesse), Psychological Man (Freud), the Modern Pragmatist (James Dewey, Mead, Sullivan, Fromm), the Existentialist (Nietzsche, Sartre, Kierkegaard, Berdyaev, Tillich, Marcel, Camus, Buber), and Absurd Man (Beckett, Camus, Kafka, Wiesel). The conclusion is an essay on "The Image of Man and Moral Philosophy" drawing from my study of these writers).

∞

Martin Buber and the Theater. Edited, translated, and with three essays by Maurice Friedman. New York: Funk & Wagnall, 1969.

This book came into being because of my interest in Buber on drama and that of the editor of Funk and Wagnall. I include in it three essays of my own, in particular Buber's interchange with the great Austrian playwright Hugo von Hofmannsthal concerning the latter's play *The Tower* and the biblical and philosophical background to Buber's "mystery play" *Elijah*. I had translated *Elijah* without Buber's knowing it and sent it to him shortly before his death in 1965. At Pendle Hill, the Quaker Study Center in Wallingford, Pennsylvania, we had a reading of the play with myself reading the part of Elijah and Eugenia the Voice [of God]. At Manhattanville College of the Sacred Heart a full-scale play was mounted with musical accompaniment and chorus. Unfortunately, midway through rehearsals the director fired the actor who was playing Elijah and took over the part himself, rendering Elijah with a Yiddish accent and Brooklyn-Jewish mannerisms that could not have been further from the Tishbite prophet of the desert! Unfortunately, too, just after publication of the book, Funk and Wagnall ceased to be a trade press so *Martin Buber and the Theater* never received adequate distribution and shortly went out of print. *Elijah, ein Mysterianspiel* has recently been republished by Verlag Lambert Schneider in Germany with an essay of Elie Wiesel's on Elijah; but *Martin Buber and the Theater* will never be re-published because of the attitude of Buber's son Rafael, who considered his father's play the worst of his works.

∞

Touchstones of Reality: Existential Trust and the Community of Peace. New York: Dutton, 1972; Dutton paperback, 1973.

In this book I put forward my new metaphor of "touchstones of reality" an approach to the philosophy of religion but also to all the events of our lives. It is a way of remaining in the present yet again and again bringing the past into the present. Chapters 2 to 5 of Part I—"An Opening Way" are autobiographical, going from my high school days to my return to the world after three and a half years service in Civilian Public Service camps and units during the Second World War. Part II—"In Dialogue with the Religions" includes my encounters with Hinduism, and Jesus plus Zen, Taoism, the Biblical Covenant, Hasidism, and Jesus plus a discussion of Jewish-Christian Dialogue, the Working Party for the Quaker Movement (to which I belonged), the Religious Symbolism. Part III includes chapters on the crisis of religious values, psychology and religion, a new social ethic, and the "covenant of peace." Part IV concludes with "The Partnership of Existence," "Existential Trust: the Courage to Address and the Courage to Respond," and "A Meaning for Modern Man."

∞

The Hidden Human Image. New York: Delacorte, Delta Books, 1974.

This was my third book on the image of the human. It applies the conclusions of *Problematic Rebel* and *To Deny Our Nothingness* to science and psychology, the meeting of literature and religion, anxiety and death, sex, love, and women's liberation, education, encounter groups and the human potential movement, social witness and social change. It proceeds on the assumptions that the human image is the hidden ground of all these fields and that this hidden ground needs to be made manifest even while remaining hidden.

∞

The Human Way: A Dialogical Approach to Religion and Human Experience. Chambersburg, PA: Anima, 1982.

My original title for this book was the *Via Humana*, which I posited in conscious contrast to the *via positiva* and the *via negativa* of traditional religious symbolism. I saw as the special task of this book making explicit the new philosophy of religion implicit in *Touchstones of Reality*. The first chapter, accordingly, is "Approaching Religious Reality through Touchstones." *The Human Way* is also a phenomenology of religious experience and a study of religious communication, solitude and community, tradition, and modernity, religious leadership, world view, and existential trust.

∞

The Confirmation of Otherness: In Family, Community, and Society. New York: Pilgrim, 1983.

This book devotes four chapters to Buber's ontology of the "between" and then develops Buber's seminal idea of "confirmation"—first in terms of my own thoughts on the problematic of confirmation (in the four chapters of Part II), second in its application to family, again four chapters, and third in relation to community—still another four chapters in which I develop my contrast between the "community of affinity" or like-mindedness and the "community of otherness," as well as my reflections on the learning community, "dialogue in mentoring and research," and intentional community. The largest part of the book is the six chapters on the confirmation of otherness in society, ranging across women's liberation, aging, transcultural nursing, un- and underemployment, the covenant of peace and violence/non-violence. The book concludes with "Restoring Relational Trust" as the necessary step toward a community of communities.

∞

Contemporary Psychology: Revealing and Obscuring the Human.
Pittsburgh: Duquesne University Press, 1984.

Contemporary Psychology continues my concern with the human image, applied specifically to psychology and psychotherapy. It begins with
the assumption that while psychology has done much in our time to
reveal the hidden human image, it has also contributed a good deal to
obscuring it. After introductory chapters on my image of the human by
Richard Stanton and myself, there is a dialogical critique on the three
forces of contemporary psychology followed by chapters on Rollo May,
phenomenology and existential analysis, R. D. Laing, and family psychiatry (Wynne and Boszormenyi-Nagy). Part Four takes from *Problematic
Rebel* and elsewhere material on anxiety, freedom and compulsion, the
divided self, the crisis of motives and the problematic of guilt, and sex
and love.

∞

Martin Buber's Life and Work: The Early Years, 1878–1923. New York:
Dutton, 1981. Paperback Edition, Detroit: Wayne State University
Press, 1988.

The first three volumes of this book treats Buber's route to I and Thou,
dealing with his childhood and youth, his mysticism, his philosophy of
"realization," the First World War and the breakthrough to dialogue,
communal socialism and revolution, Rosenzweig and the Frankfurt
Lehrhaus, and his progression from the "easy word" to the "hard word."
It concludes with four chapters on *I and Thou*: knowledge and art, love,
marriage, politics, and the community, psychologism and psychotherapy, and the "eternal Thou." The notes include critiques of Walter
Kaufmann's translation of *I and Thou* and of writers who have tried to
show Buber as influenced by Franz Rosenzweig and Ferdinand Ebner.

∞

Martin Buber's Life and Work: The Middle Years, 1923–1945. New York:
Dutton, 1983. Paperback Edition—Detroit: Wayne State University
Press, 1988.

The first part of *The Middle Years* sketches Buber's enormous productivity during the Weimar Republic, including chapters on Zionism, education, the Buber-Rosenzweig translation of the Hebrew Bible into German, Buber & Rosenzweig's dialogue on Jewish law, Religious Socialism and the remarkable Protestant-Catholic-Jewish journal *Die Kreatur*, Buber at fifty, and Buber's "Work Folk" disciple Hermann Gerson. The second part deals with Nazi Germany, including Buber's response to the Nazi challenge in essays, in attempts at Jewish-Christian dialogue, and in re-organizing the whole system of Jewish education in Nazi Germany. Part III includes the immigration of Martin, Paula, and their grandchildren to Jerusalem, Palestine, the Second World War, and discussions of Buber's philosophical treatises *What is Man?* (in *Between Man and Man*) and his Hasidic chronicle-novel *For the Sake of Heaven*.

∞

Martin Buber's Life and Work: The Later Years, 1945–1965. New York: Dutton, 1984. Paperback Edition—Detroit: Wayne State University Press, 1988.

Part I on Palestine/Israel deals with Jewish-Arab rapprochement and conflict, Buber's books of interpretation of the Hebrew Bible and his mature retelling of the tales of the Hasidism, his work with kibbutz socialism, and the school for the teachers of the people that Buber directed in Israel after the Jewish-Arab war. Part II discusses Buber's *Two Types of Faith* and the Jewish-Christian dialogue that centered around it, German pilgrimages of guilt to Buber in Israel, and the Peace Prize of the German Book Trade (1953). Part III deals with Buber's three visits to America, his dialogue with Americans, encounters with American psychotherapists, the death of Paula, and Buber's replies to critics, including Gershom Scholem's attack on his interpretation of Hasidism. Part IV treats Buber's dialogues with Dag Hammarskjöld and Ben Gurion. Part V includes the Erasmus Prize conferred on Buber in 1963, Buber's last years, and his death.

In giving me the National Jewish Book Award for Biography in 1985 the judges said that it was for all three volumes of this "dialography," as I called these 1500 pages.

∞

The Healing Dialogue in Psychotherapy. New York: Jason Aronson, 1985. Paperback edition, Northvale, NJ: Jason Aronson, 1994. Published in German translation as *Der Heilended Dialog in der Psychotherapie,* translated by Brigitte Stein. Edition Humanistische Psychologie im Internationale Institut zur Forderung der Humanistische Psychologie, Köln: Moll & Eckhardt, 1987.

This is the first book to try to make an inclusive and systematic presentation of Dialogical Psychotherapy, which is also the name of the Institute founded in San Diego in 1984 and co-directed by Richard Hycner, Maurice Friedman, and James DeLeo. The first part discusses therapists from various schools who are in significant ways dialogical, even if they do not single-out the name: Robert Langs (Freudian), James Hilman and Hans Trüb (Jungian), Harry Stack Sullivan, Erich Fromm, and Frieda Fromm-Reichmann (Interpersonal), Carl Rogers (Humanistic), Fairbairn, Kohut, and Guntrip (Object Relations and Self Psychology), Rollo May and Leslie Farber (existential), Laura Perls and Erving and Miriam Polster (Gestalt), and Lyman Wynne and Ivan Boszormenyi-Nagy (Intergenerational Family Therapy). Part II treats significant elements of Dialogical Psychotherapy: confirmation, the unconscious and dreams, existential guilt, the "problematic of mutuality" between therapist and client, empathy, identification, inclusion, and intuition, and my own "dialogue of touchstones" as an approach to psychotherapy.

∞

Martin Buber and the Eternal. New York: Human Sciences Press, 1986.

This little book brings together a lot of my thoughts on Buber in relation to the philosophy of religion and religion in general, as witnessed by its chapter headings: "Dialogue and the 'Eternal Thou,'" "Biblical Existentialism: Creation, Revelation, Redemption," "Revelation and Reason," "Religion and Ethics," "Existential Guilt, Existential Trust, and the Eternal Thou," "The Comparative and the Unique: An Approach to the History of Religion," "Dialogue with Oriental Religions," "Religious Education as Dialogue," "Existential Trust and the Eclipse of God."

∞

Abraham Joshua Heschel and Elie Wiesel: "You Are My Witness." New York: Farrar, Straus, & Giroux, 1987.

This book is both a study of the main elements in the writing of Heschel and Wiesel and a personal statement of my relationship with Judaism. As the title implies, we are God's witnesses. But it also means to me that Heschel and Wiesel (and, of course, Buber too) are *my* witnesses. My introduction deals with "Biblical Covenant, Hasidic Fervor, and American Judaism." I begin the Heschel section with a chapter on my almost thirty year friendship with Heschel, and I say a good deal about my friendship with Wiesel in my chapter on "The Holocaust as Touchstone of Reality." Aside from their friendship, what united Heschel and Wiesel was the Hebrew Bible, the Covenant, Hasidism, and *Shoah*. I make my own witness to the Covenant here, but not as a theologian or even an observant Jew but simply as a person of *emunah*—unconditional trust in the relationship with God.

∞

A Dialogue with Hasidic Tales: Hallowing the Everyday. New York: Human Sciences Press, 1988.

This book is not a study of Hasidism or even of Buber's *Tales of the Hasidim* but the record of almost forty years of *dialogue* with the Hasidic tales in the classic form which Buber has given them. As such, it grows in no small part out of the discussion groups on Hasidic tales that Eugenia and I led at Pendle Hill and that I have continued to lead for the last twenty years in San Diego—a "basic Hasidic tale" that "speaks to one's condition" from the master, or *zaddik*, we are focusing on at that time—one gives a personal response to it, and then the rest of the group responds to that tale and to that person's response. In contrast to Buber's grouping of the tales under the *zaddik* to whom they are attributed, in *A Dialogue with Hasidic Tales* I have grouped the tales and my personal commentary on them under three topical headings, first, "The Hasidic Way of Life": uniqueness, serving God with the evil urge, *kavana*, overcoming dualism; second, "The Bond between Spirit and Spirit": teaching and learning, love and community, healing and helping, the limits of helping; third, "To Be Humanly Holy": trust, prayer, death, hope.

◌◌

Encounter on the Narrow Ridge: A Life of Martin Buber. New York: Paragon House, 1991. Paperback edition, New York, Paragon House, 1993. Published in Spanish translation as *Encuentroel Desfiladero: La Vida de Martin Buber*, translated by Daniel Zadunaisky. Buenos Aires, Argentina: Planeta, Espeja del Mundo, 1993.

This book represents an abridgement of the three volumes of *Martin Buber's Life and Work*. I have tried to emphasize the life more than the works and to add what I could to flesh out the life. For this purpose I did research on Buber's unpublished letters at the Martin Buber Archives of the Jewish National and University Library at the Hebrew University during 1987–1988—the year that I was Senior Fulbright Lecturer at the Hebrew University of Jerusalem. *Encounter on the Narrow Ridge* has five parts: I—"The Road to I and Thou," II—"The Weimar Republic and Nazi Germany," III—"Prewar Palestine and the Early Years of the State," IV— "Postwar Germany and America: Replies to Critics," V—"Hammarskjold, Ben Gurion, and Last Years."

◌◌

Dialogue and the Human Image: Beyond Humanistic Psychology. Newbury Park, CA: Sage, 1992.

This book grew out of a panel at the American Psychological Association Convention at Atlanta, Georgia, in August 1988 titled, "After Maslow and Rogers, What?" After a critique of humanistic psychology, the book is divided into two parts, namely, "Dialogue" and "The Human Image." These are the two elements that have not been sufficiently empha-sized and that are essential for any humanistic psychology in the root meaning of the term. In the "Dialogue" part of the book, the chapter on "Therapists of Dialogue" deals with quite a number of psycho-gists who have elements of dialogical psychotherapy in their writings whereas the chapter on "Dialogical Psychotherapists" deals with three psychologists who have made healing through meeting central to their writings: Hans Trub, Leslie H. Farber, and Richard Hycner. (If I were writing today, I would add my wife Aleene Friedman because of her book *Treating Chronic Pain: The Healing Dialogue* and William Heard because of his book *The Healing Between: A Clinical Guide to Dialogical Psychotherapy.*) There is also a chapter on Buber and Ivan Boszormenyi-Nagy—"The Role of Dialogue in Contextual (Intergenerational Family) Therapy." "The Image of the Human" part of the book draws again on what I have gained from my intensive study of Melville, Dostoevsky, Kafka, and Camus in *Problematic Rebel* dealing with anxiety, sex and love, freedom, compulsion, and the divided self, the crisis of motives, and the problematic of guilt. It closes with a chapter on "The Image of the Human and Psychotherapy."

∽

Religion and Psychology: A Dialogical Approach. New York: Paragon House, 1992.

Although *Religion and Psychology* touches on subjects that have great relevance for religious psychology, psychology of religion, and pastoral psychology, it is centrally concerned with the *meeting* of religion and psychology and with the issues that grown out of that meeting, such as attitudes toward anxiety, existential trust, the limits of the psyche as touchstone of reality, neurotic and existential guilt, and the limits of the responsibility of the helper. Even the critiques of the psychology of religion of Jung, Fromm, Maslow, and Frankl in Part II serve to illuminate these issues. Part I expounds the foundations of the book's dialogical approach in biblical, existential, and relational trust, Hasidic healing and helping, the philosophy of dialogue and dialogical psychotherapy, ad the double approaches of touchstones of reality and the image of the human. Part III deals with issues such as psychologism and the cult of experience and the interpretation of myth. Part IV deals with healing through meeting, Contextual Therapy, neurotic and existential guilt, and the dialogue of touchstones.

∽

A Heart of Wisdom: Religion and Human Wholeness. Albany, NY: State University of New York Press, 1992. Hardcover and paperback.

This is the third book I published in the same year, which in retrospect seems a bit much. *A Heart of Wisdom* brings together more of my thought on religion and the religions than any of my earlier books and does so from the perspective of the relation of religion to human wholeness. To this purpose I took over into this book a number of chapters from *Touchstones of Reality* and *the Human Way* plus the chapter on literature and religion from *The Hidden Human Image*, all three of which books were out of print by then. Here too I use the approach of touchstones of reality in discussing the religions with which I have been in dialogue (Hinduism, Buddhism, Zen, Taoism, Sufism, the biblical covenant, Hasidism, and the teachings of Jesus).

∞

Intercultural Dialogue and the Human Image: Maurice Friedman at the Indira Gandhi National Centre for the Arts. New Delhi, India: 1995.

This book grew out of my stint as the first visiting professor at the Indira Gandhi National Centre for the Arts in New Delhi. It includes my four public lectures and the discussion that follows each of them, my wife Aleene Friedman's public lecture plus discussion and the transcript of a two-day seminar on "Dialogue and the Human Image" attended by noted scholars from many fields from all over India. The titles of my four lectures are "Martin Buber's Philosophical Anthropology," "Dialogical Psychotherapy," "the Dialogue of Touchstones," and "The Healing Partnership: Biofeedback Pain Therapy." Except for a short position paper by me, the two-day seminar had no formal papers or speeches but a very active participation by most of the twenty-seven people who were present.

∞

Martin Buber and the Human Sciences. Maurice Friedman—Editor-in-Chief, Pat Boni—Executive Editor, Lawrence Baron, Seymour Cain, Virginia Shabatay, and John Stewart—Associate Editors. Albany: State University of New York Press, 1996.

This book grows out of an International Interdisciplinary Conference on Martin Buber's impact on the Human Sciences initiated and directed by me and held at San Diego State University, October 21–23,

1991. With three exceptions, *Martin Buber and the Human Sciences* is made up of essays selected by the editorial committee over two years of work from the wealth of papers presented at the conference. This selection, like the conference itself, presents a broad spectrum of Buber's impact on the human sciences, which we have defined so as to include not only the traditional humanities but also much that is traditionally classified as psychology and the social sciences. It demonstrates that Buber's influence thirty years after his death is still a powerful one in many countries and many fields. After my long introductory essay the book contains four parts—Philosophy and Religion; the Written and the Spoken Word: Hermeneutics, Aesthetics, and Literature; Economics, Politics, and History; and Dialogical Psychotherapy and Contextual (Intergenerational Family) Therapy. I include this book here not only because of my own three essays in it but also because it is an enormous and impressive piece of work of which those of us who worked on it have reason to be proud.

☙

The Affirming Flame: A Poetics of Meaning. Amherst, NY: Prometheus, 1999.

This book is the conclusion to my published dialogue with modern literature, begun in my M.A. thesis on "The Search for Faith in Ten European Novels" and continued in *Problematic Rebel* and *To Deny Our Nothingness*. Beginning with "mystics of the particular" and "Poets of the Here and Now," the book proceeds to the abandonment that comes in the face of the threat of meaninglessness and of that evil that destroys the meaning that is found in the particular. It concludes with four chapters on the "Dialogue with the Absurd" in which meaning is found again but not without the threat of abandonment and not through any harmonic world-view. The ultimate Dialogue with the Absurd takes place in the confrontation with the *Shoah*.

Through a dialogue with many nineteenth- and twentieth-century works of literature, mostly poetry, I try to find meaning moving from the meeting with the particular, through insecurity and doubt, and the demonism of nature and human beings, to a final position of holding the tension between affirming where we can affirm and withstanding where we must withstand. The conclusion, "Confronting Death," is followed by a "hermeneutical appendix": "Toward a Poetics of Dialogue."

∞

Community on the Narrow Ridge
(Work in Progress)

This book does not start with a description of genuine community as a finished product but with an in-depth plumbing of the types of relationships that make real community possible. "The Life of Dialogue" and "The Confirmation of Otherness" form the foundation and the necessary steps on the road toward bringing into being "Genuine Community." In this book I take over some chapters from *Touchstones of Reality*, e.g., "The Partnership of Existence," and several from *The Confirmation of Otherness: In Family, Community, and Society*—both books long out of print. I particularly wanted to redeem *The Confirmation of Otherness* that never received proper distribution or attention.

    The Affirming Flame sums up one aspect of my philosophy, *Community on the Narrow Ridge* another. Taken together they represent a summation and conclusion of my life's teaching.

∞

The "Creative House: A Memoir
(Completed but not yet published).

This book portrays in novel form, without being itself fiction, my life as a conscientious objector in the Second World War. It moves from my last years at Harvard through three and a half years in Civilian Public Service Camps for C.O.s to the group "psychodrama" that broke me out of my immersion in mysticism to a shattering of all security followed by some form of "basic trust" and a life devoted to "hallowing the everyday" (1939–1946).

∞

My Friendship with Martin Buber
(currently being reviewed for publication).

Springing from my relation with Buber, beginning in the summer of 1950 and ending with Buber's death in 1965, this work takes the reader from my earliest contact with Buber, through Buber's three visits to America, his wife's death, my stay in Jerusalem, and the articulation of Buber's culminating philosophy of the interhuman. To trace this chronology, I draw extensively—particularly in chapters between Buber's visits to America—on my personal collection of letters to and from Buber. These letters preserve the substance of our dialogue, bringing into focus subjects of mutual interest and opening a window on our shared intellectual concerns. The chapters drawn primarily from my fifteen years of correspondence with Buber retain the form of dialogue that was close to Buber's heart.